The First Book of
WordPerfect® 6

The First Book of
WordPerfect® 6

Kate Miller

alpha
books

A Division of Prentice Hall Computer Publishing
11711 North College Avenue, Carmel, Indiana 46032 USA

To Jeff and "the girls." Still living happily ever after.

International Standard Book Number: 1-56761-022-6

Library of Congress Catalog Card Number: 92-75142

95 94 93   8 7 6 5 4 3 2 1

Interpretation of the printing code: the rightmost double-digit number is the year of the book's printing; the rightmost single-digit number is the number of the book's printing. For example, a printing code of 93-1 shows that the first printing of the book occurred in 1993.

Screen reproductions in this book were created by means of the program Collage Plus from Inner Media, Inc., Hollis, NH.

Printed in the United States of America

Publisher:
Marie Butler-Knight

Associate Publisher:
Lisa A. Bucki

Managing Editor:
Elizabeth Keaffaber

Acquisitions Manager:
Stephen R. Poland

Development Editor:
Faithe Wempen

Manuscript Editor:
San Dee Phillips

Interior Design
Roger Morgan

Cover Design
Susan Kniola

Indexer
Craig Small

Production Team
Diana Bigham, Katy Bodenmiller,
Scott Cook, Tim Cox,
Mark Enochs, Linda Koopman,
Tom Loveman, Beth Rago,
Carrie Roth, Greg Simsic

Special thanks to C. Herbert Feltner for ensuring the technical accuracy of this book.

Contents

9 The Professional Touch: Headers and Footers 167

10 Using the Writing Tools 177

Introduction

The *First Book of WordPerfect 5.1 Bestseller Edition* helped almost 100,000 people learn WordPerfect quickly. Now, the edition has been updated for WordPerfect's exciting 6.0 version and improved to provide even more help.

Popular word processors usually have hundreds of features for you to learn to use. This is more than the average user needs or wants, and for the beginning user, the sheer bulk can be intimidating. What *The First Book of WordPerfect 6.0 Bestseller Edition* does is glean only the "most used" features. It focuses on those features you'll need to use in the great majority of your work. This way, you save time and eliminate the frustration of trying to sort out what you need from what you don't need.

Conventions Used in This Book

Read "In This Chapter" at the beginning of each chapter for a brief idea of what you'll learn in the chapter. The most important procedures are summarized at the beginning of every chapter, too, so if you're in a hurry, you don't need to wade through any text to find what you need. Throughout the chapter, tables, notes, tips, cautions, FYI Ideas and steps make learning easy.

Once you have learned WordPerfect, you may need an occasional reminder. The tear-out quick reference card repeats the Quick Steps from the book in handy, take-along form. The inside back cover of the book summarizes the WordPerfect codes that you may encounter most often.

Several special icons are used in this book:

The generous number of Quick Steps give you the at-a-glance steps to quickly perform an operation. These numbered steps describe both the actions you perform and the result of those actions. The inside front cover provides a list of Quick Steps for fast reference.

TIP: Hints and shortcuts for using the program more effectively.

NOTE: Additional features that provide background information you need to understand special terms.

Alert you to potential pitfalls and help solve common problems.

Describe practical ways that you can use Word Perfect at work and at home to create projects and documents you may not have imagined.

Entering Commands

WordPerfect allows you to select commands with the mouse or keypresses. The instructions in this book cover both options. Work with whatever approach is most comfortable for you. Keystrokes to be made in combination are separated by a plus (+) and in this book, are represented by small key cap illustrations meant to replicate the common keyboard key appearance. For example, Ctrl + Q indicates you should press Ctrl and Q simultaneously.

When an operation is described as follows:

Press ⇧Shift + F8, or choose **L**ine from the Layout menu.

it means that there are two different methods of accomplishing the same thing. The first method would be to hold down the ⇧Shift key and press F8. The second method would be to pull down the Layout menu (you'll learn how to do this later in the book) and select the **L**ine option from it. (The bold letter in the command indicates that you can choose it by typing that letter.)

Acknowledgments

Many thanks to the continued excellent support from the staff at Prentice Hall Computer Publishing. Special thanks to Marie Butler-Knight, Faithe Wempen, Liz Keaffaber, and San Dee Phillips.

Trademark Acknowledgments

All terms mentioned in this book that are known to be trademarks or service marks are listed below. In addition, terms suspected of being trademarks or service marks have been appropriately capitalized. Alpha cannot attest to the accuracy of this information. Use of a term in this book should not be regarded as affecting the validity of any trademark or service mark.

Lotus and 1-2-3 are registered trademarks of Lotus Development Corporation.

WordPerfect is a registered trademark of WordPerfect Corporation.

MS-DOS is a registered trademark of Microsoft Corporation.

Starting WordPerfect

1. Type **cd\wp60**, and press `↵Enter`.
2. Type **wp**, and press `↵Enter`.

Using a Mouse

- *Point*—Move the mouse until the on-screen mouse pointer touches the desired object.
- *Click:*—Press and release the left mouse button once.
- *Double-click:*—Press and release the left mouse button twice quickly.

Selecting a Command from a Pull-Down Menu

1. Press `Alt` or click the right mouse button.
2. Type the selection letter of the menu name, or click on the name with the mouse.
3. Type the selection letter of the command name, or click on the command with the mouse.

Getting Help

1. Press `F1`, or select Help from the menu bar.

Switching the Screen to Graphics Mode

1. Open the View menu.
2. Select Graphics Mode.

Ways to Exit WordPerfect

- Press `Home`, `F7`.
- Select Exitwp from the File menu.

1

Getting Started with WordPerfect 6.0

Welcome to the quick and easy way to learn WordPerfect. If you're not sure how to get started, this chapter will provide some help. In it, you'll learn how to start WordPerfect, how to move around and enter commands, and how to use the on-line Help feature.

TIP: If you're a newcomer to computers (or want to review the basics) take a look at Appendix A, "Getting Ready to Use WordPerfect." If WordPerfect has not been installed on your computer, refer to Appendix B, "Installing WordPerfect" for instructions.

Starting WordPerfect

Once WordPerfect is installed, you are ready to begin using the program.

Make sure the computer is turned on. From the drive that holds the WordPerfect program files (probably drive C:) type in

```
wp
```

and press `⏎Enter`. If you get the message

```
Bad command or filename
```

then you may need to change to the WordPerfect directory by typing in the change directory (cd) command, followed by the path to the directory, and press `⏎Enter`. For example, you would type this command line if WordPerfect was installed as suggested by the program:

```
cd\wp60
```

and press `⏎Enter`. Then you can try again typing wp to start the program.

A First Look at the Screen

The opening screen appears, followed by the WordPerfect document screen shown in Figure 1.1. Don't be alarmed at the many menu options across the top of the screen. This chapter will show you how to access WordPerfect's menu system and how to speed up your work with mouse techniques and keyboard shortcuts.

Menu bar

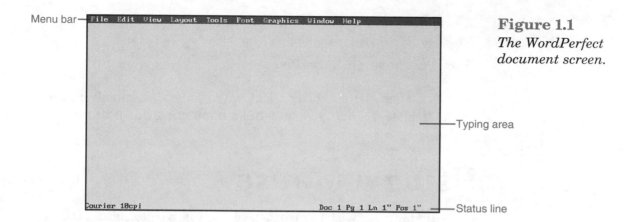

Figure 1.1
The WordPerfect document screen.

Typing area

Status line

The WordPerfect screen is plain and uncluttered, so there is plenty of room for you to work. All you see are the status line, the menu bar, and the typing area. The typing area is pretty self-explanatory; it's where you type your text. The menu bar will require some explanation; we'll look at it in a moment. But first, let's examine the status line, and find out what information it contains.

In Figure 1.1, notice the status line on the last line of the screen. On the right, this appears:

```
Doc 1 Pg 1 Ln 1" Pos 1"
```

This information indicates which of nine possible WordPerfect documents with which you are working. Then, information about your cursor position appears. Shown are the page (Pg) number, the line (Ln) position in inches from the top of your page, and the position (Pos) in inches from the left of the page.

On the left, this appears:

```
Courier 10cpi
```

This information tells you the font the characters will print and the size of the font (in this case, 10 cpi or characters per inch). A *font* is a style of lettering. Here are some examples of common fonts.

```
This text is printed in Courier font.
```
This text is printed in Helvetica font.

This text is printed in Times Roman font.

Messages about WordPerfect operations also appear on the status line, so keep an eye on what's happening down there.

Using a Mouse

If you are familiar with mouse use, you can skip this section. Using a mouse seems simple after you've become familiar with it but can be intimidating for the beginner.

A mouse is an input device the approximate size and shape of a bar of soap. To use a mouse, simply roll it across your desk or mousepad. The roller on the bottom of the mouse causes the pointer to move across the screen. If you run out of desk space, just pick up the mouse and reposition it; the pointer position will remain unchanged on your screen.

Table 1.1 explains the basic mouse actions and the special terms used to describe them.

Table 1.1
Mouse Terms

Term	Mouse Action
Point	To move the mouse until the on-screen pointer is over the desired item.
Click	To press and release the left mouse button once.
Double-click	To press and release the left mouse button twice rapidly.
Drag	To hold down the left mouse button and move the mouse pointer to another location, then release the button.

Making WordPerfect Selections

When you work with WordPerfect, you usually have two options for selecting WordPerfect functions. You can:

- Make a menu selection from the menu bar (with the keyboard or a mouse).

  OR

- Press a function key alone or in combination with the [Alt], [⇧Shift], or [Ctrl] keys. The function keys are labeled [F1] through [F10], or [F12]. They are assigned special uses in WordPerfect.

Because the menu bar provides an easy way for a beginner to access commands without memorizing function keys, we'll start our discussion there.

Using the Menu Bar

A menu on a computer screen is similar to a menu in a restaurant. For example, in a restaurant you might select a steak from the menu and then be asked how you want it cooked, what side dishes you want, and what kind of dressing you want on your salad. Likewise, in WordPerfect, each menu offers several selections, and once you make a choice, you are often asked to make additional decisions about how you want the command to execute.

For example, Figure 1.1 shows the menu bar. If you select File, the options for handling a file appear. The File menu is shown in Figure 1.2. The menus that appear from the menu bar are often referred to as pull-down menus, since they appear to be pulled down from the menu bar. Notice that from the File menu, you can print, exit WordPerfect, or select any other option related to file handling.

Figure 1.2

*The File menu (a
pull-down menu).*

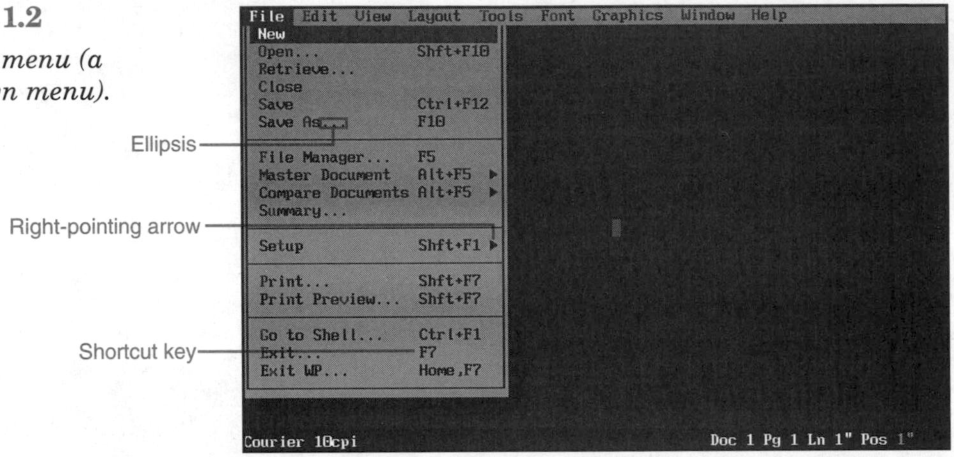

```
 File  Edit  View  Layout  Tools  Font  Graphics  Window  Help
 New
 Open...            Shft+F10
 Retrieve...
 Close
 Save               Ctrl+F12
 Save As...         F10

 File Manager...    F5
 Master Document    Alt+F5   ►
 Compare Documents  Alt+F5   ►
 Summary...

 Setup              Shft+F1  ►

 Print...           Shft+F7
 Print Preview...   Shft+F7

 Go to Shell...     Ctrl+F1
 Exit...            F7
 Exit WP...         Home,F7

 Courier 10cpi                          Doc 1 Pg 1 Ln 1" Pos 1"
```

Ellipsis ———

Right-pointing arrow ———

Shortcut key ———

Each of the menu bar items has a different colored, bold, or
underlined letter, indicating what letter you would type to select
it. These are called *selection letters*. When you open a menu, you'll
see that each item on the menu has a selection letter, too. You'll
see how these selection letters come in handy in the next section.

> **TIP:** If the menu bar does not appear, it may be turned
> off. To turn it on, hold down the [Alt] key and press [=].
> Then type [V] (for **V**iew), then [P] (for **P**ull-Down Menus).

Choosing Commands with Pull-Down Menus

To use WordPerfect's pull-down menus, you activate the menu
bar, select a pull-down menu, and then select a command from the
menu. Depending on the command you select, it will either open
a *cascading menu*, open a *dialog box*, or execute immediately.

You can tell by looking at a menu command what will happen
when you select it (see Figure 1.2). Menu commands with right-
pointing arrows to their right open additional menus called

cascading menus. Commands followed by ellipses open *dialog boxes.* A dialog box is a special window that appears to prompt you to perform a specific operation. Commands with neither of these things beside them execute immediately.

Some commands may not be available at all times. For example, you cannot access the **P**aste command until you have used **C**ut or **C**opy to mark something to be pasted. Options that are temporarily unavailable appear in lighter (*grayed-out*) text. (There aren't any grayed-out commands shown in Figure 1.2; all **F**ile menu commands are available.)

Getting Started

Most of the menu commands have shortcut key equivalents, such as pressing F10 to save a file. The shortcut keys are listed on the pull-down menus next to the command names (see Figure 1.2). Users who are already familiar with a previous version of WordPerfect may prefer the shortcut keys to using the menus.

However, the menu bar is the best tool for beginners. Menu actions are grouped on the menus logically. If you are unsure of the keys to press to perform a function, browse through the menus. Even sophisticated word processing users will hunt for commands as they become familiar with a new word processing system. Then, once you are more familiar with WordPerfect, you may want to begin using the key combinations to speed up your work.

You can use either the keyboard or a mouse to choose a command from the menu bar. Experiment with both methods to see which you prefer. The following Quick Steps show how to choose a menu command with the keyboard.

TIP: If the following Quick Steps do not work for you (that is, if pressing Alt does not activiate the menu bar), hold down Alt, and press = to activate it. To force Alt to activate the menu bar, select Screen Setup from the View menu, select Screen Options, and then choose Alt key to activate menus.

QUICK STEPS

Choosing a Menu Command with the Keyboard

1. Press Alt.

File is highlighted.

2. Type the selection letter (the bold, underlined, or highlighted letter) in the desired menu name. For example, type F for the File menu.

The selected pull-down menu appears. Each command on the pull-down menu has a selection letter.

3. Type the selection letter for the command you want to select.

The command is executed, or WordPerfect opens another menu or dialog box to request more information.

4. If prompted, provide additional information in the dialog box that appears, or choose a command from the cascading menu that appears.

Getting Started with WordPerfect 6.0

TIP: You can press Alt and the selection letter simultaneously, combining steps 1 and 2 to make the procedure quicker.

If you get into a menu and then decide you want to exit from it without selecting a command, just press Esc until you're back to the regular editing screen.

Follow these Quick Steps to select a menu command with the mouse.

Choosing a Menu Command with a Mouse

1. Move the mouse on your desk until the pointer is over the menu name you want.

The mouse pointer appears as a small rectangle on your screen.

2. Click the left mouse button to pull down the menu.

The menu appears. For example, if you clicked on File, the File menu would appear, as shown in Figure 1.2.

3. To make menu selections, point at the item and click the left mouse button.

The command is executed, or WordPerfect opens another menu or dialog box to request more information.

4. If prompted, provide additional information in the dialog box that appears, or click on a command from the cascading menu that appears.

If you open a menu and then decide you want to escape from it without selecting any command, just click the mouse anywhere outside of the menu.

Special Markings on Menus

You may have already encountered some of WordPerfect's special markings on menus that help you get around, such as an ellipsis after a command. Here's a quick rundown of the marks.

Right-pointing arrows indicate that the command opens a smaller menu called a *cascading menu*. For example, the Setup command on the File menu opens a cascading menu (see Figure 1.3). You select commands from a cascading menu exactly as you do regular menu commands: either click on them or type their selection letter.

Figure 1.3

The File Setup cascading menu.

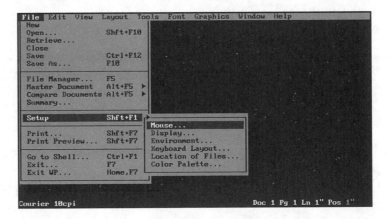

Another visual prompt on a menu is a check or an asterisk before the command. When you see one, it means the command is selected. For example, in Figure 1.4, the View menu has the Text Mode and Pull-Down Menus options marked.

Asterisks ──

Figure 1.4
Menu commands selected.

An ellipsis (...) after a command indicates that a dialog box or window will appear, allowing you to check or change option settings or type in information to complete the command. See "Dialog Boxes" later in this chapter for more information.

Using Shortcut Keys

Shortcut keys circumvent the sometimes lengthy route through several menus to a particular feature. For example, to block some text you can select the **E**dit menu, and then select **B**lock. Or you can simply use the keyboard shortcut Alt + F4.

> **NOTE:** Shortcut keys primarily involve function keys (the "F" keys: F1, F2, and so on). Occasionally, other keys are used, such as Ctrl + B to insert [Bold On][Bold Off] codes.

When using a shortcut key, you might press a function key alone or in conjunction with one or more other keys (usually some combination of Ctrl, ⇧Shift, or Alt). To use a key combination, such as Alt + F4, just hold down the keys simultaneously. If you find that difficult, hold down the first key while pressing the second.

The Keyboard Template

The quickest way to perform an operation or command is with a shortcut key combination. But how do you remember all those combinations? Each function key has a separate operation for it by itself, with the ⟨⇧Shift⟩ key, with the ⟨Ctrl⟩ key, and with the ⟨Alt⟩ key—in total, more than 40 commands.

Luckily, WordPerfect comes with a keyboard template. The template shows you which keys to press, alone or together, to perform a specific operation. The template fits on your keyboard, and provides a quick reference of all the function key combinations and their meanings. The functions listed under ⟨F1⟩ through ⟨F12⟩ indicate which keys to press for which functions.

TIP: Some computer keyboards have only the ⟨F1⟩ through ⟨F10⟩ keys. The ⟨F11⟩ and ⟨F12⟩ keys may be assigned by pressing a key combination specific to your computer. Check your computer manual for details.

If you lose your template, or find yourself on someone else's computer without one, don't lose hope! WordPerfect's on-line Help feature can show you the template. Also, you can view a list of all the shortcut keys through Help. See the "Help!" section later in this chapter.

Let's look at a couple of template examples. Take a look at the operations under ⟨F7⟩ on your template. It looks something like this:

Ctrl	Notes
Alt	Columns/Tables
Shift	Print/Fax
	Exit
	F7

Starting at the bottom of the template:

- To exit a document, just press F7.

- To print or fax a document, press ⇧Shift+F7.

- To open the Columns/Tables dialog box, press Alt+F7.

- To open the Notes dialog box, press Ctrl+F7.

The template is color coded to make it easier to read each line across and identify which key to press.

Don't be intimidated by the number of key options on the template. Use this book to get started, and you will learn the most useful functions first. Concentrate on learning key combinations for the functions you use most. The more you use them, the more the key combinations will become second nature to you.

Moving the Cursor

The cursor is the insertion point for any text you type. You can move it around the screen and use it to designate where you want certain commands to take effect. By default, it appears as a blinking line.

> Don't confuse the cursor with the mouse pointer. You can move the cursor by using the mouse, however, as you'll learn later.
>
> CAUTION

Cursor Movement with the Keyboard

Some keyboard actions enable you to move the cursor quickly. These are called *quick movement keys*. Table 1.2 summarizes the quick movement keys. You will probably want to refer to this table frequently as you begin working in WordPerfect.

Table 1.2
Quick Movement Keys

Move	Keys to Press
One character left	←
One character right	→
Left a word	Ctrl with ← (Word Left)
Right a word	Ctrl with → (Word Right)
Left side of screen (even when characters go "off" the screen)	Home, then ←
Left end of line, after codes	Home, Home, then ←
Right end of line, before codes	Home, Home, then →
Right side of screen (even when characters go "off" the screen)	Home, then →
Up a single line	↑
Down a single line	↓
Top of the screen	Home, then ↑
Bottom of the screen	Home, then ↓
First line on previous page	PgUp
First line on next page	PgDn
Up a paragraph	Ctrl+↑
Down a paragraph	Ctrl+↓
Beginning of document (after WordPerfect codes)	Home, Home, ↑
Beginning of document (before codes)	Home, Home, Home, ↑
End of document (before WordPerfect codes)	Home, Home, ↓
End of document (after WordPerfect codes)	Home, Home, Home, ↓
To a page number you type in	Ctrl+Home

Cursor Movement with the Mouse

Don't want to bother with all those cursor movement keys? Table 1.3 gives some simple tips for moving the cursor.

Screen Movement	Mouse Action
Move the cursor to a spot	Point to the spot and press the left button.
Move to parts of the document that are off the screen	Press and hold the right button, and drag the mouse to the edge of the screen; release the button to stop the screen movement.

Table 1.3
Moving with the Mouse

Dialog Boxes

Dialog boxes are special windows that appear to perform specific operations. Dialog boxes allow you to enter required information or select from options.

Selection and movement in dialog boxes is a little different than in menus. Figures 1.5 through 1.7 illustrate the common methods to supply information in dialog boxes. Don't worry about what the boxes shown here do; just look at the various ways they provide for you to make decisions.

To move around a dialog box with the keyboard, use the Tab⇅ key to move forward or ⇧Shift + Tab⇅ to move backward. Once you're in a section, use the arrow keys to select among the choices. Moving around with the mouse is easy; just click on the option you want.

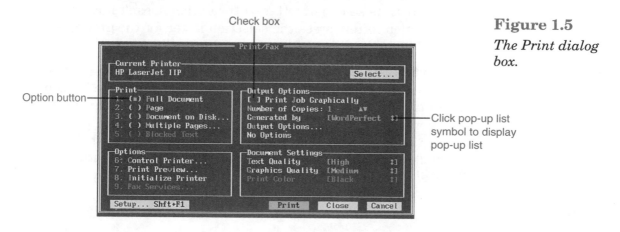

Figure 1.5
The Print dialog box.

Figure 1.6

The Retrieve Document dialog box.

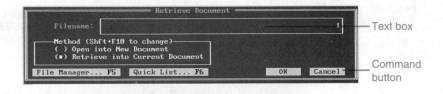

Text box

Command button

Figure 1.7

The File List dialog box.

List box

Selections

Scroll bar

Check boxes: Check boxes are used for situations where a feature is either on or off. If the check box has an X in it, the option is on; if it doesn't, the option is off. Click on the check box, or press its selection letter to change its status.

Option buttons: Option buttons are sometimes called radio buttons because just like on a car radio, only one button can be selected at a time. When you press a second button, the first one pops back out. Option buttons are used for multiple-choice questions like, "Which of these four layouts do you want?" Click on the option you want, or press its selection letter. If the option doesn't have a selection letter, press the selection letter for the group, and individual letters for each option will appear.

Lists: Lists allow you to select a single choice from a list. Sometimes, just like pull-down menus, the lists are hidden until you select the menu name. A double-headed arrow symbol indicates a hidden pop-up list. A downward pointing arrow indicates a pull-down list. Open these lists by clicking on the arrow or by pressing the selection letter. Make a selection from the list by clicking on it or by using the arrow keys to highlight it.

Text boxes: Text boxes are used to type in information, such as a file name. If an arrow appears at the end of the text box, you may click on it to reveal a list from which to choose.

Command buttons: Command buttons are used to get away from the dialog box. For example, OK closes the dialog box and puts your changes into effect. Cancel closes the dialog box and ignores the changes you may have made to the dialog box settings. Other buttons, such as File Manager...F5 in Figure 1.6, take you temporarily away from the dialog box without closing it.

List boxes: List boxes are used to select one item from a list. They're like pull-down lists except they're always visible. If the list is long, scroll bars are used to help navigate through it. In Figure 1.7, the item selected appears about halfway through the list.

Selections: Some dialog boxes contain numbered selections you can pick. To select them, you can click on one, or press either the selection letter or the number beside the option. For example, pressing S or 1 (for Select) would both have the same effect.

Scroll Bars

You may have noticed in the list box in Figure 1.7 that a scroll bar appeared when there were more options than could be shown in the fixed area allotted for the list box. Scroll bars help mouse users move quickly through a list or document.

To use a scroll bar with the mouse:

- Drag the bar in the scroll box to the approximate point in the list where you want to be. For example, drag the box to the bottom of the scroll bar to go quickly to the end of the list.

- Click on the arrows at the end of the scroll bar to move a line at a time.

- Click and hold on an arrow to move continuously.

- To move a screen up or down, click above or below the scroll box on the vertical scroll bar.

- If there is a horizontal scroll bar, to move a screen right or left, click to the right or left of the scroll box on it.

Using Scroll Bars in Documents

If you like, you can set up WordPerfect to use scroll bars in your documents. You can choose a horizontal scroll bar, a vertical scroll bar, or both.

1. Open the View menu.

2. Select Horizontal Scroll Bar or Vertical Scroll Bar. The selection is displayed when an asterisk (*) appears in front of the selection.

3. If you want both scroll bars, repeat steps 1 and 2 to enable the second scroll bar type.

You can repeat the procedure to disable the scroll bars.

The Button Bar

WordPerfect comes with a Button Bar set up to quickly access commonly used commands on each button. The Button Bar is one more option, besides the menus or pressing keys, for selecting a few of the WordPerfect commands. Figure 1.8 shows the Button Bar. Chapter 17, "Editing Tools," covers the Button Bar in detail, but we'll cover some of the basics here. To display the Button Bar:

1. Open the View menu.

2. Select Button Bar.

When an asterisk or a check appears before Button Bar, it is displayed. Remove the asterisk and the Button Bar disappears.

Figure 1.8
The Button Bar

To make a selection from the Button Bar, click on the appropriate button with the mouse. (You cannot use the keyboard to make a Button Bar selection.) If a selection is not available, it appears grayed. This indicates that some operation needs to be completed before you can choose the button.

The Button Bar, which appears in Figure 1.8, is the default Button Bar, the one that comes with WordPerfect. You can also create your own Button Bar containing the commands you use most often.

The Button Bar has more buttons than can be displayed across the screen at one time. Notice that at the left end of the button bar there are arrows. If you click on the arrow, more buttons are displayed. The buttons in the default Button Bar include:

File Mgr: Brings up the File Manager screen. This button gives the same effect as pressing F5 or selecting File File Manager.

Save As: Allows you to name and save the document. This button gives the same effect as pressing F10 or selecting File Save As.

Print: Allows you to send a document to be printed. This button is the same as pressing ⇧Shift+F7 or selecting File Print/Fax.

Preview: Shows you how the document will appear when printed. This button is the same as selecting File Print Preview or pressing ⇧Shift+F7, and then selecting Print Preview on the Print/Fax dialog box.

Font: The Font dialog box appears. This button is the same as selecting pressing Ctrl+F8 or selecting Font Font.

GrphMode: Switches to graphics mode. This button is the same as pressing `Ctrl`+`F3` and then selecting Graphics in the screen display box. Or you can select Graphics Mode from the View menu.

TextMode: Switches to text mode. This button is the same as pressing `Ctrl`+`F3` and then selecting Text to reach text mode or selecting View Text Mode.

Envelope: The Envelope dialog box appears. This button gives the same effect as selecting Layout Envelope or pressing `Alt`+`F12`.

Speller: Starts the speller. This button is the same as pressing `Alt`+`F1`, and then Speller or selecting Tools Writing Tools Speller.

Gramatik: Starts the grammar checker Grammatik. This button is the same as pressing `Alt`+`F1`, and then Grammatik or selecting Tools Writing Tools Grammatik.

QuikFndr: Starts the QuickFinder index to find a word, word pattern, or phrase. This button is the same as pressing `F5` then selecting the QuickFinder button or selecting File Manager from the File and then selecting the QuickFinder button.

Tbl Edit: Takes you to table editing mode. This button is the same as pressing `Alt`+`F7` and then selecting Tables and Edit or selecting Tables and then Edit from the Layout menu.

Search: Brings up the Search dialog box to begin a search. This button is the same as pressing `F2` or selecting Search from the Edit menu.

BBar Sel: Brings up the Select Button Bar dialog box to select an existing Button Bar. This button is the same as selecting Button Bar Setup and then Select from the View menu.

BBar Opt: Brings up the Button Bar Options dialog box to change the Button Bar options. This button is the same as selecting Button Bar Setup and then Options from the View menu.

Displaying and Using the Button Bar

1. Select View Button Bar.   The Button Bar appears.

2. Click on a button.   The operation of the button
                                    is performed.

3. To deselect the Button Bar,   The Button Bar
   select View Button Bar   disappears.
   again.

Help!

WordPerfect can answer your cry of Help! Just select Help from
the menu bar. The first three options on the pull-down menu allow
you to choose:

- **Contents:** Select Contents to see the full contents of help.
  As shown in Figure 1.9, you may choose from the following
  options: Index (for a list of features), How Do I (to learn by
  task), Glossary (terms and their meanings), Keystrokes
  (keys and their result), Shortcut Keys (list of actions),
  Template (actions arranged according to function key), and
  Using Help (how to use help).

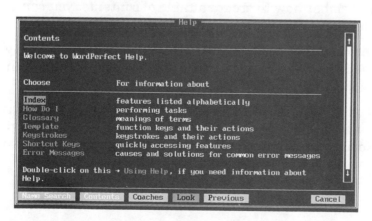

Figure 1.9
Help Contents.

> **NOTE:** Pressing F1 at WordPerfect's document screen, unless you are executing a command or using a feature, will take you directly to the Contents help screen. If you're in the middle of something, pressing F1 will take you to a Help screen that deals with the topic at hand. This is called *context-sensitive help*. To leave Help, press Esc.

- **Index:** Select Index, and the same screen accessed through the Contents help screen described in the preceding NOTE will appear. You can choose from an alphabetical list of features. When you choose a feature, the keystrokes to use the feature, along with the steps and other referenced information, appears.

- **How Do I:** Select How Do I to see a list of typical tasks to be performed in WordPerfect, such as Change justification or Create a Graphics Line.

From within Help, you can double-click on an underlined word (or choose Look) to see a glossary definition. Double-click or choose Look for a bolded word to jump to a related topic. Don't worry about getting lost, you can always use the Previous button to move back a topic.

The Help pull-down menu also includes these options:

- **Coaches:** Choose Coaches, and you can select a task to receive prompting as you work. For example, if you can't remember how to create a table of contents, you can use a coach to walk you through the process.

- **Macros:** Select Macros to get special help about using macros which allow you to automate keypress and other WordPerfect activities.

- **Tutorial:** Choose Tutorial to work with your own, private teacher. The tutorial has lessons about common activities such as editing text and formatting text. You may also choose from a topic list.

Take some time to play with the Help feature. It can answer your questions and save you some frustrating moments.

NOTE: If you exhaust the help alternatives within your immediate control (including referring to the reference manuals provided), a call to WordPerfect Corporation's technical support group will usually clear up any lingering problems. Current phone numbers are listed in the WordPerfect Reference Manual. Before calling, prepare yourself. Be ready to provide a detailed description of the problem and know the type of computer and version of WordPerfect you are using.

Switching Between Screen Modes

You may have noticed that the Button Bar has a button for Graphics Mode and wondered what that means. WordPerfect 6.0 comes with a "graphics mode" that lets you see on your screen exactly what will be printed. This is called WYSIWYG (pronounced "WHIZZ-ee-wig"), and it stands for "what you see is what you get." When you install WordPerfect, however, the program is set up to run in text mode, because not all monitors support graphics mode.

The entire screen, especially the button bar, is more attractive in graphics mode. (The drawback of graphics mode is that it makes the program run a little slower than normal.) All the pictures in the rest of this book will be shown in graphics mode. If you want your screen to be displayed in graphics mode too, either click on the GraphMode button on the Button Bar, or follow these steps:

1. Open the View menu.

2. Select Graphics Mode.

Wow! Your screen changes to graphics mode. If you decide later that graphics mode is too different or makes your computer work too slowly, you can change back to text mode by selecting View Text Mode.

As you'll learn later in this book, there are other screen modes that have special purposes, such as Print Preview. Print Preview shows what columns and borders will look like when printed. There is also a page mode, which is very similar to graphics mode. You can use page mode by selecting View Page Mode.

Here's a quick summary of the various screen modes and their uses:

- Text Mode: The characters are monospaced (all the same size). Special fonts or graphics are not displayed. Attributes like bold and underline appear in a different color rather than the actual appearance. For fast response in editing, use this mode for most of your work.

- Graphics Mode: The characters appear closer to what they'll look like when printed. For example, italics appear as italics, not as regular characters in a different color. Because this mode is slower than Text Mode, many users like to edit on this screen rather than enter a lot of text.

- Page Mode: This mode is the same as Graphics Mode except that the contents of an entire page (including top margins, headers, and footers) are displayed. This mode is the closest to what the document will look like when printed.

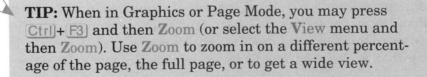

TIP: When in Graphics or Page Mode, you may press Ctrl + F3 and then Zoom (or select the View menu and then Zoom). Use Zoom to zoom in on a different percentage of the page, the full page, or to get a wide view.

Exiting WordPerfect

Later in the book, you'll learn various ways of exiting from WordPerfect after you have saved a document. But for now, here's a quick way, in case you want to leave and come back to learn more later. Just open the File menu, and select Exit WP, as shown in the following Quick Steps.

Exiting WordPerfect

1. Press [Home] and then [F7], or select Exitwp from the File menu.

   The Exit WordPerfect dialog box appears.

2. Place a check in the check box for each file you want to save. To mark or un-mark all files, select the (Un)mark All button.

   The files to save are marked.

3. Select the Exit button that appears if there are no files to save, (or the Save and Exit button if there are files to be saved).

   If you chose to save files, a saving message appears. Then, you are returned to the DOS prompt (such as C>).

Turning on Reveal Codes

1. Press `Alt`+`F3`, or select Reveal Codes on the View menu.
2. Repeat step 1 to remove the Reveal Codes screen.

Toggling Between Insert and Typeover Modes

1. Press `Ins` to toggle between insert and typeover modes.

Ways to Delete Text

- Press `Backspace` or `Del` to delete a character.
- Block the text, and then press `Del`.
- Press `Ctrl`+`F4`, or choose Select from the Edit menu, and then choose Sentence, Paragraph, or Page.

Canceling a Deletion

1. Press `Esc`, or select Undelete from the Edit menu.
2. Select Restore, or select Previous Deletion to view other recent deletions.

Using Undo

1. Press `Ctrl`+`Z`, or select Undo from the Edit menu.

Creating a Block of Text

- With the keyboard: position the cursor, press `Alt`+`F4`, or select Block from the Edit menu, and complete block highlight by moving the cursor.
- With the mouse: press the left mouse button, hold it down, and drag it across the text to block.

Creating Your First Document

Now that WordPerfect is set up and ready to go, you can start typing a document. This chapter covers how to create a new document and how to enter codes to control the appearance of text in the document. Unless you never make a mistake, you'll find an opportunity to use the typeover and insert modes to edit your work. You'll also learn some editing basics such as deleting, blocking, moving, and copying, and a couple of important safeguards—undelete and undo—that can save you when you make mistakes.

Just Start Typing!

When you start WordPerfect, an empty document file appears automatically for your use. The cursor appears in the upper left corner of the screen. As you type, the characters appear on-screen at the cursor.

Do not press Enter until you reach the end of a paragraph. Just continue typing, and the text will move automatically to the next line. This is called *word wrapping*. Then, when you edit the text later, the lines of text within the paragraph will re-adjust automatically to fit within the margins.

TIP: If you want to keep words together on a line (such as a person's first and last name), you can enter a *hard space*. Delete any existing space between the words. Then, with your cursor on the first letter of the second word, press Home + Spacebar. A space appears on your screen, and two brackets ([ ]) are placed as a code in the text. Codes are covered in the next section.

To practice entering text, type in the following example. [Enter] at the end of a line indicates that you should press ↵Enter. [Left Tab] indicates that you should press Tab⇆. When you are done, your screen should look like Figure 2.1.

```
Mr. David Randolph [Enter]
Vice President [Enter]
Bennington Corporation [Enter]
45 Superstition Highway [Enter]
Phoenix, Arizona 85251 [Enter]
[Enter]
Dear Mr. Randolph: [Enter]
[Enter]

[Left Tab] I am interested in pursuing a career with
the Bennington Corporation.
```

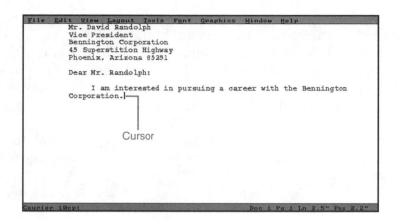

File Edit View Layout Tools Font Graphics Window Help
Mr. David Randolph
Vice President
Bennington Corporation
45 Superstition Highway
Phoenix, Arizona 85251

Dear Mr. Randolph:

 I am interested in pursuing a career with the Bennington
Corporation.|

Cursor

Courier 10cpi   Doc 1 Pg 1 Ln 2.5" Pos 2.2"

Figure 2.1
Sample text entered into the document screen.

Codes in Your Document

When you create a document, as you saw in entering the example text, you not only type letters and numbers, but you also press special keys, such as ⏎Enter and Tab⇥, that affect the text.

 Some word processing programs put codes on the screen to symbolize such actions, but having all those codes among your text can get confusing. WordPerfect hides its codes, without odd symbols scattered around. You can see the codes through Reveal Codes. Handling the codes in this way provides two major benefits:

- There are no confusing symbols on your screen.

- Longer codes (instead of short but cryptic symbols) can be used, which fully explain the action taken.

Revealing and Hiding Codes

To see the codes, press Alt+F3 or F11, or select Reveal Codes from the View menu. The Reveal Codes area appears on the bottom of your screen. It not only shows the text in the document but also each code entered. You can repeat the procedure to hide the codes again.

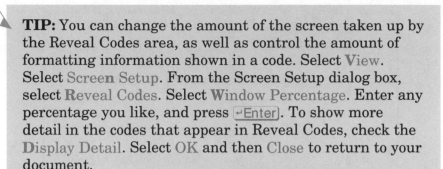

TIP: You can change the amount of the screen taken up by the Reveal Codes area, as well as control the amount of formatting information shown in a code. Select View. Select Screen Setup. From the Screen Setup dialog box, select Reveal Codes. Select Window Percentage. Enter any percentage you like, and press ⏎Enter). To show more detail in the codes that appear in Reveal Codes, check the Display Detail. Select OK and then Close to return to your document.

Let's look at an example. The address entered for a letter, along with Reveal Codes, is shown in Figure 2.2. When Reveal Codes is active, the regular document text is shown at the top of the screen. The same text, along with the codes, appears at the bottom of the screen. Notice these codes:

```
[HRt]
[Lft Tab]

[SRt]
```

Figure 2.2
The address shown in the document screen and Reveal Codes.

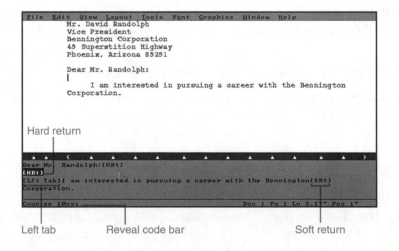

The [HRt] code stands for a hard return. This shows each place you have pressed Spacebar) or ⏎Enter). The [Lft Tab] code shows where Tab ⇥) was pressed. The [SRt] code stands for a soft return.

This code is automatically entered by WordPerfect and shows where each line wraps around.

It's a good idea to use Reveal Codes when you want to insert, cut, or copy text. This way, you can make sure the codes are handled properly along with the text. Reveal Codes is also helpful in tracking down formatting problems. If your text looks odd, you may have entered a code inadvertently. Just check Reveal Codes, and remove any unwanted codes.

Saving Time

If you want to use the same codes over and over in a document, it may be faster to enter the keystrokes for the codes, and then copy the codes and paste them where you want them. For example, you may enter complex settings for a particular line or graphic that you want repeated. Instead of setting up the line or graphic from scratch later in the document, copy the code, and paste it later in the document. (Copy, paste, line, and graphic functions are all covered in later chapters. For now, just keep this possibility in mind.)

Inserting and Deleting Codes

Although codes appear to be made up of individual characters, each is really a single entity. Therefore, you cannot edit codes the same way that you edit regular text. You can, however, insert and delete codes very easily.

- **To insert a code**, move the cursor to the desired location, and then perform the action. The action's code appears. For example, to insert a [HRt] code at the cursor location, just press ⏎Enter.

- **To delete a code**, move the cursor on the code, and press Del.

To close the Reveal Codes screen, press Alt + F3 again, or select Reveal Codes from the View menu.

Insert and Typeover Modes

When you type text in Insert mode, existing text moves to the right to make room. Insert mode is WordPerfect's default mode. For example, in the sample letter shown in Figure 2.3, the phrase As I mentioned in our conversation today, was inserted after the tab and before the beginning of the existing sentence. The original sentence moved to the right and wrapped around automatically.

Figure 2.3

In insert mode, old characters move over to make room for newly typed ones.

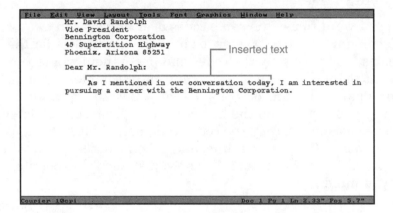

If you prefer, you can switch to Typeover mode, which means any characters you type will replace existing characters. Take a look at the letter in Figure 2.4. The word mentioned in As I mentioned . . . was typed over with the word discussed. Notice that the word Typeover appears in the bottom left corner of the screen.

To switch between insert mode and typeover mode, just press [Ins]. This key is called a *toggle key* since pressing it toggles you between one option and another.

Figure 2.4

In typeover mode, old characters are replaced by new ones.

Typeover prompt

TIP: Text that you type will never replace a code, even in typeover mode. The code will simply move over, just as text does in insert mode. The text is inserted before the code.

Deleting Text

One way to get rid of text one character at a time is to press `◆Backspace`; the character, space, or code to the left of the cursor is deleted as the cursor moves left. On many computers, you can hold down `◆Backspace` to continue deleting text until you release the key.

TIP: When you delete text, it is removed from the document. Because text in WordPerfect may contain codes as well as text and spaces, it is a good idea to turn on Reveal Codes when you delete. This way you can be assured that you're deleting precisely the text, spaces, or codes you want to delete.

Another way to delete text is to use the Delete key, marked `Del` on many keyboards. When you press `Del`, the character, space, or code at the cursor is deleted and all remaining text on the page moves one position to the left. As with `◆Backspace`, holding down `Del` on most keyboards repeats the delete. Your cursor stays in position, and the text to the right of the cursor moves to the left as you delete one character at a time.

TIP: To delete a word at the cursor, press `Ctrl`+`◆Backspace` or `Ctrl`+`Del`. To delete to the beginning of the word, press `Home` `◆Backspace`. To delete to the end of the word, press `Home` `Del`. To delete from the cursor to the end of a line, press `Ctrl`+`End`. To delete to the end of the page, press `Ctrl`+`PgDn`.

Deleting a Sentence, Paragraph, or Page

You can delete a sentence, a paragraph, or a page quickly with WordPerfect. The command to use is a little misleading because it is called Move. Bear with me; soon you will see the delete option behind this command.

Put your cursor anywhere on the sentence, paragraph, or page you want to delete. For example, suppose you want to delete Vice President in Figure 2.5. You would position the cursor somewhere on the Vice President line. Then you press Ctrl+F4, or choose Select from the Edit menu. Options to move a sentence, paragraph, or page appear.

Figure 2.5
Deleting a sentence.

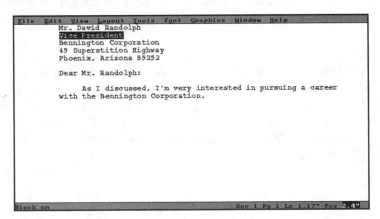

Select the option that identifies the amount of text you want to delete. For our example, you would choose to delete the paragraph, because the title line is a paragraph.

TIP: Each hard return signifies the end of a paragraph. It is easier to see where paragraph breaks occur if you turn on Reveal Codes.

When you select the paragraph option, the entire sentence is highlighted, as shown in Figure 2.5. If you used Ctrl+F4, the Move dialog box gives you these additional options:

Cut and Paste

Copy and Paste

Delete

Append

Delete and Append

Choose **De**lete. The highlighted text and spaces are deleted. If you use the Edit menu, no dialog box appears. Just press Del.

The following Quick Steps summarize the process.

Deleting a Sentence, Paragraph, or Page

1. Put the cursor on a sentence, paragraph, or page to delete.

Your cursor marks the text.

2. Press Ctrl+F4, or choose Select from the Edit menu.

The options to delete a sentence, paragraph, or page.

3. Choose Sentence, Paragraph, or Page.

The sentence, paragraph, or page is highlighted. If you press Ctrl+F4, the dialog box presents you with **D**elete as an option. If you used the menus, no dialog boxes appear.

4. If you used Ctrl+F4, select **D**elete from the dialog box. Otherwise, press Del.

The text is deleted.

Blocking Text

To delete, cut, or copy large pieces of text, you'll need to *block* the text. Blocking text is sometimes referred to as selecting text. Blocking text marks the characters, spaces, and codes you want to manipulate. Blocking text is also used to perform other functions such as centering a large amount of text. You can block text using the keyboard or with a mouse.

Once you have blocked the text, you must immediately perform the delete, cut, or copy action.

TIP: Always use Reveal Codes when you are blocking text that may involve codes. That way you won't miss important formatting in your selection.

Blocking Is Important

Many WordPerfect functions can be performed on blocked text. Delete and copy were used as examples earlier in this chapter, but there are many more. These include, but are by no means limited to:

- Character size and appearance
- Spell checking
- Printing
- Saving
- Searching
- Replacing
- Line spacing
- Indenting

You can use blocking whenever you want to perform a given action on a block of text, no matter what that action is.

The following Quick Steps detail how to block text with your keyboard.

Blocking Text with the Keyboard

1. Put the cursor on the first character, space, or code in the block.

   The cursor is in the position you choose.

2. Press Alt + F4, or select Block from the Edit menu.

   Block on appears in the lower left corner of the screen.

3. Move the cursor to the last character of the block of text.

   The text is highlighted. For example, Figure 2.6 shows the Reveal Codes screen when Vice President is blocked. Notice the code [Block] appears before Vice President.

4. Perform the desired operation (such as delete, copy, or cut).

   The text in the block is altered, and Block on disappears. In Figure 2.7, the block was deleted.

Note that in Figure 2.7, where Vice President was deleted, the code was deleted as well as the text, since the cursor was after the return code at the end of the line.

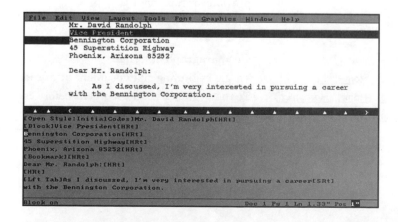

Figure 2.6
Blocked text.

Figure 2.7
Result of deleting a block of text.

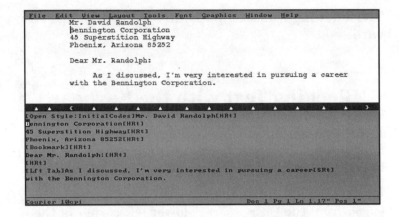

If you press Alt + F4 to block text and then decide you don't want to block text, just press Alt + F4 again. Block on disappears, and you can continue with other activities.

Table 2.1 lists other options to quickly block text once Alt + F4 is pressed.

Table 2.1
Other Keyboard Blocking Techniques

Press	To block
← or →	One character at a time
↑ or ↓	A line at a time
End	To the end of a line after codes
Home	To the beginning of a line before codes
PgUp or PgDn, then continue pressing PgUp or PgDn	To the top or bottom of the screen, then screen by screen
Alt + PgUp or PgDn	To the first line of the previous or next page
Ctrl + ← or →	One word at a time
Ctrl + ↑ or ↓	One paragraph at a time
Home, Home, ↑	To the beginning of a document after codes
Home, Home, Home, ↑	To the beginning of a document before codes
Home, Home, ↓	To the end of a page after codes

You can also block text with a mouse. Point to one end of the text to be blocked. Hold down the left mouse button, and drag the insertion point to the other end of the selected text. As you drag, the selected text appears highlighted. When you have the correct text highlighted, release the left mouse button. The text is selected. The following Quick Steps cover how to block text with the mouse.

Blocking Text with a Mouse

1. Point at one end of the text to highlight.	One end is identified.
2. Press the left button, and drag the mouse to the other end of the text.	The text block is highlighted.
3. Release the left button.	The text is blocked.
4. Perform the desired operation on the block.	The blocked text is manipulated.

TIP: If you decide you no longer want the text blocked, just click outside the blocked area.

Canceling Deletions (Undelete)

With WordPerfect, you can afford an "oops" when you delete, as long as you restore the text before making three other deletions. WordPerfect stores the most recent three deletions.

To restore a deletion, follow these steps:

1. Place your cursor where you want the text to be restored.

2. Press Esc, or select Undelete from the Edit menu. When you undelete, you can select among the last three deletions and restore your selection. On the Undelete dialog box, these options appear: **R**estore and **P**revious Deletion.

3. Continue to select Previous Deletion until the deletion you want to restore appears. Then, select Restore to insert that deleted text.

There's a limit to the amount of deleted material WordPerfect can remember. If you make an unusually large deletion, WordPerfect will ask you:

```
Delete without saving for Undelete?(Y/N)
```

This message means you can go ahead and make your deletion, but it won't be available to be undeleted through Esc or Undelete from the Edit menu.

Quick and Dirty Copying or Moving

Some WordPerfect users like to employ the Esc option as a "quick and dirty" way to move or copy text. For example:

1. Delete the text you want to move or copy.

2. Position the cursor in the first location to move or copy to. (If you are copying, you will copy the text back into its original position then continue to make other copies.)

3. Press Esc to cancel the delete.

4. Identify the text you want, and restore it.

Because a deletion is stored even after you have restored it, you can repeat a restoration as often as you like. This gives the effect of copying the text.

Using Undo

Undo can be used to reverse your last editing activity, such as entering or deleting text, adding graphics, or changing format-ting. Text is restored to its original location. To undo, press [Ctrl]+[Z], or select Undo from the Edit menu.

> **TIP:** Don't confuse Undo with Undelete. They are very different. Undo reverses your last editing action and restores text to its original position. When you use Unde-lete, any of the last three deletions can be restored at the current location of the cursor.

You might want to turn off Undo to save memory or disk space or speed up some WordPerfect operations. To turn Undo on or off, press [Shift]+[F1], or select Setup from the File menu. Select Environment. Place a check in the **A**llow Undo check box to turn Undo on, or remove the check to turn Undo off.

> Not all activities can be undone with Undo. Complex activities like sorting, generating lists, and the like cannot be undone. To protect your original work before performing a complex editing activity, save your file before performing the work. Then, if you don't like the result, you can "undo" the work by exiting your file without saving it and then using the original, saved file. Learn more about saving documents in the next chapter.
>
> CAUTION

Moving Text

You can move a sentence, paragraph, page, or block of text at a time. When you move text, it is cut (removed) from the location from which you are moving and is pasted (inserted) in the location to which you are moving. To move an unusual amount of text (not a complete sentence, paragraph, page), you can block the text with Alt + F4 , or select Block from the Edit menu before starting the move procedure.

The quickest way to move blocked text is to first block the text, then select Cut and Paste from the Edit menu, or press Ctrl + Del . This prompt appears:

```
Move cursor; press Enter to retrieve.
```

Place your cursor on the character before which the text should be inserted. (It's okay to edit text along the way; just don't press ↵Enter until you are ready to retrieve the moved text.) Press ↵Enter to retrieve the cut text at the new cursor location.

You can also move text by sentence, paragraph, or page, rather than blocking it first. To begin the move, press Ctrl + F4 . Options for moving a Sentence, Paragraph, and Page appears. Once you have selected the amount of text to move, select Cut and Paste when it appears. Move your cursor, and press ↵Enter to retrieve the text.

Using the menus involves a few more keystrokes but is equally effective. Choose Select from the Edit menu. The options for moving a Sentence, Paragraph, and Page appears. Select the amount of text to move. Use the Edit menu to choose Cut and Paste. (Alternatively, you can press Ctrl + F4 , and choose Cut and Paste.) Move the cursor, then press ↵Enter .

Moving a Block of Text

1. Use Alt + F4 , or select Block from the Edit menu to block the text.

   The blocked text is highlighted.

2. Press Ctrl + Del or choose Cut and Paste from the Edit menu.

   The highlighted text disappears. A prompt appears.

3. Put the cursor where the text should go, and press ⏎Enter.	The text is moved.

Moving Unblocked Text

QUICK
STEPS

1. Press Ctrl+F4, or choose Select from the Edit menu.	Options to move a sentence, paragraph, or page appear.
2. Choose whether you want to select a sentence, paragraph, or page.	The text is selected.
3. If you used the Edit menu, press Ctrl+F4.	The Move dialog box appears.
4. On the Move dialog box, select Cut and Paste.	The highlighted text disappears. A prompt appears.
5. Put the cursor where the text should go, and press ⏎Enter.	The text is moved.

Copying Text

You can copy a sentence, a paragraph, a page, or a block of text. When text is copied, the original remains in place. A copy is stored by WordPerfect for you to retrieve at another spot in the document.

The process for copying text is very similar to moving text. If you want to copy a block of text, highlight it with Alt+F4. Select

Copy from the Edit menu. With your cursor in the location where you want the text copied to, press ⏎Enter.

Like the move feature, you can copy by block, sentence, paragraph, or page with a longer process. Follow the next Quick Steps.

Copying Blocked Text

1. Mark the block with Alt+F4, or select **Block** from the **Edit** menu.

The blocked text is highlighted.

2. Press Ctrl+Ins.

The highlight on the text disappears. A prompt appears.

3. Put the cursor in the spot to copy text, and press ⏎Enter.

The text is copied.

Copying Unblocked Text

1. Press Ctrl+F4, or choose **Select** from the **Edit** menu.

Options to move a sentence, paragraph, or page appear.

2. Choose whether you want to select a sentence, paragraph, or page.

The text is selected.

3. If you used the **Edit** menu, press Ctrl+F4, otherwise, go on to the next step.

The Move dialog box appears.

4. On the Move dialog box, select Copy and Paste.	The highlighted on the text copied disappears. A prompt appears.
5. Put the cursor where the text should go, and press ↵Enter.	The text is copied.

CAUTION

The results of copying, deleting, or moving can be surprising. Whenever you work with copying or moving text and you are unsure of the outcome, save your work first with F10. Then, if the outcome isn't as you expected, your original document is available. Chapter 3, "Saving, Opening, and Exiting Documents," covers the ways to save a document.

FYI
IDEAS

Hidden Uses for Copying

There are several "hidden uses" for copying. Copy to reduce mistakes, to repeat a line of text for a particular effect, or to streamline formats represented by codes.

Copying is handy when you want to make sure you don't introduce mistakes when existing information is repeated in a document. For example, it is easy to incorrectly enter an address, account numbers, or an unusual proper name. Assuming the first occurrence of the text is correct, copy that occurrence to ensure the other occurrences are correct, as well. Just enter the first occurrence of the text, then copy the text as needed.

Copying can also be useful to repeat a particular line of text. For example, if you are making a sign-in sheet for a

continues

continued

meeting, create a line with tabs and underlines for the
necessary information (such as name, phone number, and
so on). Then copy that line to add a second line. Next, copy
two lines to make four lines and so on until you create a
complete page of underlines for the sign-in sheet. This
approach saves you the tedium of setting up the tabs and
underlines in each line and ensures all lines are the same
length.

Finally, save time and use copying to repeat format or
other settings held in codes. For example, you might have
created a particular tab setting, then changed to a new tab
setting later in the document. If you want to go back to the
original tab setting later, just copy the `[Tab Set:]` code to
the desired spot.

Creating Another New Document

WordPerfect allows you to have more than one document available at a time. Documents are stored in document windows. As mentioned earlier, how to handle the up to nine windows possible is covered in detail in Chapter 12, "Managing Documents." For now, just be aware that the New command on the File menu can be used to create a new document without having to exit other documents. To create a new document, select New from the File menu. WordPerfect takes you to a new, blank document window. You can tell that you are in a new document by looking at the right text in the status line. For example, if you had one document available and then chose New, the status line reflects:

```
Doc 2 Pg 1 Ln 1" Pos 1"
```

This indicates you are in document 2 or the second document window.

You can move between the two documents by pressing ⇧Shift+F3. For more information about handling multiple documents, see Chapter 12, "Managing Documents."

Ways to Save Your Work

- Press `F10`, or select Save As from the File menu.
- Select Save from the File menu.
- Press `F7`, or select Exit from the File menu.
- Press `Home`, `F7` or select Exit wp from the File menu.

Rules for Saving

- Name a document to save using up to eight characters (optionally followed by a period and a three-character extension).
- Get in the habit of saving your work often.

Opening a Document

- Press `⇧Shift`+`F10`, or select Open from the File menu, and enter the path and file name.
- To select from existing documents, press `F5`, highlight the document, and select Open into New Document.

Retrieving a Document

1. Position your cursor where the document should appear.
2. Press `⇧Shift`+`F10` twice, or select Retrieve from the File menu, and enter the path and file name.

Using the File Manager to Open or Retrieve

1. If retrieving, position your cursor where the document should appear.
2. Press `F5`, or select File Manager from the File menu.
3. Enter the directory and select OK.
4. Select the file and Open into New Document or Retrieve into Current Doc.

Saving, Opening, and Exiting Documents

Once you have learned how to create a document, you will want to protect your document. The best way is to know how to properly save a document and exit the program. (Hint: turning the computer's power off is *not* the proper method of exiting the program!)

Why You Must Save Your Work

Save your work or you lose it. As you work on a document, it is stored in a temporary storage space called RAM, which is only available as long as there is power to the computer. When the power is cut off (even accidentally for a split second), the data in RAM is lost. When you save a document, you copy it from RAM to a disk, where the data remains safe even when the power is off.

> **TIP:** Because accidents happen to disks, too, saving a document to more than one disk is your insurance that the document will be available, even if one disk is lost or damaged.

Nearly every computer user can tell you a story of working for hours or days on an important document but forgetting to save it, then losing the entire document when the power flickered or the wrong keys were accidentally pressed. Always take time to save your work. Develop these good habits:

- Periodically save your work as you go. That way, if the power to your computer fails, you will have a recent, complete version of your work. Any time you have entered edits that are significant (and that you wouldn't want to lose), save your work.

- Always save more than one copy of your document on more than one disk. Disks can be damaged or lost.

- Use WordPerfect automatic backup options. WordPerfect has options that automatically make copies of your most recent edits as you work. They're explained later in this chapter.

Choosing a Name for Your Document

Before you save a document, you must choose a unique name for it. Follow these guidelines.

Names can be up to eight characters long. If you enter a name longer than eight characters, WordPerfect automatically cuts off the characters beyond eight.

The eight-character name can be followed by a period and an extension of three characters. For example, a document might be named MYDOC123 with an extension of WPP. Its full name is MYDOC123.WPP.

When naming a document, you can use:

- Letters A through Z

- Numbers 0 through 9

- Special characters such as ! @ # $ % ^ & ( ) - _ ' { }

Some special characters cannot be used in file names because they have other specific purposes. They are:

* + = [ ] : ; " ~ < > ? / \ , (space)

Do not use a period in a file name because it will be mistaken for the divider between the name and the extension.

Each document must have a unique name. You can save the same document under many different names if you want multiple copies. It's a good idea to give a document a name that suggests the use of the document. Here are some examples:

LETDAVE1.WPP: The first letter to Dave.

LETDAVE2.WPP: The second letter to Dave.

IBBRPTV1.WPP: IBB Report, Version 1.

ME060893.WPP: Memo of 6/8/93.

File extensions are important because they help you distinguish among types of files. You'll notice that in these examples, I've assigned an extension of WPP to all my files. Use the same extension for all WordPerfect documents you create. By using an extension unique to only your WordPerfect documents, you will be able to identify WordPerfect documents when they are stored on a disk with documents created with other software.

Saving Your Work

Save your work as you go. Save every time you have performed edits you would hate to lose. Most users save their work every 15 minutes or so. Here's how to do it.

From the document, select Save from the File menu or press Ctrl + F12. A dialog box like the one shown in Figure 3.1 appears.

Figure 3.1
Dialog box to save a document.

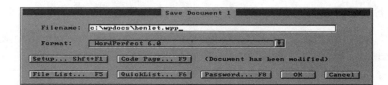

Type in the drive, path, and document name, if needed, and press ↵Enter. (The drive, path, and document name will appear automatically if the document has already been saved or retrieved.)

In this example, to save the letter to the Bennington Corporation, we use drive C:\WPDOCS as the directory (the default document subdirectory set up when WordPerfect is installed), and BENLET.WPP as the document name.

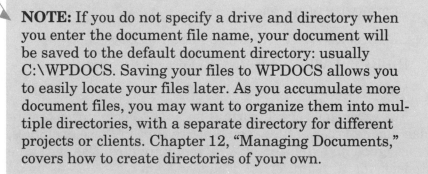

NOTE: If you do not specify a drive and directory when you enter the document file name, your document will be saved to the default document directory: usually C:\WPDOCS. Saving your files to WPDOCS allows you to easily locate your files later. As you accumulate more document files, you may want to organize them into multiple directories, with a separate directory for different projects or clients. Chapter 12, "Managing Documents," covers how to create directories of your own.

If this is the first time you are saving the document, this message appears as the document is saved:

```
Saving C:\WPDOCS\BENLET.WPP
```

You're done! If the document had already existed on disk, this message would have appeared:

```
Replace: C:\WPDOCS\BENLET.WPP?
```

Select the No button if you want to specify a new name (and then do so), or select the Yes button to replace the "old" version on disk. A similar message to this one appears as the document is saved:

```
Saving C:\WPDOCS\BENLET.WPP
```

The following Quick Steps summarize the process of saving a document.

Saving a Document

1. Select Save from the File menu or press `Ctrl`+`F12`.

   A prompt appears for the document name.

2. Type the drive, path, and document name, as necessary, and press `⏎Enter`, or select OK.

   The document is saved. If a dialog box with a Replace message appears, press Y.

Using Save As

After you've saved a document once, WordPerfect remembers its name and location and saves the new version on top of the old one each time you save. If you want to save the new version under a different name, or in a different location, use Save As instead.

To use Save As, press `F10`, or select Save As from the File menu. A dialog box identical to the one in Figure 3.1 appears. You can enter a new drive, path, and file name, and then press `⏎Enter`, or just press `⏎Enter` to keep the old name.

Creative Uses of Save As

If you need multiple versions of the same document, use F10 or Save As from the File menu to create them. Simply give each version a related name. For example, if you are working on a budget report and want to save three different versions each with a different organization, you could name them BRPTVER1.WPP, BRPTVER2.WPP, and BRPTVER3.WPP.

You can also use Save As to create a backup of a file. To do this, save the same document to multiple locations. For example, you may want to save to a floppy disk, as well as to your hard disk. First, save to your hard disk with F10 or Save As from the File menu. Then, use F10 or Save As from the File menu again, this time entering the path for the floppy disk drive. In effect, you have just created a floppy disk backup of the file on the hard disk.

Saving Documents in Other Formats

If you exchange work with other users of personal computers or send documents over the phone lines via a modem, you may need to put your document file in another format. You may also need to convert a different format into WordPerfect.

To convert a WordPerfect file to another format, just use the Save As command with an additional step. After pressing F10 or selecting Save As from the File menu, type in a name for the document that suggests its format. For example, while the last three characters of benlet.wpp suggests a WordPerfect document (if you used that convention), benlet.txt would suggest the file is saved in ASCII Text (Stripped) format for a modem transmission. Once the name is typed in, select the Format option and choose from one of the over 30 formats available. After selecting a format, continue with the Save As as usual.

Saving and Closing the Document

Instead of saving the document and continuing, you can save the document, and then:

- Close the document and exit WordPerfect

  or

- Close the document and work with a different document.

To do either of these things, follow these Quick Steps.

Saving and Closing a Document

1. Press F7, or select Exit from the File menu. | A dialog box appears asking for confirmation.

2. To save the document under a new name, select the Save As button. To save the document under the current name, select Yes. | A Saving message appears.

3. If you get the Replace message, press Y. | A Saving message appears.

4. When the Exit dialog box appears, follow the prompts to leave the document (and WordPerfect if no other document is active) or stay in the document (or WordPerfect). | The action is completed.

CAUTION Never turn off the computer while in Word-Perfect. This can damage your document or WordPerfect software. Always use Home, F7 or File Exit WP to leave WordPerfect. Turn off your computer only if you are at the DOS prompt.

Saving Part of a Document

You can save just a part of a document, if you want. This is useful when you want to delete the rest of the document. It is also useful when you want to place part of a document in a new document with a unique name. The result is to create a new document made up of a portion of the existing document. Follow these Quick Steps:

Saving Part of a Document

1. Use Alt+F4 or Block from the Edit menu to block the part of the document you want to save.

2. Press F10 or select Save As from the File menu.

   The Save Block dialog box appears.

3. Type in the name of the document, including any extension, and press Enter or select OK. (Include the drive and path designation, if necessary.)

   The blocked portion of the document is saved under the new name, and you are returned to your document.

Using Automatic Backup

If you regularly save your documents, they will be protected from power loss or system failure. To provide additional protection for the forgetful, WordPerfect has an automatic backup option. (You will still want to use **S**ave often in order to save your entire document.) There are two automatic backup functions:

- **Timed Document Backup:** The document on your screen is saved every 10 minutes or at time intervals you specify. It is saved in a temporary file. When you exit WordPerfect properly, all temporary files are deleted, but if the power is accidentally cut off, the temporary files remain, and you can often retrieve a portion of your work from them.

- **Original Document Backup:** When you save a document or exit WordPerfect, the last disk version of the document is saved in a file with a .BAK extension rather than replaced by the new version.

To set up automatic backup options, follow these Quick Steps.

Backup Options Setup

1. Press ⌖Shift+F1, or select Setup from the File menu.

Setup options appear.

2. Select Environment.

The Environment dialog box appears.

3. Select Backup Options.

The Backup dialog box shown in Figure 3.2 appears.

continues

continued

4. To use the Timed Backup feature, check the Timed Document Backup option. Then after Minutes Between Backups, identify the new timed backup interval in minutes.

The Timed Backup options are set.

5. Select Back Up Original Document (.BK!) on Save or Exit to create backup files of each document. Or deselect the option to omit keeping backup files for each document.

The option is set.

6. Select OK twice, and then Close to return to your document.

Figure 3.2
The Backup dialog box.

Recovering an Automatically Saved Document

If you use timed backup and you experience a computer power failure, you may be able to recover the timed backup copy of your document. Just restart WordPerfect. The Backup File Exists dialog box (see Figure 3.3) automatically appears if there any files available to recover.

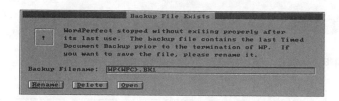

Figure 3.3
*The Backup File
Exists dialog box.*

Select **R**ename to rename the file, and save it for future reference; **D**elete to delete the backup file; or **O**pen to open the file. If you select **R**ename, type in the file name after Backup File-name, and press ⏎**Enter**. The backup file is renamed and WordPerfect is available for use.

Don't give the recovered backup file the same name as the original file in which you were working, in case the original file is a more complete copy.

CAUTION

Open and Retrieve: What's the Difference?

Opening or retrieving a document refers to moving the document from disk storage into RAM (and onto the screen). *Opening* a document inserts it into a new document window. *Retrieving* a document inserts it into the current document window, which may or may not include existing text. You can also *view* a document without either opening or retrieving it.

TIP: If you've used WordPerfect, version 5.1, you'll be happy to know that your documents are automatically converted to WordPerfect 6.0 format when you open them in WordPerfect 6.0.

Opening a Document

To open a document, follow these steps.

Opening a Document

1. Press ⇧Shift+F10, or select **O**pen from the **F**ile menu.

The Open Document dialog box appears.

2. In the Open Document dialog box, enter the path and file name of the document you want to open.

3. Make sure the Method radio button on the dialog box is set to Open into New Document. Select OK.

The document is opened into a "blank" document window.

TIP: In step 2, click on the down arrow in the Filename text box to see the default directory. If the drive and directory is what you want, only enter the document name.

If you don't know the name of the file, you can either select the File Manager button (or press F5) or the QuickList (or press F6) on the Open Document dialog box. Identify the drive, directory, and select the file you want to open. There is more information about selecting files with File Manager later in this chapter.

Retrieving a Document

You can retrieve a document into a "blank" document window or into an existing document. Follow these Quick Steps.

Retrieving a Document

1. Place your cursor where you want the document to be inserted.

2. Press ⇧Shift+F10 twice or select **R**etrieve from the **F**ile menu.

   The Retrieve Document dialog box appears.

3. Type in the path and document name. You can use the File Manager button (or F5) or the QuickList (or F6) to select the path and file.

   The file you enter can be something like this: `C:\WPDOCS\BENLET.WPP`

4. Ensure the Method radio button is set at Retrieve into Current Document, and select OK.

   The document is retrieved.

In the example just shown in the Quick Steps, `C:` shows the drive, `WPDOCS` is the directory, and `BENLET.WPP` is the document name. The directory and document name are always set off by backslashes.

When you type in a file name to open or retrieve a file and select OK, you may see a dialog box with a message like this:

continues

continued

`File not found - `*`filename`*

This means that one of the following has occurred:

- You have made a typographical error in the document drive, directory, or name.

- The information is incorrect.

- The file does not exist on the disk.

Whatever the reason, WordPerfect cannot match the information you provided with a document on the disk. If, after carefully checking your typing accuracy, you cannot determine the problem, it may be that you've forgotten the document name. Use the File Manager or QuickList to locate the document.

Using the File Manager to Open or Retrieve

Sometimes you'll want to retrieve a document whose name you don't remember. Or you'll attempt to retrieve a document by name and get a message like this:

`ERROR: File not found BENLET.WPP`

In either case, the File Manager can help you find your document. As seen earlier in this chapter, the File Manager is available via selecting the button after using Shift+F10 or the Open or Retrieve option on the File menu. You can also access the File Manager more directly. Read on to learn how.

Figure 3.4 shows the File Manager dialog box. It contains an alphabetical list with the document BENLET.WPP highlighted. To select from the list, use the arrow keys or a mouse to highlight the desired document name. The drive and directory for these files appears at the top of the screen. Selections you can make are shown at the side of the screen and numbered. Notice that **O**pen into New Document and **R**etrieve into Current Doc are the first two selections.

Open

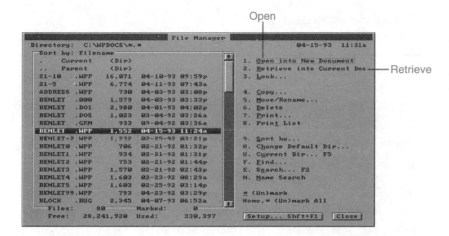

Figure 3.4
List of documents with BENLET.WPP highlighted.

To open or retrieve a document from the File Manager, follow these Quick Steps.

Using the File Manager to Open or Retrieve a Document

QUICK STEPS

1. Press F5, or select File Manager from the File menu.

The Specify File Manager List dialog box appears with the current directory, path, and *.* for file names (for example, C:\WPDOCS*.*).

2. Enter a new drive and directory, if necessary (keep the *.* notation in place of a document name), and select OK.

The File Manager dialog box appears, showing the contents of the drive and directory you entered. (See Figure 3.5.)

continues

continued

3. Highlight the document to be opened or retrieved, and then select **O**pen into New Document or **R**etrieve into Current Doc.

The document is opened or retrieved.

TIP: If you are sure about the document's first letter, or extension, or some other portion, you can narrow the search by specifying some parameter other than *.* for the document name on the Specify File Manager List dialog box . For example, if you remembered that the document started with D, you could use `D*.*`; if you knew the extension was WPP, you could use `*.WPP`.

From the File Manager dialog box, you can move to another directory. For example, on the screen shown in Figure 3.5, the Parent directory is highlighted. Parent directory is another name for the superior or higher directory. For example, the root directory `C:\` is the parent directory of `C:\WP60`. If you press `Enter` with the name of a directory highlighted, the files in it appear. You can then select files from this screen, or select Close to change your mind and exit the File Manager screen.

Figure 3.5

Parent directory highlighted.

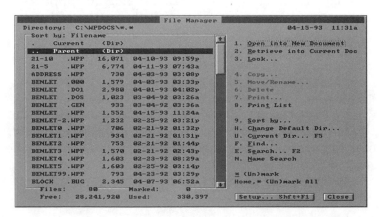

> Do not press ⏎Enter after highlighting a document in the File Manager unless you want the command selected on the right of the box to be executed for that file. Typically, Open into New Document is selected so pressing ⏎Enter has the same effect as making that selection.

CAUTION

Saving Typing with Retrieving

If you have a document on the screen, and then retrieve another document, the document you are retrieving is placed into the current document at your cursor position. This feature is useful for loading boilerplate text into a document. *Boilerplate* is any text that you use over and over, such as an address or greeting.

Let's say you've typed a letter and want to retrieve the boilerplate text: Sincerely, Barbara J. Wiley from a document called CLOSE.WPP. Just position the cursor at the end of the letter and use File Retrieve.

Changing the Designated Drive and Directory

The drive and path that WordPerfect automatically brings up is the *default* directory. That is, if no other drive and directory path is indicated, the default directory is used.

Each time you save a document, open or retrieve a document, or search for a document, the default directory name appears when you press F5 or select File Manager from the File menu. If you consistently use a drive and path different from the one that automatically appears, you can enter that drive and path to come up each time until you exit WordPerfect. Follow these Quick Steps.

Changing Designated Drive and Directory

1. Press F5, or select File Manager from the File menu.

The Specify File Manager List dialog box appears.

2. In the Directory text box, press = (equals sign).

The Change Default Directory dialog box appears.

3. Change the drive and directory as desired and select OK.

The Specify File Manager List dialog box appears with the new drive and directory.

4. Select Cancel.

The new drive and directory are set.

TIP: Here's another method to change the default drive and directory. Press F5, select OK, select Change Default Dir, type in the new path, select OK twice, and then select Close.

The next time you use the File Manager, open documents, retrieve documents, or save a document, the new default is used if no other drive or directory is designated.

Permanently Changing the Default Directory

The method to change the default directory described earlier is good for that WordPerfect session only. In other words, when you exit WordPerfect and re-enter, the old default drive is in place. To make the change last even after exiting and re-entering WordPerfect, follow these steps.

1. Press ⇧Shift + F1 or select Setup from the File menu, then select Location of Files.

2. Select Documents, and enter a new drive, path, and directory as the default.

3. Select OK.

Viewing a Document Without Retrieving It

If you have many documents or a number of documents with similar names, the File Manager listing can be confusing. Opening or retrieving the incorrect document and then repeating the process to find the correct one is time consuming and frustrating. WordPerfect gives you a way to avoid this situation by letting you look quickly at a document before retrieving it. The following Quick Steps detail how to view a document without retrieving it.

Looking at a Document

1. Press F5, or select File Manager from the File menu.

   In the Specify File Manager List dialog box, the current directory, path, and *.* for file names appears.

2. Type in drive, path, and file name information, if needed, and select OK.

   A screen listing the documents appears.

3. Highlight the document name to be opened or retrieved, and then select Look.

   The document appears on-screen along with the Look at Document dialog box (Figure 3.6).

4. View the document, using the arrow keys to scroll (move backward or forward) its text.

5. Select OK when done.

   You're returned to the File Manager dialog box.

The Look at Document dialog box (Figure 3.6) gives you more options. Some will be familiar to you and others are covered in more depth in later chapters. For now, just take a look at what's available. **N**ext and **P**revious lets you look at the next or previous document in the File Manager list. This is really handy when you want to skim document contents quickly. You can also **O**pen the document, **D**elete a document, mark the document with an asterisk (*), **S**croll down through the document, or Search the document using F2.

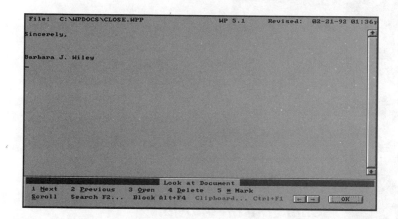

Figure 3.6
The Look at Document dialog box.

If you are running WordPerfect from the Shell program that comes with WordPerfect, you can also Block text (Alt+F4) from the Look screen and copy it to the Clipboard (Ctrl+F1). For more information about Shell, see the WordPerfect Shell User's Guide that came with WordPerfect.

Selecting Paper Size and Type

1. Press `⇧Shift`+`F8`, and select Page, or select Page from the Layout menu.
2. Select Paper Size/Type.
3. Select the paper size and type.

Changing the Margins

1. Press `⇧Shift`+`F8`, and select Margins, or select Margins the Layout menu.
2. Enter the new margin settings.

Changing the Unit of Measure

1. Press `⇧Shift`+`F1`, or select Setup from the File menu.
2. Select Environment.
3. Select Units of Measure.
4. Select Display/Entry of Numbers.
5. Enter the type of measurement.
6. Identify the unit for the Status Line Display.
7. Select OK twice.

Types of Alignment

- Left Indent: Press `F4`, or select Layout, Alignment, Indent→.
- Right and Left Indent: Press `⇧Shift`+`F4`, or select Layout, Alignment, Indent→←.
- Hanging Indent: Select Layout, Alignment, Hanging Indent.
- Back Tab: Press `⇧Shift`+`Tab⇆`, or select Layout, Alignment, Back Tab.
- Center Text: Press `⇧Shift`+`F6`, or select Layout, Alignment, Center.
- Flush Right: Press `Alt`+`F6`, or select Layout, Alignment, Flush Right.

4

Margins and Alignment

Where the text appears on the page is easy to control with WordPerfect. You can set the size of margins, control the size and type of paper, use a variety of units of measure, and print "sideways" on a page. You can also control the alignment of the text in relation to those margins. This chapter will teach you how to do all these things and more.

What's a Margin?

Margins are the amount of space from the edge of the paper to the text in your document. WordPerfect allows you to determine the size of your margins document by document. You can change margins within a document as often as you like.

NOTE: Most WordPerfect users like to use inches to measure the margins. You may enter other units of measure, however, as described at the end of this chapter.

Controlling margins is a two-step procedure:

- **Enter the paper size and type.** This tells WordPerfect the dimensions of your paper. (A printer must be selected before you can do this. Typically, a printer is selected when WordPerfect is set up. If not, see Chapter 6, "Printing.")

- **Identify the size of each margin:** top, bottom, left, and right. WordPerfect will leave the margins as "white space."

WordPerfect fits your text in the space that remains. As a result, the line length of the text you enter is determined by the measurement from the left to the right of the page minus the left and right margins. The number of lines that WordPerfect fits on a page is determined by the length of the page minus the top and bottom margins.

Figure 4.1 shows the edge of the paper, the margins, and the area for WordPerfect to use for the letter.

Figure 4.1

Margins are the areas between the paper edge and the document area.

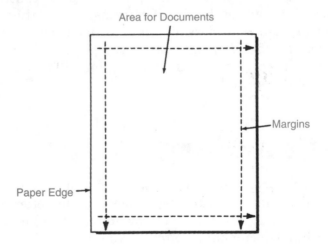

Setting the Paper Size and Type

The first step in controlling margins is to set the paper size and type. WordPerfect's default (the setting that comes already established in WordPerfect) is 8.5" x 11" paper of standard weight. This default handles most common stationery and computer or typing paper, as well as common envelope sizes. For most work, you won't need to change the default settings. In fact, you will only need to change the paper size or type if you happen to use paper of a size other than 8.5" x 11" or a different type, such as envelopes, letterhead, transparencies, labels, or cardstock.

TIP: More than one Paper Size/Type can appear in a document. The code affects all the text that follows. You could, for example, have a letter on a page and then switch the Paper Size/Type to include the envelope on the next page. Just make sure the correct paper or envelope is available when printing.

To specify a different paper size or type for the document you are creating, follow these Quick Steps.

Changing the Paper Size or Type

1. Place the cursor at the top of the page for which the new paper size will take effect.

2. Press ⇧Shift + F8 and **P**age. Or select **P**age from the **L**ayout menu.
   The Page Format dialog box appears.

3. Select Paper **S**ize/Type.
   The Paper Size/Type dialog box shown in Figure 4.2 appears.

continues

---

continued

4. In the Paper Size/Type dialog box, highlight the Paper Name.

The details describing the paper appear at the bottom of the dialog box.

5. Choose **S**elect, OK, and then Close.

You are returned to your document.

A code like the following one is placed in your document and may be viewed using Reveal Codes with the cursor on the code:

```
[Paper Sz/Typ:8.5" x 11",Standard]
```

Figure 4.2

The Paper Size / Type dialog box.

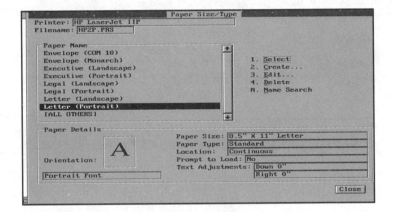

Understanding Landscape Printing

All printers print in portrait orientation (such as a typical business letter where text is parallel to the short edge of the paper or envelopes that are fed with the wide edge first). Yours may also allow for landscape orientation (or sideways, with print parallel to the long edge of the paper). This is useful for printing text that needs to be in wide columns or envelopes fed with the narrow edge first. Figure 4.3 illustrates these two print orientations: a typical letter and an envelope that accompanies the letter.

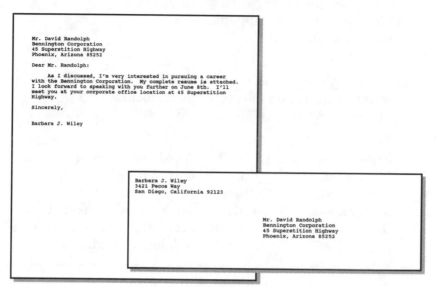

Figure 4.3

Portrait printing for a letter, and landscape printing for its envelope.

TIP: Landscape printing is useful for a document such as a list or chart with a left margin that is too long to fit on an 8.5" wide sheet of paper. If you landscape print the document, more text is allowed on a line.

Setting Margins

In WordPerfect, the right, left, top, and bottom margins are all set to 1" unless you change them. The following Quick Steps detail the procedure.

Setting Document Margins

1. Place the cursor where you want margin settings. To affect the entire document, place the cursor at the beginning.

   The code will be inserted at this spot.

2. Press ⇧Shift+F8, and select **M**argins, or select **M**argins on the **L**ayout menu.

   The Margin Format dialog box appears.

3. Enter all settings for **L**eft Margin, **R**ight Margin, **T**op Margin, and **B**ottom Margin, select OK, and then Close.

   A code is inserted in your document like this: `[Lft Mar:2"]`, and the margins take effect. Text occurring after this code will be affected.

Figure 4.4 shows our letter with 1" margins, WordPerfect's default. Figure 4.5 shows the letter after the margins have been changed to 2". The lines in the letter are shortened and wrap around to accommodate the new, wider margins.

Here's a quick guide to printing on letterhead paper. Measure how far down from the top of the letterhead the text must fall. Set your top margin at this measure. Measure how far from the bottom of the letterhead text should stop for a pleasing effect. This is the length to enter for your bottom margin.

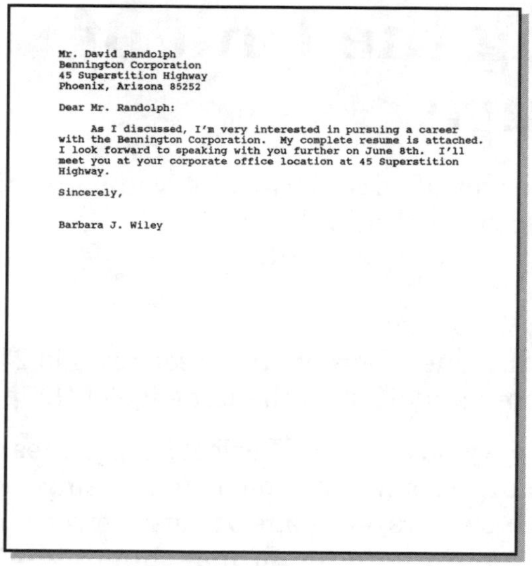

Figure 4.4
A letter with 1"
margins.

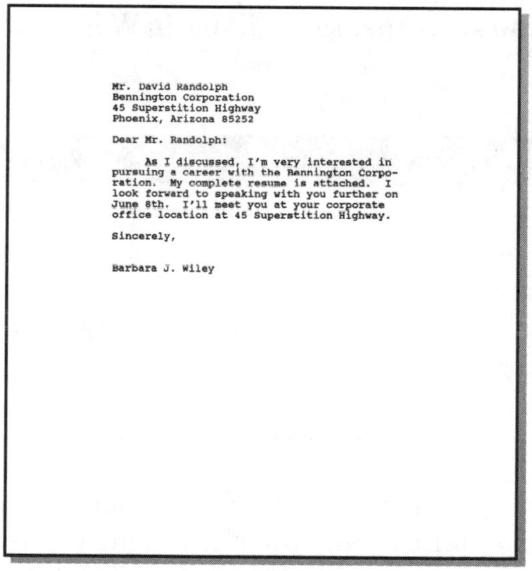

Mr. David Randolph
Bennington Corporation
45 Superstition Highway
Phoenix, Arizona 85252

Dear Mr. Randolph:

As I discussed, I'm very interested in pursuing a career
with the Bennington Corporation. My complete resume is attached.
I look forward to speaking with you further on June 8th. I'll
meet you at your corporate office location at 45 Superstition
Highway.

Sincerely,

Barbara J. Wiley

Figure 4.5
A letter with 2"
margins.

Mr. David Randolph
Bennington Corporation
45 Superstition Highway
Phoenix, Arizona 85252

Dear Mr. Randolph:

As I discussed, I'm very interested in
pursuing a career with the Bennington Corporation. My complete resume is attached. I
look forward to speaking with you further on
June 8th. I'll meet you at your corporate
office location at 45 Superstition Highway.

Sincerely,

Barbara J. Wiley

Setting the Unit of Measure

The status line identifies the location of your cursor in inches. For example, these status line values:

```
Ln2" Pos 5"
```

indicate that the line where your cursor rests is 2" from the top edge of the paper and 5" from the left edge of the paper.

Most people who use WordPerfect keep inches as the default measure for margins and other measures. Using inches makes it easy to place characters on a page because you can pick up a ruler and measure margins or other format options.

You may have a special need for another unit of measure, though. The units of measure available in WordPerfect are shown in Table 4.1.

Table 4.1
WordPerfect's Measurement Unit Options

Measurement	Notation
Inches	i or "
Centimeters	c
Millimeters	m
Points	p
1200ths of an inch	w
Units for lines and columns	u

When you type in a type of measurement (such as a margin entry), you can enter the amount of the measurement followed by its notation. If inches is set as the default, the entry is converted to inches. For example, if you want a right margin to be 4 centimeters, enter 4c in the Right Margin field. If the default is inches, WordPerfect converts 4 centimeters to 1.58" and displays that amount. Points is a special measurement used with particular type styles. If you are using a laser printer, you may want to use points occasionally.

WordPerfect allows you to control the measure used on menus along with the measure displayed in the status line. You can change the default for the unit of measurement.

To change the unit of measurement default, follow these steps:

1. Press ⇧Shift+F1, or select Setup from the File menu.

2. Select Environment.

3. From the Environment dialog box, select Units of Measure. The Units of Measure dialog box appears.

4. Select Display/Entry of Numbers.

5. Enter the type of measurement (i or ", c, m, p, w, or u).

6. Identify the unit for the Status Line Display (typically the same unit).

7. Select OK twice and then Close to return to your document. The new defaults are set.

Overview of Aligning Text

Though you can align text the old-fashioned way (using the Spacebar to place characters), there are faster methods yielding more pleasing results that are more easily altered. A few key presses allow you to indent, center, justify, and place text flush right. You can also control line spacing and set initial codes to create your own default settings to save more time when new documents are created.

Indenting Text

Using WordPerfect's indent feature is different from using the Tab↹ key. When you use Tab↹, only the first line is indented. When you use WordPerfect's indent feature, you indent the entire paragraph. You can type as many lines as you want and then press ↵Enter to end the paragraph (and the indention).

There are four types of indents you can use in WordPerfect:

- **Left indent:** The entire paragraph is indented a certain distance from the left margin.

- **Left and right indent** (*double indent*)**:** The entire paragraph is indented a certain distance from both the left and the right margins.

- **Hanging indent:** The first line of the paragraph aligns with the left margin but subsequent lines are indented.

- **Back tab:** The text does a "reverse indent," aligning to the left of the current setting, even further left than the left margin.

These four types of indents are shown in Figure 4.6.

Figure 4.6
Text with indents.

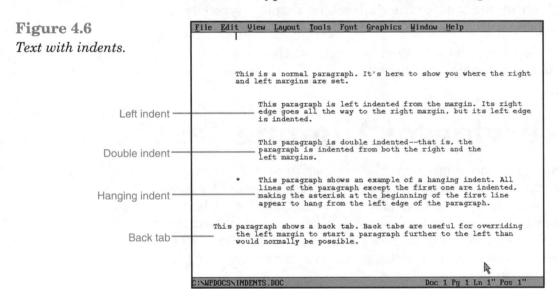

All indents align with the tab settings in WordPerfect. For now, you should work with the default tab settings. (Chapter 7, "Tabs, Columns, and Tables," covers how to change tab settings.)

The following Quick Steps summarize each kind of indent.

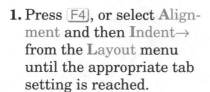

Setting the Left Indent

1. Press F4, or select Alignment and then Indent→
from the Layout menu
until the appropriate tab
setting is reached.

An Indent code is embed-
ded in your text. The
[Lft Indent] code appears.

2. Type in the text you want
indented.

The text automatically
aligns with the last indent
entered.

3. Press ↵Enter to complete
the indent.

Any text in the paragraph
immediately following the
indent is indented.

Setting Left and Right Indents

1. Press ⇧Shift+F4. Or
select Alignment and
Indent→← from the
Layout menu.

The code [Lft/Rgt Indent]
is placed in your text.

2. Type in the text.

The text aligns along the
left tab setting and an
equal distance from the
right side.

3. Press ↵Enter to complete
the indent.

The text in the paragraph
following the Left/Right
indent is set in from the
left and right margins.

Setting a Hanging Indent

1. Select Alignment and then Hanging Indent from the Layout menu.

The codes [Lft Indent] [Back Tab] are placed in your text.

2. Type in the text.

3. Press ⏎Enter.

The first line remains at the left margin and subsequent lines are indented.

Setting a Back Tab

1. Press ⇧Shift+Tab↹. Or select Alignment and then Back Tab from the Layout menu.

The code [Back Tab] is placed in your text.

2. Type in the text.

3. Press ⏎Enter.

The first line moves to the left, possibly past the left margin.

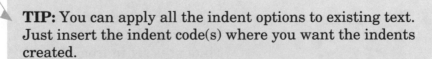

TIP: You can apply all the indent options to existing text. Just insert the indent code(s) where you want the indents created.

Centering Text

The old-fashioned way of centering text was to count the number of characters in the text to be entered, subtract that number from the number of characters possible in the line, divide by two, space in that number of spaces, and begin typing. This tedious operation is replaced with the ⇧Shift+F6 key combination or by selecting Alignment and Center from the Layout menu. A code is placed in your text, and the cursor goes to the center of the line. Type in your text. As you type, the characters move to the left or right to even the centering. When you are done, press ↵Enter. To remove centering, delete the code.

You can also center existing text or multiple lines. Just block the text and press ⇧Shift+F6. Or select Alignment and Center from the Layout menu. The text in the block is centered, and the appropriate codes are inserted.

Placing Text Flush Right

Figure 4.7 demonstrates the Flush Right option on the date line. You don't have to count text or backspaces; just press Alt+F6, or select Alignment and Flush Right from the Layout menu. The cursor goes to the right margin. As you type in the text, it moves left. Press ↵Enter, and the text aligns with the right margin. Press ↵Enter to stop typing text that is flush right.

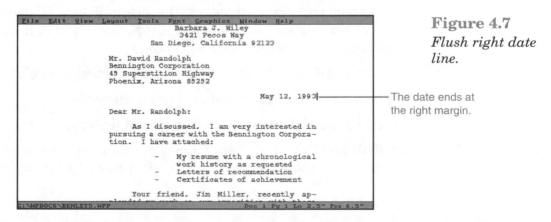

Figure 4.7
Flush right date line.

The date ends at the right margin.

To make existing text flush right, place the cursor before the text and press Alt + F6 .

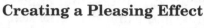

Creating a Pleasing Effect

You can create a pleasing effect by combining tab, indent, center, and flush right capabilities. For example, you may want a top of a report to have the name of the report indented on the left, the date in the center, and the page number flush right. Just indent, type in the name of the report, center and type in the date, flush right, and enter the page number. The effect might look like this:

```
Bennington Report        January 10, 1992             Page 6
```

Later chapters in this book cover how to make such a heading appear on each page of the document and how to have WordPerfect consecutively page number for you. For now, just consider how you can combine alignment capabilities for the result you want.

Justifying Text

Justification refers to the even horizontal alignment of text between margins in a document. When you enter a justification code, all the text that follows that code will be justified until a new justification code is entered or the original one is deleted. WordPerfect's default is called *full justification*, which lines up text evenly between right and left margins.

WordPerfect makes five types of justification possible:

- **Left justification:** Used for most documents.

- **Right justification:** Used for special layouts.

- **Full justification:** Text aligned evenly between the left and right margins, except for the last line of paragraphs.

- **Full justification, all lines:** Text aligned evenly on left and right margins including the last line of paragraphs. Some people find that this option puts too much white space in the last line of paragraphs.

- **Center justification:** Text centered on every line for special layouts.

Figure 4.8 illustrates an advertising piece with each type of justification applied.

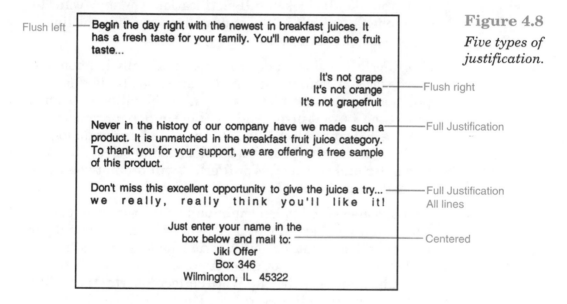

Flush left

Begin the day right with the newest in breakfast juices. It has a fresh taste for your family. You'll never place the fruit taste...

It's not grape
It's not orange
It's not grapefruit
— Flush right

Never in the history of our company have we made such a product. It is unmatched in the breakfast fruit juice category. To thank you for your support, we are offering a free sample of this product.
— Full Justification

Don't miss this excellent opportunity to give the juice a try...
we really, really think you'll like it!
— Full Justification All lines

Just enter your name in the
box below and mail to:
Jiki Offer
Box 346
Wilmington, IL 45322
— Centered

Figure 4.8
Five types of justification.

To justify text:

1. Place the cursor where you want to begin the justification.

2. Press ⇧Shift+F8, and select Line. The Line Format dialog box appears where you can select Justification. Or choose Justification from the Layout menu.

3. Select the type of justification you want. A justification code is placed in your document at the cursor location.

To remove or change the justification, delete the first code or enter the code for another type of justification.

TIP: To quickly change justification, you can use the Justification list on the Ribbon. Access the Ribbon via the View menu, and select Ribbon. The justification set at the current cursor position appears and can be changed.

If you like the look of full justification, you may want to hyphenate words at the ends of lines to make the lines appear more uniform.

WordPerfect is smart enough to automatically hyphenate words for you; simply turn hyphenation on. To do this, position the cursor where you want hyphenation to begin. Select the Layout menu and the Line option, or press ⇧Shift+F8, and select Line. On the Line Format dialog box, check the Hyphenation check box, and select OK. As you enter and edit text, WordPerfect will prompt you when it needs some help in hyphenating a word.

You can also type hyphens manually. One way is to use the - (minus) key. The hyphen will be in place even if you edit your document, however, it may no longer be at the end of a line. This is not good. A preferable course is to use a soft hyphen (like the one WordPerfect inserts) that will "disappear" when the word is no longer at the end of a line. To do this, hold down Ctrl and press - (the hyphen key). The hyphen only appears on your screen when the word is at the end of a line.

Controlling Line Spacing

Line spacing refers to the number of lines between each printed line. The default is single spacing. However, you can double or triple space or space by any number of lines you want to enter. For fine detail in your layouts, you even can enter fractions of a line in the setting. The following Quick Steps detail how to set line spacing.

Setting Line Spacing

1. Press ⟨⇧Shift⟩+⟨F8⟩ and Line, or select Line from the Layout menu.

   The Line Format dialog box appears.

2. Select Line Spacing, and enter the number of lines.

3. Select OK and Close to return to your document.

   A code like this is placed in the document: [Ln Spacing:1.2]. The text following the inserted code follows the new line spacing setting.

If you will be printing on a preprinted blank form, line spacing can be frustrating if the lines don't "line up." Avoid frustration by creating a text document first. Enter the line spacing and place a character followed by a hard return on each line (numbering the lines 1, 2, 3, 4, is a good way to go). Print your test documents on a plain piece of paper. Hold it and the preprinted form up to the light to see how close you've come. Adjust the line spacing, if needed, and repeat the process until you see that the lines will match.

Initial Codes

When you looked at the codes in your documents, you may have noticed one that got there all by itself and cannot be deleted. That code is [Open Style:InitialCodes]. This code stands for the defaults, which you can change. For example, you may want to change WordPerfect's default of single line spacing. If you typically use double spacing, you may get tired of having to set the line spacing for each document. You can change this initial code (and others) through the Initial Code option.

You can change the initial codes in one of two ways, depending on the outcome you want. The Initial Codes Setup affects all documents you create. The Document Initial Codes affect only the document you are using at the time.

To set either type of initial codes, follow these steps:

1. Press Shift+F8, and select Document. Or select Document from the Layout menu.

2. On the Document Format dialog box, select Document Initial Codes or Initial Codes Setup.

3. Enter new line spacing or any other codes you want as the new default(s). You can also delete or edit existing codes.

4. Save the entries by pressing F7, selecting OK, and then selecting Close.

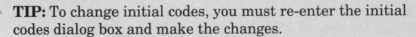
TIP: To change initial codes, you must re-enter the initial codes dialog box and make the changes.

You should be aware that when you use initial codes (instead of just putting the codes in the document screen), the codes are stored on your computer, not in the document. If you give the file to someone else, the codes will not transfer. If you need to send the file "plain" to someone via modem, this can be a benefit, but if you need to give the file to someone complete with its fancy formatting, you'll need to put the codes in the document manually rather than using initial codes.

TIP: Any codes you enter directly in the body of a document take precedence over the Initial Codes.

If a document is retrieved into another document, the initial codes for the retrieved document are not retrieved along with it; instead, the document takes on the initial codes of the document into which it was retrieved.

Change the Size or Appearance of Characters

1. Press `Ctrl`+`F8`, or select the Font menu.
2. Select the size or appearance attributes that you want.

Change the Initial Font for All New Documents

1. Press `⇧Shift`+`F7`, or select Print from the File menu.
2. Choose Select, highlight the printer, and select Edit.
3. Choose Font Setup, and then select Initial Font.
4. Select Font, and choose the font that you want.

Change the Font for a Document

1. Press `⇧Shift`+`F8`, and select Document. Or select Document from the Layout menu.
2. Select Initial Font.
3. Select Font, and choose the font that you want.

Change the Font for Part of a Document

1. Press `Ctrl`+`F8`, or select Font from the Font menu.
2. Select Font.
3. Highlight the font that you want.

Display the Ribbon

1. Select Ribbon from the View menu.

Chapter 5

Giving Characters a New Look

Changing the look of your characters can add emphasis, interest, and clarity to your documents. The available character enhancements possible depend not only on WordPerfect but on your printer. Not all printers are capable of printing all of WordPerfect's character options. You can experiment with your printer to see which results are possible.

WordPerfect's **F**ont menu controls the look of your characters. With the Font options, you can control the typeface, type size, placement, and appearance of characters. Figure 5.1 shows some of the options available.

Figure 5.1
Some effects you can create through the Font menu.

Bold:	Bold can **emphasize**.
Underline:	Underline can add <u>interest.</u>
Double Underline:	Double underline can add <u>even more interest</u>.
Redline:	Redline text can set off text.
Strikeout:	~~Strikeout~~ does the same.
Shadow:	Shadow is another look.
Small Caps	SMALL CAPS gives this appearance.
Superscript:	Use superscript in footnotes.[2]
Subscript:	Subscript is good for text like H_2O.
Fine:	Fine text is one size.
Large:	Large is another
Extra Large	Extra large is another.
Some type styles:	Helvetica, Roman, Courier

This chapter will explain the various options available and will provide tips for using character appearance effectively.

Fonts

Your printer has specific typeface and type size capabilities. On many printers, it is possible to print in more than one typeface and more than one type size. For example, Figure 5.2 shows a sample résumé printed with the headings in a large Helvetica font and the body in a smaller Roman font.

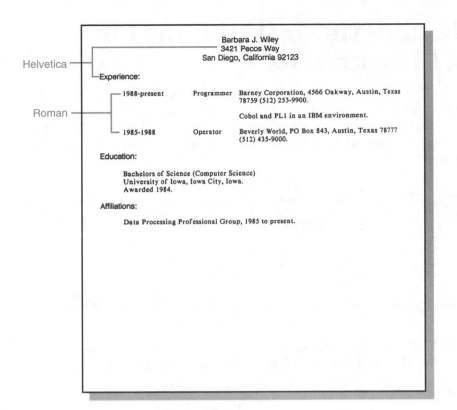

Helvetica

Roman

Figure 5.2
*A résumé with
Helvetica and
Roman fonts.*

NOTE: *Typeface* refers to the general "family" of the letters. Helvetica is an example of a typeface; Times Roman is another. (This book is printed in New Baskerville.)

Text in a particular typeface can appear in a variety of type sizes, from about 6 points (6/72 of an inch) to as high as 70 points or more, depending on the printer's capabilities. For our purposes, the term *font* means the combination of typeface and type size.

WordPerfect offers several ways to control fonts. Each method allows you to choose from the same list of fonts, which is determined by the fonts available to your particular printer.

Setting the Initial Font for All Documents

An initial font can be set up to be the default for all documents you create. This font is used unless another font is specified using one of the other two methods (discussed later in this chapter). To change the initial font (in the printer file), follow these Quick Steps.

QUICK STEPS

Setting the Initial Font

1. Press ⇧Shift + F7 , or select **Print** from the **File** menu.

   The Print dialog box appears.

2. Choose **Select**.

   The Select Printer dialog box appears.

3. Highlight the printer from the list, and choose **Edit**.

   The Edit Printer Setup dialog box appears.

4. Choose **Font Setup**.

   The Font Setup dialog box appears.

5. Choose **Select Initial Font**.

   The Initial Font dialog box appears (see Figure 5.3).

6. Select the **Font**, **Size**, and make the initial font good for **All New Documents**. Select **OK** three times and **Close** twice to return to your document.

   The initial font for all documents is set.

Figure 5.3
Initial Font dialog box.

Setting the Document Initial Font

If you want to use a different font for one document, you don't need to change the initial font for all documents to do it. You can set the document initial font. The document initial font setting is valid for the active document only and overrides the default font. To set the Document Initial Font, use these Quick Steps.

Setting the Document Initial Font

1. Press ⇧Shift+F8, and Document. Or choose Document from the Layout menu.	The Document Format dialog box appears.
2. Choose Initial Font.	The Initial Font dialog box appears.
3. Select the Font, Size, and make the initial font good for Current Document Only. Select OK.	The initial font for the document is identified.
4. Select OK and Close to return to your document.	The initial font for the current document is set.

Changing the Font Within a Document

You're not limited to one font in a document; you can use as many fonts as your printer supports, changing as often as you want. Just use the Font option, which overrides any fonts set through the other methods. It inserts a font code at the beginning and end of the selected text, just as when you select a size or appearance attribute (as you will see later in the chapter). You can use Reveal Codes (F11) to see it.

To change the font, use the following Quick Steps.

Changing the Font
Within a Document

1. Place your cursor where the font is to change. (All text from the cursor forward will be affected.) *Or* block the text to be changed. (Only the blocked text will be affected.)

2. Press Ctrl+F8, or select Font from the Font menu.

   The Font dialog box appears (see Figure 5.4).

3. Select Font.

   A drop-down list of available fonts appears.

4. Select a font from the list. Select Size from the available drop-down list, along with any other selections desired.

   The settings for the font are in place.

5. Select OK.

   You are returned to your document. A code for the font is placed in the document.

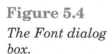

Figure 5.4
The Font dialog box.

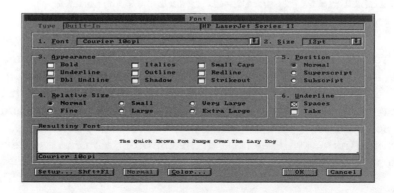

When you choose a font (using any of the methods we've discussed), you are defining a combination of typeface and type size to be the "normal" font for your document. Once you have defined what is "normal," you can concentrate on creating variations to make your document more interesting.

Controlling Character Size

No matter how carefully you choose your font, there will be times when you want to make certain words larger or smaller. WordPerfect offers several options for changing the size of text for emphasis, aesthetic appeal, or simply to fit more text on a page.

WordPerfect offers an easy way to change the size of selected text without messing up your font selection: it lets you change the size attribute of text. This is different from changing the size of a font.

Font size is measured in points. There are 72 points in an inch. When you change font size, you change from one point size to another. That's what you did when you were setting the font in the preceding section.

In contrast, when you change the size attribute of text, you don't specify a point size; you specify, in words, how you want the size to change. For example, you might specify "very large." When you do this, WordPerfect examines the size of the currently selected font and multiplies its size by a fixed percentage to determine how big "very large" would be in comparison to it. You can use the following words to change the size attribute: Fine, Small, Large, Very Large, and Extra Large.

NOTE: The dialog box that displays the size choices also displays options for superscript and subscript. These are not really size attributes, but rather position attributes. They are discussed in the next section.

TIP: Some fonts are scalable, and the size can be controlled with the Relative Size feature. Not all printers support scalable fonts.

To assign a size attribute to already-typed text, use the following Quick Steps.

Selecting Font Size for Existing Text

1. Use Alt+F4 and the arrow keys, or select **B**lock from the **E**dit menu to block the text you want to alter.

    The text is highlighted.

2. Press Ctrl+F8, and choose **R**elative Size.

    The size attributes become available.

3. Select the size attribute you want, and select OK.

    Codes reflecting your selection are placed in your document on either side of the selected text.

To change the size of text you are about to type, follow these Quick Steps.

Selecting Font Size for New Text

1. Press Ctrl+F8, and then choose **R**elative Size.

    The size attribute choices are made available.

2. Select the desired size and OK, and return to your document.

A code for the size appears in Reveal Codes.

3. Type the text.

4. Press Ctrl+ F8 again, and choose **R**elative Size and then **N**ormal. Or press the right arrow key to move past the end code for the font size.

The size attribute is set back to normal (the size of your document's font).

Figure 5.5 shows the various sizes available, as well as examples of superscript and subscript (covered in the next section).

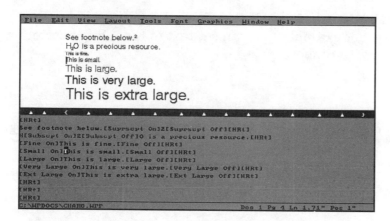

Figure 5.5

Character size and position attributes in both the document and Reveal Codes screen.

Controlling Character Position

In some instances, you may want characters to appear slightly above or below the normal line of text. WordPerfect offers two common options for positioning text:

Superscript: Superscript characters are placed somewhat above the line of normal text. Text in superscript is often used for footnotes and formulas. Most printers are capable of printing superscript text.

Subscript: Subscript characters are placed slightly lower than the line of text. Formulas often require subscripted text. Common printers can handle this option.

You set subscript or superscript exactly the same way that you set size attributes (see the preceding section). You can either set it for existing text or for new text, just as you can with size attributes. Briefly, press Ctrl+F8, or select Font from the Font menu. On the Font dialog box, select Position, and select Superscript or Subscript.

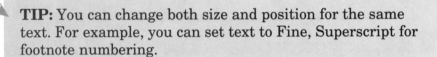

TIP: You can change both size and position for the same text. For example, you can set text to Fine, Superscript for footnote numbering.

Altering the Appearance of Characters

NOTE: *Appearance*, as WordPerfect uses it, means the presence or absence of attributes such as bold, italic, underline, redline, and strikeout.

WordPerfect's appearance options have something for everyone. Figure 5.6 shows some of the appearance options you can select. The options available are:

Bold: Bold text is heavier than normal text. Usually, bold text is displayed on-screen as brighter or in a different color than other text.

Underline: Text may be printed with a single underline. For underlines to be continuous across spaces, select Underline from the Font dialog box and Spaces. The alternative is Tabs for continuous underlining across tabs. Select neither and underlining will stop at spaces and tabs.

Double underline: Text may be printed with two underlines. Some printers do not handle this option. If your printer does, it can give your documents an unusual touch.

Italics: If your printer handles italic text, you can introduce a typeset quality to your documents. Use it sparingly to emphasize key words or phrases. Use it throughout invitations or announcements to give them an elegant appearance.

Outline: This special style is useful as an attention-getter, although many printers do not handle the style.

Shadow: This creates a shadow effect by offsetting a character from itself. Shadow is effective for use in flyers and advertisements.

Small Caps: Regardless of whether you enter the text in upper- or lowercase letters, the text is printed in small uppercase (capital) letters.

Redline: This option is often used to display edits that should be reviewed. Text to be added can be shown in redline.

Strikeout: When showing edits made to a document, you can use strikeout to illustrate text to be removed.

Figure 5.6
*Examples of
character
appearance
options.*

Normal
Bold
<u>Underline</u>
<u>Double Underline</u>
Italics
Shadow
SMALLCAPS
Redline
~~Strikeout~~

TIP: The appearances may also be selected directly from the Font menu. If you are entering a single appearance, it may be faster to use the menu. Also, some appearances have shortcut keys. Press `F6` for Bold, `F8` for Underline, `Ctrl`+`I` for Italics, and `Ctrl`+`N` for Normal.

The process for changing an appearance is similar to that for changing a size attribute. The following Quick Steps detail the procedure for existing text.

Setting Appearance Attributes for Existing Text

QUICK STEPS

1. Use Alt + F4, or select **Block** from the **Edit** menu to block the text you want to alter.

   The text is highlighted.

2. Press Ctrl + F8, or select **Font** from the **Font** menu.

   The Font dialog box appears.

3. Select **Appearance**.

   The options become available.

4. Select the appearance attributes desired and select OK.

   Codes are placed in your document before and after the text block.

After the appearance is set, codes are placed around the text in your document. Figure 5.7 illustrates the document and Reveal Codes screen for the appearances in Graphics mode. If you have a color monitor, redline appears in red.

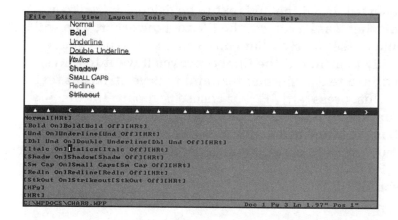

Figure 5.7
Appearances in the document and in Reveal Codes.

To change the appearance for text you are about to enter, press Ctrl + F8, or select **Font** from the **Font** menu. Select

Appearance on the Font dialog box, choose the appearances you want, and then choose OK. Type the text. Select a different appearance, or press the right arrow key to move beyond the ending appearance code.

As with size choices, you can combine appearances, or you can combine size and appearances. For example, you can select Very Large Bold Italic text. Just make the necessary selections.

TIP: With WordPerfect, you can block text and convert it to uppercase, lowercase, or initial caps. (Initial caps changes the first letter in each word to a capital letter.) Block the text to convert, including the punctuation, and press ⇧Shift+F3. Identify whether you want the result in Uppercase, Lowercase, or Initial Caps.

Redline and strikeout have a nifty bonus. When you use them to edit files, you can later strip the strikeout text from the document automatically. First, enter text to be inserted in redline and text to be deleted in strikeout. You can then pass a copy of the file to a coworker, who will be able to see clearly what edits you made. When you're ready to print out the final copy, you'll want to convert redlined text to normal text and remove strikeout text. To do this, press Alt+F5, or choose Compare Documents from the File menu. Choose Remove Markings. On the Remove Markings dialog box, select Remove Redline Markings and Strikeout Text, and choose OK. (If you chose to Remove Strikeout Text Only, the redline markings would still be in place.)

Additional Fonts

If your printer comes with only a few fonts, you're not stuck. There are several ways to get extra fonts to use in WordPerfect. One method, WordPerfect's graphic fonts, is free and requires only that your printer be capable of printing graphics. (Nearly all printers except daisywheel models can do this.) Other options are cartridges and fonts that you can buy separately from WordPerfect.

WordPerfect's Graphic Fonts

With WordPerfect, you're not limited to the fonts that come with your printer. WordPerfect comes with additional graphic fonts that can be used to print on printers that support graphics.

To add a graphic font to your list of available fonts, follow this process. Press ⇧Shift+F7, or select Print from the File menu. On the Print dialog box, choose Select. From the Select Printer dialog box, choose Edit. From the Edit Printer Setup dialog box, select Font Setup. On the Font Setup dialog box, choose Select Graphics Fonts. Mark the fonts to use with an asterisk (*), and select OK. Return to your document.

The available fonts were set up by WordPerfect when the printer was installed. Each font has a different look. When you use the font, the look appears on the Font dialog box. You will want to experiment with your printer to see the printed result.

Font Cartridges and Soft Fonts

Many printers, particularly laser printers, will print additional fonts (combinations of typefaces and sizes) that you purchase separately as a cartridge (that plugs into the printer) or as software that you install on your computer (also called downloadable fonts or soft fonts).

If you have a cartridge installed, you need to tell WordPerfect what cartridge you want to use. If you have soft fonts installed, you need to indicate where (in what directory) your soft fonts are stored and which fonts you want to use. Do this using the following steps:

1. Press ⇧Shift + F7 , or select Print from the File menu.

2. On the Print dialog box, choose Select to go to the Select Printer dialog box.

3. Highlight the printer from the list, and choose Edit.

4. Check the Directory for Soft Fonts. Enter the drive, path, and directory of soft fonts (if any).

5. Choose Font Setup.

6. On the Font Setup dialog box, choose Select Cartridges/ Fonts/Print Wheels to display the font sources.

7. Highlight a source to use, and select Edit to go to the Select Fonts dialog box shown in Figure 5.8. The same dialog box shows you what fonts may be built into your printer (you cannot make changes in these). It also identifies the number of cartridges or print wheels your printer handles and the space available for soft fonts.

8. If you selected Soft Fonts, the Font Groups dialog box appears. Highlight the group of soft fonts you want, and select Edit.

Figure 5.8

The Select Fonts dialog box for soft fonts.

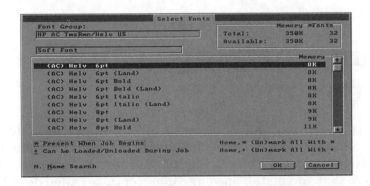

9. Highlight the cartridge, font, or print wheel to use.

NOTE: You can only select the number of cartridges that your printer will handle or number of soft fonts that consumes the available space.

10. Follow the prompts to select * (Present When Job Begins) or + (Can be Loaded/Unloaded During Job). For soft fonts, if you use the * option, you must choose Initialize Printer in the Print dialog box every time you turn on your printer. Use the + option if you want WordPerfect to load and unload the soft fonts during the print job.

Repeat the steps, as needed, to set up all fonts. If you set up soft fonts with an asterisk (*), don't forget to run the Initialize Printer option every time you turn on your printer. To do this, press ⇧Shift + F7 , or select Print from the File menu. On the Print dialog box, select Initialize Printer.

The steps given here are the basic ones for selecting a cartridge or soft font for use. Dealing with cartridges and soft fonts can become very complex. If you run into trouble, consult your WordPerfect Reference or a more advanced book.

CAUTION

Using the Ribbon

The Ribbon (Figure 5.9) can be used to quickly access options to affect the size and appearance of text in a document. The settings are effective for the current document only. You must have a mouse to use the Ribbon.

If the Ribbon is not displayed, select Ribbon from the View menu. To set up the Ribbon so it always displays, press Ctrl + F3 .

Choose the Setup button (or ⬆Shift+F1), or select Screen Setup from the View menu. On the Screen Setup dialog box, select Ribbon from the Screen Options group.

The ribbon can be used to change the font and point size. It can also be used to affect options that will be discussed in more depth in later chapters, such as viewing the size of a document, changing the paragraph level in an outline, changing the number of columns, and changing text alignment. Figure 5.9 explains the purpose of each of the Ribbon's buttons.

Figure 5.9
The Ribbon.

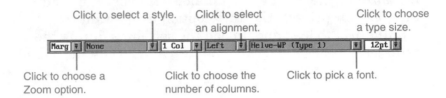

WordPerfect Characters

WordPerfect Characters are characters that are not available on your keyboard. You can print out these special characters if you have a graphics printer or if you have a font that contains the characters.

WordPerfect Characters include diacritics (for phonetic values such as accent e (é) and tilde n (ñ)). To use one of the over 1,500 characters available:

1. Position your cursor where you want the character, and press Ctrl+W, or select WP Characters from the Font menu. The WordPerfect Characters dialog box appears.

2. Type in the number of the character set containing the character you want.

3. Type in a comma (,).

4. Enter the number of the character to create.

5. Select Insert.

For example, suppose you want an e with an accent over the e. You would press Ctrl+W. On the WordPerfect Characters dialog box, type in 1,41 and select Insert. The é appears on your screen.

Special Characters include ANSI characters and IBM PC Extended Characters such as boxes, lines, and other symbols. To use either, simply hold down Alt while typing the corresponding number on the numeric keypad (not the numbers across the top of your computer keyboard). Release Alt.

CAUTION

Not all graphic displays will show all characters possible through WordPerfect. Not all printers will print each character. Experiment with your display and printer to see what capabilities are available.

FYI
IDEAS

Create Unusual Effects

Combining keyboard characters or WordPerfect special characters with unusual fonts can create pleasing graphical effects. For example, you can use the IBM PC Extended Character Set circle (character 248) with a large font size for an unusual bullet for a bulleted list. Or you could use an extra small character size with multiple pipes (¦¦) on your keyboard for an unusual line style.

Select the Printer File to Use

1. Press ⟨⇧Shift⟩+⟨F7⟩, or select Print from the File menu.
2. Select Select.
3. Highlight a printer on the list.

Print a Document

1. Press ⟨⇧Shift⟩+⟨F7⟩, or select Print from the File menu.
2. Identify what you want to print (Full Document, Page, or Document on Disk to print a document on disk).
3. Select any other options, such as the Number of Copies.
4. Select Print.

Printing Part of a Document

1. Block the text to print.
2. Press ⟨⇧Shift⟩+⟨F7⟩, or select Print from the File menu.
3. Select Print.

Printing Your Work

For most WordPerfect users, printing is the reason for all the rest of the work—getting a paper copy to be mailed or presented. This chapter covers what you need to know to identify your printer to WordPerfect and print all or part of a document.

Setting Up Your Printer

When you installed WordPerfect, you identified the brand and type of printer you use. There are additional setup steps you can perform from within WordPerfect that help identify the printer.

Press ⇧Shift+F7, or select Print from the File menu. The Print dialog box shown in Figure 6.1 appears.

The currently selected printer is listed. If you are using only one printer and are not printing any fancy special effects, all you need to do is make sure that the name of the printer appears here.

If you installed more than one printer and need to change the printer selected, or if you need to set up options for fancy printing jobs (for example, using special fonts loaded from a disk), choose

Select. This displays the Select Printer dialog box, which shows you the printers that you have installed along with the name of the file WordPerfect uses to communicate with a particular kind of printer.

Figure 6.1
The Print dialog box.

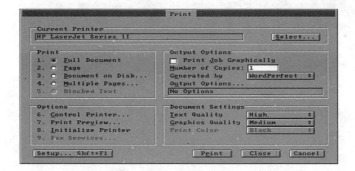

These are the options available from the Select Printer dialog box:

Select: To select a printer file other than the one highlighted.

Add Printer: To select other printer files that were installed. (See Appendix B for installation instructions.)

Edit: To see the Edit Printer Setup dialog box shown in Figure 6.2.

As you can see in Figure 6.2, you can edit:

Figure 6.2
The Edit Printer Setup dialog box.

The **D**escription of the printer (which is linked to the printer file).

The **P**ort (the connection point of the computer to the printer cable). Or you can identify the network port.

Whether you are using a **S**heet Feeder or another type of paper feeding device.

Whether you want the Printe**r** Configured for Color.

The **F**ont Setup (if your printer uses them; Chapter 5, "Character Formatting," covers more detail on this topic.) This option takes you to the Font Setup dialog box where you can change setting like the current initial font that will be used and what cartridges, fonts, or print wheels are used.

The Directory for S**o**ft Fonts that is the path to locate downloadable fonts (special character styles) or printer command files.

Delete: To delete a printer file you no longer need.

Copy: To copy a printer file for editing through 3 - Edit.

Information: To provide information important to setting print functions.

Update: To update the printer file when you get a new printer file (such as one delivered with a later version of WordPerfect).

Select Close to return to the document screen when you have set up the printer.

Previewing a Document

Some WordPerfect formats don't show up on the editing screen. For example, headers, footers, footnotes, special fonts, and other formats may not appear. Figure 6.3 shows a page break in a draft chapter of a book. A header is set up to print at the top of each page and include the book title, chapter number, and page number, but you can't see it in Figure 6.3's draft mode. Through Print Preview, the header placement can be seen (see Figure 6.4).

Figure 6.3
Pages in a document.

Double line indicates page break

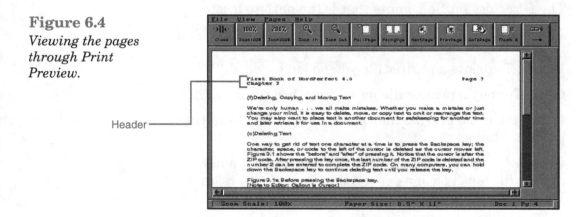

Figure 6.4
Viewing the pages through Print Preview.

Header

To use View Document, press ⇧Shift + F7 to display the Print dialog box. Select Print Preview. The following options are available from the **V**iew menu:

100% View: To increase the display by 100%.

200% View: To zoom in the maximum amount: 200%.

Zoom **I**n: To increase the display size.

Zoom **O**ut: To decrease the display size.

Zoom Area: To select the area to show in detail.

Select Area: To change the portion of the screen shown.

Reset: To restore the view and size.

Full Page: To display the entire page on the screen.

Facing Pgs: To see even numbered pages displayed on the left and odd numbered on the right.

Thumbnails: To display several pages at once.

Button Bar: To display (or not display) the Button Bar.

Button Bar Setup: To edit or change the options for the Button Bar.

These options are available from the **P**ages menu:

Go To Page: To Enter the page to which you want to go.

Previous Page: To view the page before the one displayed.

Next Page: To view the page after the one displayed.

You can move around using the scroll bar or buttons to go to a specific page, the previous page, or the next page. You can also use the mouse to drag a view box to a specific part of the page to magnify. Just point at the upper left corner of the area, hold down the button, and drag the box to mark the complete area to magnify.

TIP: If you want to stop lengthy redrawing of the screen and go on to other work, just press Esc.

When you are done viewing the document select Close and return to your document.

Printing a Document

Once you have set up the printer, make sure your printer is ready to print:

- Is the cable between the printer and computer secure on both ends?

- Is the printer turned on? If not, make sure it is plugged in, and then turn it on.

- Is the on-line light lit? If not, use the panel to put the printer on-line (which means it is ready to receive your document from the computer).

- Is there paper in the printer, and is it fed properly? If not, add paper and make sure it feeds smoothly into the printer.

When your printer is ready and the document to print is showing on your screen, press ⚈Shift + F7, or select Print from the File menu. The Print dialog box shown in Figure 6.1 appears.

To print the entire document, select Full Document. To print only the page on which your cursor rests, select Page. To print certain pages, select Multiple Pages. The **Multiple Pages** print option is covered in detail in Chapter 8.

To print more than one paper copy, select Number of Copies, and type in the number of copies you want.

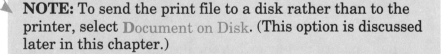

NOTE: To send the print file to a disk rather than to the printer, select Document on Disk. (This option is discussed later in this chapter.)

The following Quick Steps explain how to print a document.

Print a Document

1. With the document on the screen, press ⇧Shift+F7, or select Print from the File menu.

   The Print dialog box appears.

2. Select Full Document to print the entire document, Page to print the page the cursor is on, or Multiple Pages to print certain pages.

   The Print setting is complete.

3. Select Number of Copies and enter a number, if you want more than one copy.

   The number of copies appears.

4. Select Print.

   The document prints.

Printing on Different Paper Sizes and Types

You may have more than one paper size/type in a document. For example, you may have a letter to be printed on 8.5' x 11' paper followed by text to be printed on an envelope. In such a case, put the different paper sizes/types on different pages, and print each page separately by using ⇧Shift+F7, and then Page. This will give you time to hand-feed the paper to the printer or change the paper that is automatically fed through the printer.

Printing a Selected Part of a Document

In the previous section you saw how to use Page and Multiple Pages to print certain pages. But what if you want to print a few paragraphs, but not the entire page? Or a range of paragraphs that begins halfway down a page and ends halfway down another page?

You can block the text to print and press ⇧Shift + F7. Or select Print from the File menu. The Print dialog box Print setting is automatically set for Blocked Text. Enter the Number of Copies, and select Print.

Controlling the Print Operation

Sometimes after starting a print job, you can change your mind. To stop the printing, press ⇧Shift + F7. Or select Print from the File menu, and then select Printer. The Control Printer dialog box shown in Figure 6.5 appears. Notice that information about the Current Job (document being printed) appears at the top. Then a Job List (the list of waiting documents) appears. Notice that each waiting job is assigned a number. The options from which you can select appear in the lower right corner of the dialog box.

Figure 6.5

The Control Printer dialog box.

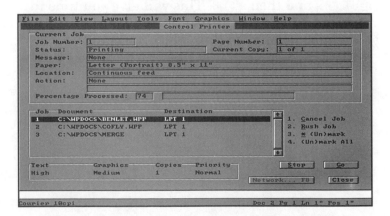

To change a print job, select one of these options:

Cancel Job(s): To cancel printing. Enter the number of the job (shown in the Job List on the screen).

Rush Job: To move a print job ahead of other documents waiting to be printed. Identify the number of the job to be printed next.

* (Un)mark: To unmark (remove the asterisk) or mark the selected job. Operations can be performed on marked jobs to speed your work.

(Un)mark All: To remove or add asterisks from all jobs.

There are also two buttons for your use. They are **G**o (to start the printer after it has been stopped) and **S**top (to stop the printer to adjust paper or perform another activity). Use **G**o to start the printer again.

Entering Tabs

1. Press `⇧Shift`+`F8` and Line. Or select Line from the Layout menu.
2. Select Tab Set.
3. On the Tab Set dialog box, enter an L, D, C, or R for new tabs, or use `Del` to clear old tabs. For dot leaders, type a period (.) over the tab setting letter.

Decimal Aligning Text

1. Press `Ctrl`+`F6`, or select Alignment Decimal Tab from the Layout menu.

Using Columns

1. Select `Alt`+`F7` and Columns. Or select Columns from the Layout menu.
2. Complete the definitions, and select OK.
3. Enter text in columns. Press `Ctrl`+`⏎Enter` to start a new column or to end a series of columns.
4. Select `Alt`+`F7` and Columns. Or select Columns from the Layout menu. Select Off.

Creating a Table

1. Press `Alt`+`F7`, select Tables and then Create. Or select Tables, and then Create from the Layout menu.
2. Enter the number of columns and rows, and select OK.
3. Select Close to go to document-editing mode. Re-enter the Table Edit dialog box any time.

Chapter 7

Using Tabs, Columns, and Tables

Arranging text on the screen can be streamlined with the use of tabs, columns, and tables. This chapter not only covers how to change WordPerfect's default tab settings but how to add a variety of tabs specific to your needs. You will also learn how to create columns and tables that can simplify working with text you want to remain together in columns or columns and rows.

Default Tabs

A tab in WordPerfect is like a tab setting on a typewriter, only better. At the basic level, you press Tab⇥ to indent the first line of a paragraph, or select F4 to indent the entire paragraph. The cursor moves to the next column marked by a tab setting, and a [Lft Tab] or [Lft Indent] code appears in your text. At a more sophisticated level, according to the type of tab setting you enter, you can align characters on the left, the right, by any character, or you can center the characters.

WordPerfect comes with defaults of tab settings every half inch. The sample resume shown in Figure 7.1 was created with WordPerfect default tab settings. (The tab settings are denoted by triangles on the Reveal Codes dividing line.)

Figure 7.1

Resume with default tabs.

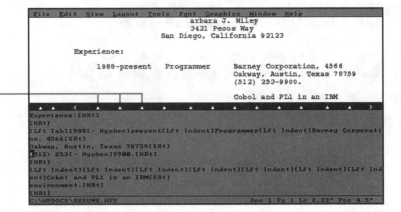

Triangles are tab markers ——

Notice that with tabs set every half inch, F4 had to be pressed several times to complete the entries. As you'll learn later in this chapter, you can set new tab settings anywhere you like. By entering your own tab settings, you can reduce the number of times you have to press Tab↹ or F4.

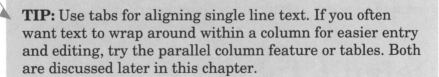

TIP: Use tabs for aligning single line text. If you often want text to wrap around within a column for easier entry and editing, try the parallel column feature or tables. Both are discussed later in this chapter.

Tab Types and Settings

WordPerfect uses four types of tabs:

- Left
- Decimal

- Center

- Right

The fund-raising activities included on the resume, shown in Figure 7.2, illustrate each type of tab setting. A description of each type follows.

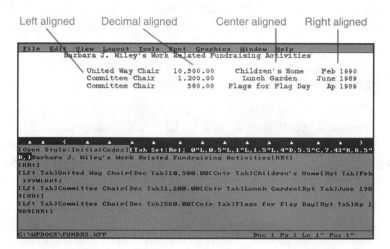

Figure 7.2
Types of tab settings.

Left Tab

The left tab setting is the default used by WordPerfect. When you use a left tab setting and begin typing, the text is entered one space to the right of the tab setting. The [Lft Tab] code is placed in your text. In Figure 7.2, the titles (such as Committee Chair) are aligned under the standard left tab setting.

Decimal Tab

You set a decimal tab to align text (usually dollar amounts) on a decimal point. When you press Tab⇄, the [Dec Tab] code is entered into the text. Text you type in is entered to the left of the decimal tab until you press the decimal point (a period). Then the text is entered to the right. This feature is especially helpful when you want to enter columns of financial figures, as in Figure 7.2, where the money raised is aligned under the decimal point.

Center Tab

The center tab is used to center text under the tab setting. As you type, the text is centered automatically, like when you use the ⟨Shift⟩+⟨F6⟩ or select Justification and Center from the Layout menu. Setting a center tab setting enables you to enter text before and after the centered text on the line, as shown in Figure 7.2. You can also see that the [Cntr Tab] code is entered into the text.

Right Tab

The right tab setting is used to align text on a rightmost character. As you enter text, it moves left until you finish typing. The code [Rgt Tab] appears in the text. In Figure 7.2, the year is entered using the right tab setting, which makes an even right margin. You can, however, place the right tab setting anywhere in a line.

To use each of these tab settings, you don't need to press special keys—just the standard ⟨Tab⟩ key. You do, however, need to set tab settings to tell WordPerfect where to place the tabs and what type of tab setting to use.

TIP: You can enter a specific type of tab for one time only as a hard tab. For example, you might want a right tab at the next tab setting only (not change the tab settings for the whole document). The tabs can be entered with or without *dot leaders*, which are a series of characters (usually dots) between tabs. To enter a hard tab, use these keystrokes:

Hard Tab	Keystrokes	Keystrokes (for Dot Leaders)
Hard Left	⟨Home⟩, ⟨Tab⟩	⟨Home⟩, ⟨Home⟩, ⟨Tab⟩
Hard Center	⟨Home⟩, ⟨Shift⟩+⟨F6⟩	⟨Home⟩, ⟨Home⟩, ⟨Shift⟩+⟨F6⟩
Hard Right	⟨Home⟩, ⟨Alt⟩+⟨F6⟩	⟨Home⟩, ⟨Home⟩, ⟨Alt⟩+⟨F6⟩
Hard Decimal	⟨Ctrl⟩+⟨F6⟩	⟨Home⟩, ⟨Home⟩, ⟨Ctrl⟩+⟨F6⟩

You can tell you've entered a hard tab by the code. Codes for hard tabs are in capital letters, such as [DEC TAB] (not [Dec Tab]). Also, the code indicates whether the tab has dot leaders: [DEC TAB (DOT)].

Changing Tab Settings

You can set up WordPerfect to use any of the four types of tabs. First, however, you need to decide where you want tab settings placed. To determine an exact location, just measure your page and identify the location of the tab settings from the left edge of the page for Absolute tab settings or from the left margin for Relative tab settings. For example, setting an Absolute tab setting at 3" means the tab setting will be 3" from the left edge of the paper, not 3" from the left margin setting. You may also just "eyeball" the tab locations and begin entering new tab settings. You will have to visualize the tab setting effect as you work.

There are several benefits to becoming familiar with how to set tabs:

- You can use all four types of tabs instead of being stuck with left tabs only.

- By setting your own tabs, you can reduce the number of times you have to press `Tab` or `F4`.

- You can use tabs to easily change the layout of your text. Simply by entering new tab settings, the text after those tab settings is rearranged.

The following Quick Steps detail how to set tabs.

Adding and Deleting Tabs

1. Place your cursor where you want the new tab settings to begin.

Text after the location will be affected.

2. Press `Shift`+`F8`, and select Line and Tab Set. Or select Tab Set from the Layout menu.

The Tab Set dialog box (Figure 7.3) appears with the current tab settings denoted by L (left), R (right), C (center), and D (decimal).

continues

continued

4. If you want to delete existing tab settings, position your cursor on one of them, and press Del or ⌫Backspace.

5. To add or change the type of tab setting, position the cursor (or click on a position) and enter L, R, C, or D.

The letters identify the tab settings.

6. Select Absolute (to measure from the page edge) or Relative (to measure from the margin).

7. Select OK, and return to your document.

A tab setting code is entered in your document, and text you enter after the code is affected.

Figure 7.3

The Tab Set dialog box.

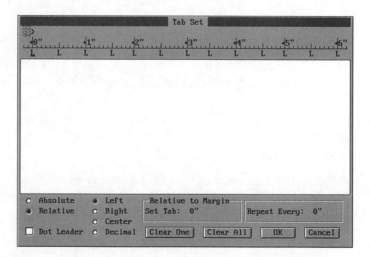

There are other handy options on the Tab Set dialog box.

- To move a tab, put the cursor on the tab setting, and press and hold Ctrl. Use the arrow keys to move the tab.

- To clear multiple tab settings, press Ctrl + End from a tab setting to clear the tab settings to the right of the cursor. To delete all tab settings, select Clear All.

- To enter regularly spaced tabs, clear all tabs, select the type of tab setting to enter, and enter the space between tab settings in the **Rep**eat Every text box. Tab settings of the type indicated are spaced appropriately.

- For very precise tab placement, type a position number in the **S**et Tab text box and press ↵Enter. A tab setting is placed at the location. To change the type of tab setting at the spot, enter a new letter (L, R, C, or D). For example, you might type in 3.01 for a tab setting at 3.01 inches from the left edge of the page if **Ab**solute was chosen or the left margin if **R**elative was chosen.

- You can use the **S**et Tab text box to tell WordPerfect where to start regularly spaced tab settings along with the spacing. First, clear all tabs. Then, enter the position for the first tab setting, a comma, and the regular spacing. For example, to go back to the original tab settings, clear the tabs with Clear All. In the **S**et Tab text box, type in 1, .5. This tells WordPerfect to start at 1" and enter a tab every .5 inches.

You may want to "try out" a new tab setting for exiting text without deleting or changing the existing tab setting. That way, if you don't like the new setting, you can delete the code and still have the old tab setting. Be careful. If you place your cursor just before the existing tab setting code and then set up the new code, the existing tab setting code will simply be edited. You will have lost the old tab settings. Instead, enter a hard return (by pressing ↵Enter) or enter some text after the "old" tab setting. Enter your new setting. Both codes will exist in your text, and you will be able to change your mind and delete the new settings.

Dot Leaders

Occasionally, you may want to enter a row of dots (called dot leaders) between the text at tab settings. In Figure 7.4, dot leaders have been added to some of the tab settings.

Figure 7.4
Dot leaders added to the text.

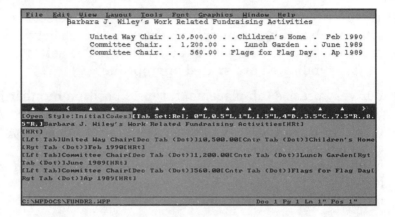

TIP: You can mix dot leader tabs with other tabs set in the same tab setting.

To enter a tab setting to include dot leaders, press ⇧Shift+F8, and select Line and Tab Set. Or select Tab Set from the Layout menu. Enter your settings. Place the cursor on a tab setting, and type in a period (.). The tab setting is in reverse video (light letter on a dark box or vice versa). When you next use the tab setting, dot leaders appear. Adding dot leaders does not affect existing tabs.

You can change the character used for dot leaders or change the amount of space between characters in a dot leader. To do this, press ⇧Shift+F8, and select Character, or select Character from the Layout menu. On the Character Format dialog box, select Dot Leader Character. Enter any Character you like, and change the Spaces Between Dots.

Entering Tabbed Headings

Often when you use tab settings, you are creating columns of text for which you want headings. You will want the headings to be aligned over the columns in most cases, rather than aligned the same way as the tabular data beneath them. If this is the case, you have several options:

- You can place your headings before the tab code (so that the earlier tab settings are used, if they are more appropriate than the newer ones).

- You can type in the headings using spaces instead of tabs.

- You can create a set of tab settings especially for the headings and create another set for the data after the headings are typed.

Of these three methods the latter is probably the most reliable, since by creating new tab settings especially for the headings, they will be exactly the way you want them.

CAUTION

If you choose to use spaces rather than tabs, be aware that some printers do not measure the spaces between tab settings and the spaces entered with the Spacebar in the same way. Thus, your headings can appear lined up on the screen but not when printed. You may need to experiment with your printer to get the outcome you want.

Changing the Decimal/Align Character

The default decimal/align character is a period (.). When you use decimal tab settings, you type in a period as the alignment character and the text lines up according to the period. You can use any character, however, not just a period to align by. For example, you might want to align text on an equal sign (=) as shown next:

```
  6+9+4=19
    8+2=10
800+310=1110
```

To change the decimal/align character, follow these steps:

1. Press ⟨⇧Shift⟩+⟨F8⟩, and select Character, or select Character from the Layout menu. The Character Format dialog box appears.

2. Select Decimal/Align Character. Type in the character you want to use for the alignment, and press ⟨↵Enter⟩.

3. Select OK, and return to your document. A code like this appears in your document identifying the decimal/align character:

```
[Dec/Align Char:=]
```

The character after Char: is the new decimal/align character that will be used in text entered after the code. In this example, it is the equal sign. You can return to the period as the decimal/align character any time by deleting the code or by setting a period as the new decimal/align character.

Tab Align

Sometimes, you might want to align characters by the decimal/align character without changing to a decimal tab setting. For example, if you want to enter only a few lines of text aligned by a decimal/align character, it would be cumbersome to change the tab setting to a decimal tab, enter the text, and then change the tab setting back to a left tab setting for the remainder of the document. Instead, you can use a key combination to use a tab setting temporarily as a decimal tab.

The Tab Align feature affects your work with a single tab setting in a single line. You can use the feature repeatedly to align multiple lines. Follow these steps:

1. Place your cursor before the tab setting under which you want to align the character.

2. Press Ctrl + F6, or select Alignment Decimal Tab from the Layout menu. The [DEC TAB] code appears in your document, and the cursor goes under the next tab setting. The message Align char== appears at the bottom left of your screen to remind you which character (in this case, the equals sign) has been chosen.

3. Type in the text. The text moves to the left.

4. Type the decimal/align character (in our example, the equals sign). The next text you type in will move to the right of the equals sign.

The decimal/align character is typically a period or decimal point. As mentioned earlier, you can change it by selecting ⇧Shift + F8 Character or Character from the Layout menu.

Columns

WordPerfect's Columns feature is useful to create any type of document with two to twenty-four columns on a page. Scripts, newsletters, and lists are popular applications.

The following are the types of columns shown in Figures 7.5a and 7.5b:

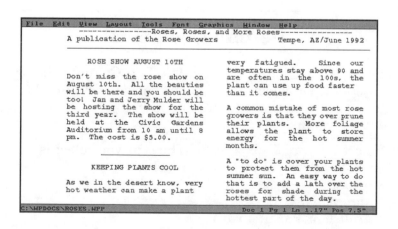

Figure 7.5a

Newspaper columns.

Figure 7.5b
Parallel columns.

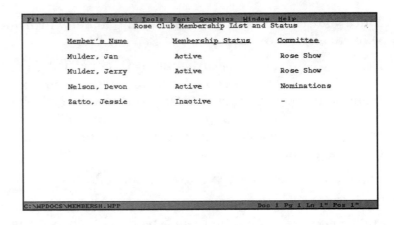

- **Newspaper** (balanced or not): Text flows from the bottom of one column to the top of the next (good for newsletters). If you choose to use Balanced Newspaper Columns, each column is adjusted to be equal in length on the page.

- **Parallel** (with or without block protect): Text is grouped across the page in rows. Related text across columns can be Block Protected to stay together on a page (good for lists where the text in each line relates).

To get started, you must define the columns you want to use. To do this, follow these next Quick Steps. Start with the cursor where you want the column to begin. Or block the text to place in the columns.

Defining Columns

1. Select Alt+F7 and Columns. Or select Columns from the Layout menu.	The Text Columns dialog box shown in Figure 7.6 appears.
2. Select Column Type, and choose the type of column you want (Newspaper, Balanced Newspaper, Parallel, or Parallel with Block Protect).	The type you select is marked.

3. Select Number of Columns, and type in the number of columns you want on the page.

The number you enter appears.

4. If you want to control the space between columns and rows, select Distance Between Columns and Line Spacing Between Rows, and enter the amount of spacing you want.

The distances between columns and rows appear.

5. To add a border, select Column Borders. Choose the Border Style and Fill Style. Press OK to return to the Text Column Dialog box.

6. Choose OK, and return to your document to begin entering text in the columns.

The [Col Def] code and, if you selected a border, the [Col Border] code appear in your document. You can begin typing in columns.

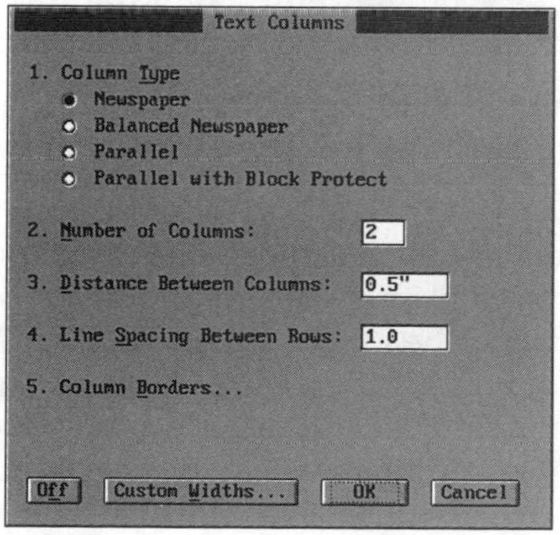

```
                  Text Columns
1. Column Type
   ● Newspaper
   ○ Balanced Newspaper
   ○ Parallel
   ○ Parallel with Block Protect

2. Number of Columns:           [2 ]

3. Distance Between Columns:    [0.5"]

4. Line Spacing Between Rows:   [1.0 ]

5. Column Borders...

   [Off]  [Custom Widths...]  [ OK ]  [Cancel]
```

Figure 7.6
The Text Columns dialog box.

WordPerfect will create columns of equal size for you unless you specify custom widths. Identify the number of columns you want on the Text Columns dialog box. Then, select the Custom Widths button. Enter the Width for each column. WordPerfect attempts to adjust widths, as necessary, to fit the measurement you identify. If you want a column to be fixed in width (and not changed by WordPerfect) check Fixed.

CAUTION   When you enter the width and distance between columns, make sure your numbers match. For example, there can't be two evenly spaced columns that are 4" wide each with a 1" space between columns on an 8.5" x 11" page. The request is for more width than is available on the page because 4"+ 4" + 1" equals 9", not 8.5".

Turning Columns Off and On

Once you have entered text in a column, you may want to turn columns off, enter text, and then turn columns back on. For example, this is helpful if you want to enter a heading horizontally across several columns and then return to using columns. To turn columns off, select Tab↹+F7, and Columns. Or select Columns from the Layout menu. On the Text Columns dialog box, select the Off button and OK. You are returned to your document where a code indicating the column is turned off is entered.

To turn columns back on, you can copy the column code and border code (if any) to the location where you want columns to start up again.

If you are using five or fewer columns and can use default WordPerfect settings, there is a faster method to control columns. Use the Ribbon. From the View menu, select Ribbon to display the Ribbon, if it is not already displayed. Place the cursor where you want the columns to start (or block the text for the columns). Click on the Col button, and double-click on the number of columns (1 Col through 5 Cols). One column gives the same effect as turning columns off.

Working with Text in Columns

The codes for a newspaper format look something like this:

```
[Col Def:Newspaper;3]
```

The definition code shows the type of column (such as Newspaper or Parallel) and the Number of Columns. Notice that the earlier text in the example is not in column format and provides the heading for our newsletter.

To enter text in a column, begin typing after the column definition code. You can use any typical editing features in columns along with fonts, graphics, and other effects.

Starting a new column is easy. The method is the same for Newspaper (not balanced) and Parallel Column (with or without Block Protect). When you want to begin a new column, press Ctrl+↵Enter to create a hard column break. You go to the next column, and a Hard Column Break code [HCol] is placed in your document. Figure 7.7 illustrates how the text wraps around to the next column in a Newspaper column format.

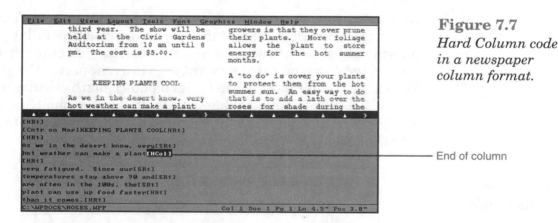

Figure 7.7
Hard Column code in a newspaper column format.

If you are using Balanced Newspaper format, you'll quickly find that the columns "balance themselves." As you type, text spreads evenly between the columns. When you want to start over at the first column (probably at the end of the page), just press Ctrl+↵Enter for a hard column break.

There are some tricks to moving your cursor around in columns. The easiest way, by far, is to use the mouse. This table summarizes the cursor movement with the keyboard:

Table 7.1
Cursor Movement in Columns using the Keyboard

Keypress	Cursor Movement
Ctrl+Home, arrow or Alt+arrow	One column in the arrow direction.
Ctrl+Home, Home, arrow	To the first or last column (left or right arrow) or top or bottom of page (up or down arrow).

TIP: Be careful when editing column text. Don't remove the important codes by accident.

Tables

An attractive way to organize information is to use the Tables feature. Rather than using tabs or parallel columns to lay out information, a table grid is created for you. Text you enter wraps around until you indicate you want to go to a new part of the grid. You can also enter formulas in tables for quick math calculations. Figure 7.8 shows a simple table. This table shows a small budget. The totals in the last line were calculated with formulas entered into the table.

Figure 7.8
A simple table.

A row

A cell

A column

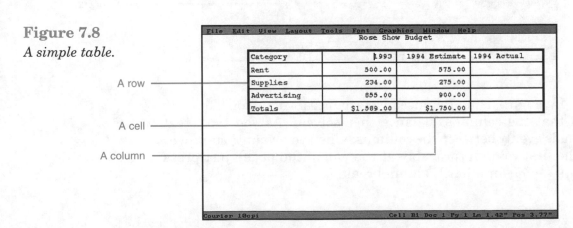

As shown in Figure 7.8, tables are organized into rows, columns, and cells. A row is a single line of boxes across. For example, Figure 7.8 shows a row for Category. A column refers to the vertical boxes in the table. In the figure, the 1994 Actual cells are in a column. A cell points to a particular rectangular space in the table. In Figure 7.8, the total for the 1993 column (1,589.00) is contained in one cell.

Creative Uses for Tables

In addition to budgets, you can use tables to create inventory lists, expense accounts, financial reports, telephone lists, class enrollments, or employee lists.

Creating a table in WordPerfect is very straightforward; you just tell it how many rows and how many columns you want. To create a table, follow the next Quick Steps.

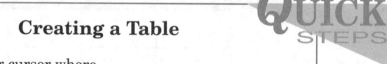

Creating a Table

1. Position your cursor where you want the top left corner of the table to begin.

2. Press Alt+F7, and select Tables and then Create. Or select Tables and Create from the Layout menu.

    The Create Table dialog box appears.

3. Enter the number of columns and rows, and select OK.

    You are placed in the Table Edit dialog box as shown in Figure 7.9.

Figure 7.9
A blank table in the Table Edit dialog box.

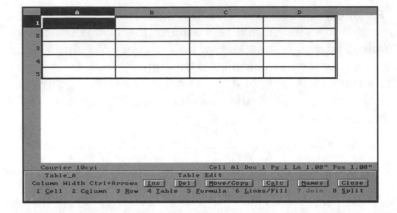

To enter text in a table, leave the Table Edit dialog box by selecting Close. Use Reveal Codes to help you place text in cells. Figure 7.10 shows the Table Definition code, the codes for rows and cells, as well as the code showing where the table is turned off. Once the grid is created, you can use regular WordPerfect features to enter information.

Figure 7.10
Reveal Codes shows the table codes.

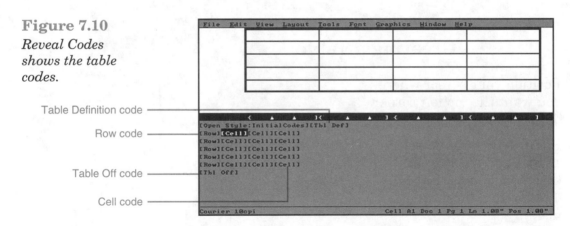

Table Definition code

Row code

Table Off code

Cell code

Enter a Formula

To add a formula, you need to understand how each cell is identified. Starting in the upper left corner, columns are represented by letters starting with A and rows are represented by numbers starting with 1. The cell in the upper left corner of the screen is A1, the next cell to the right is B1. The cell below A1 is A2 and so on. These are the *cell addresses*. See Figure 7.11.

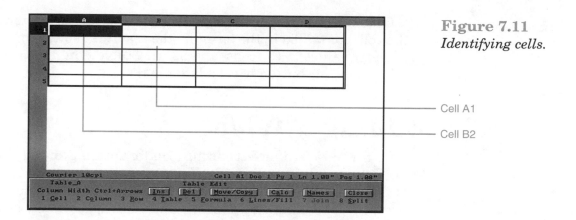

Figure 7.11
Identifying cells.

You can enter text (numbers and letters) into the table just as you type regular WordPerfect text. To enter formulas, you must leave the document editing mode by placing your cursor in the table and either pressing `Alt`+`F7` or selecting Tables and Edit from the Layout menu. The editing features appear on the bottom of the screen. To enter a formula, select Formula. The Table Formula dialog box appears. You can enter a simple formula involving cell addresses and common math symbols.

To create a total in our example, the results of the following formula would be placed in cell C5:

```
C2+C3+C4
```

The formula tells you to add the values in cells C2, C3, and C4. (Of course, you must have numeric values in these cells, not text.)

You can use these symbols in formulas:

+	Add
-	Subtract (or negative number)
*	Multiply
/	Divide

Formulas are calculated left to right, unless you put part of a formula in parentheses. In that case, the calculations in the parentheses are calculated first.

Once the formula is entered, select OK. If values are entered in the cells contained in the formula, the result is shown. Otherwise, enter values in the cells, and use the Table Edit dialog box to select the Calc button to calculate the result.

Editing a Table

Use the normal WordPerfect editing tools for entering and editing table text, as well as formatting. You can control the formatting of a single cell or a number of cells you select (for example, an entire row or column). Formatting includes appearance, size, justification, column width, and so on.

To affect a group of cells, block the cells. Otherwise, the formatting you choose will affect the entire table. From the Table Edit dialog box, select Table for most common formatting. Or select Cell, Column, or Row for formatting specific to each of those options. Depending on which you select, you are presented with different dialog boxes of options, all of which are self-explanatory.

For example, in Figure 7.12, the dollar amount cells were formatted for decimal align justification. This was accomplished by selecting Column to go to the Cell Format dialog box. Then Justify and Decimal Align were selected.

Figure 7.12
Decimal align justification.

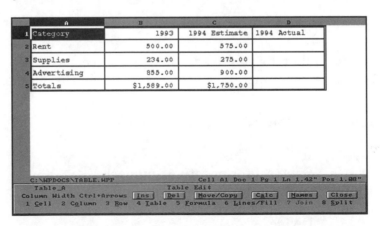

You can also add a row or column. To do this, place the cursor where you want the new row or column added. From the table editing options, select Ins. The Insert dialog box appears. Identify

Columns or **R**ows. Identify the number of columns or rows to insert after **H**ow Many? Finally, indicate the location of the insert as **B**efore Cursor Position or **A**fter Cursor Position. Select OK. The table is updated. The column or row is added. If the entire line between margins is taken up by the table, the current cell will be split when a new column is added.

To delete a row or column or the contents of a cell, place the cursor in the row, column, or cell. From the Table Edit dialog box, select Del. The Delete dialog box appears. Identify that you want to delete rows or columns or the contents of a cell. If you are deleting a row or column, you'll indicate the number of rows or columns after **H**ow Many? Select OK. The table is updated. To delete an entire table, you must select the whole table and press Del.

The Table Edit dialog box can be used to increase or decrease the width of a column by pressing Ctrl+← or Ctrl+→, respectively.

Table Shortcuts

When you begin to use very large tables, you'll want to speed up your work. There are quick movement keys for tables, methods to move and copy within tables, and over 100 math functions. You can split or join cells, as well as add lines, borders, and fill for a pleasing graphic effect.

Table 7.2 lists several of the quick movement keys.

Press	To move cursor
Alt+arrow	To move to a cell up, down, left, or right.
Ctrl+Home, *cell address*	To move to the cell address you enter.
Ctrl+Home, Home, arrow	To move to the edge of the table in the direction of the arrow.
Ctrl+Home, Home, Home, ↑	To move to the first cell.
Ctrl+Home, Home, Home, ↓	To move to the last cell.

Table 7.2
Quick Movement in a Table

Creating a Page Break

- Press Ctrl+↵Enter.

Go To a Page

1. Press Ctrl+Home, or select Go to from the Edit menu.
2. Type the page number you want and press ↵Enter.

Widow/Orphan Protection

1. Press ⇧Shift+F8 and select Other or select Other from the Layout menu.
2. Select Widow/Orphan Protection, and choose OK and Close.

Adding or Stopping Page Numbering (Not in Header)

1. Press ⇧Shift+F8, and select Page. Or select Page from the Layout menu.
2. Select Page Numbering, and complete the options.

Forcing an Odd or Even Page

1. Press ⇧Shift+F8, and select Page. Or select Page from the Layout menu.
2. Select Force Page, and then select Odd, Even, New or None.

Suppressing a Page Number on a Single Page

1. Press ⇧Shift+F8, and select Page. Or select Page from the Layout menu.
2. Select Suppress and then Page Numbering.

Working With Multiple-Page Documents

As you become skilled with WordPerfect, you will use it for pages and pages of work. In this chapter, you will learn not only how to create multiple pages, but also how to control what amount of text appears on the pages, how to go to a specific page, and how to print a group of pages. You'll also learn all about page numbering in WordPerfect.

Creating Multiple Pages

So far, you've learned to create and print a document, complete with the tab settings of your choice. Now you're ready to create a document that is more than one page long.

WordPerfect allows you to create lengthy documents; the maximum length depends only upon your computer's storage and memory capacity. Usually, though, any document over fifty pages seems a bit cumbersome because it takes too long to move around the document and make the frequent saves necessary to protect the document.

In a long document, the pages appear on-screen one after another. Think of your document as a long scroll with lines marking the pages.

FYI IDEAS

Using Different Page Formats in One Document

The pages in a document do not necessarily have to be printed on the same type of paper, nor do they need to have the same formatting. For example, one document may have a letter to be printed on letterhead on the first page. The margins would be set up to fit the letter on the letterhead. The second page of the document may contain the address for an envelope and have a paper size/type code for an envelope, different margins, and a copy of the address from the letter to be printed on the envelope. The last page of the document may be a multiple-page report for regular 8.5' x 11' paper. A new paper size/type code would be used along with margins and page numbering specific for the report.

There is more than one way to break a page. If you've been experimenting on your own, you may have already created an extra page by using WordPerfect's automatic page break feature.

Automatic Page Breaks

WordPerfect knows how many lines of text can fit on a page. It is a careful deduction of the paper size minus the margins; both are set through the Layout menu or by pressing ⬆Shift + F8 (Format) and covered in earlier chapters. The ln amount in the lower right corner of the screen shows how many inches of the page have been filled with text up to your cursor position.

On a typical 11" piece of paper with 1" top and bottom margins, you will be able to type to about the 9" mark before

WordPerfect automatically inserts a page break. The exact measure varies according to the line spacing you're using (such as single or double) and the line height. Both are set through the **L**ayout menu or by pressing ⇧Shift + F8 . If you edit the page and add or delete lines of text, the page break remains at the same line. The text, in effect, "moves" to fill the page.

On your screen, an automatic page break appears as a line, as shown in Figure 8.1. Notice that on the Reveal Codes screen, the automatic page break is shown as [HRt-SPg] (for a soft page break). Soft page break is WordPerfect jargon for an automatically inserted page break. If you insert a page break manually, this is referred to as a hard page break.

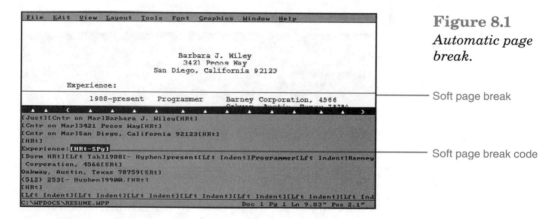

Figure 8.1
Automatic page break.

Soft page break

Soft page break code

Manual Page Breaks

You will often want a page break before WordPerfect enters one. For example, when you create a letter with several attachments, you may want to put the letter on the first page of the document and the attachments on subsequent pages, keeping all the related material in one WordPerfect document. When you print, you can insert letterhead for the first page and plain sheets after that.

Of course, you can press ↵Enter enough times to take advantage of WordPerfect's automatic page break, but editing the text later could throw off the pages. Instead, use a manual (hard) page break.

To manually break a page, place the cursor on the line and column where you want the page to be broken. Press Ctrl+⏎Enter or select **A**lignment from the **L**ayout menu, and then Hard **P**age. A double dashed line as shown in Figure 8.2 is inserted, and the [HPg] (hard page break) code is inserted in your document. Text starting with the character your cursor is on appears after the manual page break. If you want to get rid of the manual page break, just delete the code.

Figure 8.2
Manual (hard) page break.

Hard page break ——————

Hard page break code ——————

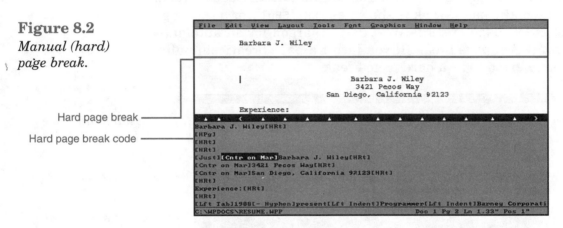

You may want a blank page in your document as a separator, or to later paste up an exhibit. To create a blank page, just enter two hard page breaks. For more blank pages, enter as many hard page breaks as you need.

Moving Between Pages

Once you have multiple pages, you will want to be able to move from page to page quickly. The number of the page appears in the bottom right corner of your screen. In this sample line:

```
Doc 1 Pg 4 Ln 8" Pos 3"
```

your cursor is shown to be on page 4. To go directly to page 15, press Ctrl+Home, or select **G**o to from the **E**dit menu. A dialog box appears for you to enter the page to which you want to go. Type **15**, and press ⏎Enter. Your cursor goes to the upper left corner of the first line of page 15.

```
Doc 1 Pg 15 Ln 1" Pos 1"
```

To move only one page, press PgUp (to go up or "back" in the document) or PgDn (to go down or "forward" in the document). When you use either of these keys, you are taken to the upper left corner of the first line of that page.

Preventing Widows and Orphans

To many beginning users, the terms *widows* and *orphans* have to do with women who have lost their mates and children who have lost their parents. In word processing, the terms also have to do with losses: specifically, when a single line of a paragraph has been lost from the rest of its paragraph by being split off by a page break. A widow is the first line of a paragraph alone at the end of a page. An orphan is the last line of a paragraph isolated at the top of a page.

If you don't like the appearance of widows and orphans, you can ask WordPerfect to prevent them. The following Quick Steps detail how to protect against widows and orphans.

Enabling Widow/Orphan Protection

1. Put the cursor where you want protection to start. Press ⇧Shift+F8, and then select **O**ther. Or select **O**ther from the Layout menu.

The Other Format dialog box appears.

continues

continued

2. Place a check in the **W**idow/Orphan Protect check box, select OK and Close to return to your document.

A code is inserted in your text.

TIP: To protect an entire document, place the widow/ orphan code at the beginning of the document.

Conditional End of Page

Sometimes you will want to keep several lines together in a document, even if it means letting a page run a little short. For example, in Figure 8.3, part of the sample resume is split by a soft page break automatically inserted by WordPerfect. The split is inappropriate. To keep the lines together, you could insert a manual page break above the lines. The problem with this is that if you edit text, the hard page break may end up cutting the page too short. A better solution is to enter a *conditional end of page*, which keeps together the number of lines you specify so that they can't be split between pages.

Figure 8.3
Resume lines split by soft page break.

Soft page break ———

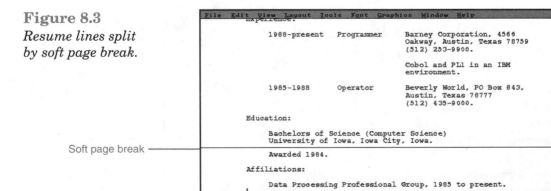

The following Quick Steps detail how to enter a conditional end of page. For our example, we'll keep the six lines at the bottom of Figure 8.3 together.

Entering a Conditional End of Page

1. Identify the number of lines to keep together, and place the cursor before the first line.

   The lines after the cursor will be affected.

2. Press ⇧Shift + F8 , and select Other. Or select Other on the Layout menu.

   The Other Format dialog box appears.

3. Select Conditional End of Page, enter the number of lines to be kept together, and press ↵Enter .

   The lines are kept together on a page.

4. Select OK and Close to return to your document.

   You are returned to your document.

The code `[Condl EOP:5]` appears, indicating that five lines are to be kept together. The text that was split is automatically moved past the page break. Figure 8.4 shows the resume after the conditional end of page code has been inserted. Notice the code placement.

Figure 8.4

Resume lines after inserting conditional end of page.

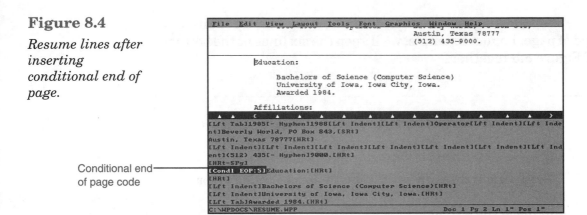

Conditional end of page code

Block Protection

You may want to keep a given block of text together (versus specifying a particular number of lines). If so, use the block protect feature instead of the conditional end of page feature. With block protect, you can change the number of lines in the block through editing, and the block will remain together on a single page.

This feature is especially useful for tables or any block that can be edited to a different number of lines. For example, Figure 8.5 shows text in a block protect. The entire block was moved to the start of a page. Notice the [BlockPro:On] and [BlockPro:Off] codes that mark the beginning and end of the block.

Figure 8.5

Block protected text.

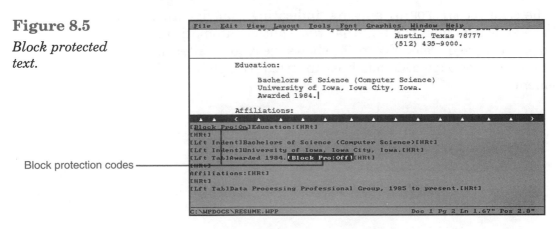

Block protection codes

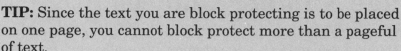

TIP: Since the text you are block protecting is to be placed on one page, you cannot block protect more than a pageful of text.

The following Quick Steps detail how to block protect text.

Using Block Protection

1. Block the text with Alt+F4, or select **B**lock from the **E**dit menu.	The blocked text is highlighted.
2. Press ⇧Shift+F8 and choose **O**ther. Or select **O**ther from the **L**ayout menu.	The Other Format dialog box appears.
3. Check the **B**lock Protect check box, and then select OK and Close to return to your document.	The block protection codes are inserted.

Page Numbering

Once you develop documents with multiple pages, you will want to be able to number the pages. With just a little setup, WordPerfect does this for you automatically. You'll be able to select from a variety of page number appearances or develop your own unique look. In addition, you can insert a page number automatically in the body of a page to reference the page.

Page Number Choices

Numbering pages is handy for short documents and essential for most long documents. But don't tediously number each page in the document by hand. Instead, have WordPerfect automatically number your pages. WordPerfect allows you to select the following:

- Position of the number on the page.
- New page number (including the number with which to start consecutive numbering) and the method–Roman, numbers, and letter.
- Format (number alone or accompanied by text).

You can change these options on any page you like and as often as you like in a document. A new code is inserted each time you enter page numbering options. The code affects the page on which it is entered and all following text until a new code is encountered.

CAUTION   Place the codes controlling page numbering at the top of a page. If you put text before the page codes, the page numbers may not print as you anticipated. If you accidentally put conflicting page numbering codes on a page, the page numbers won't number as you anticipated.

Adding a Page Number

Let's start with a basic, no-frills page number. Here are the steps.

1. Place the cursor before any existing text at the top of the page where you want page numbering to begin.

2. Press ⇧Shift+F8, and then select Page. Or select Page from the Layout menu. The Page Format dialog box appears.

3. Select Page Numbering. The Page Numbering dialog box appears (see Figure 8.6).

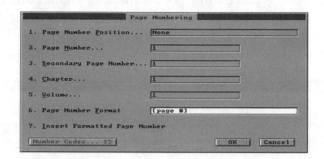

Figure 8.6

The Page Numbering dialog box.

4. Select the positioning of the page number (or no page number) by choosing Page Number Position. The Page Number Position dialog box shown in Figure 8.7 appears.

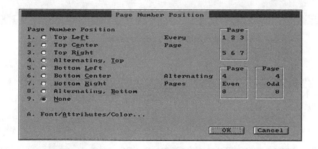

Figure 8.7

The Page Number Position dialog box.

5. Select a page position and then OK. You are returned to the Page Numbering dialog box.

6. To enter the number of the page to use and the method of numbering (Roman, numbers, or letter), select Page Number. The Set Page Number dialog box appears.

7. Enter the New Number, the Numbering Method, and select OK. You are returned to the Page Numbering dialog box.

8. To enter text before, after, or around the page number, select Page Number Format. Type in the text, and then select OK and return to your document.

You may want to check Reveal Codes to ensure that all the selections are as you want. In the example shown in Figure 8.8, you can see codes placed in the document to yield a top, centered page number beginning with Roman numerals after the text (Preface - i). The codes govern the page numbering until you enter new codes.

Figure 8.8

Page numbering codes in Reveal Codes.

```
File   Edit   View   Layout   Tools   Font   Graphics   Window   Help

                  Status of Reorganization Report Background

                 This report begins a series of monthly reports on the status
            of the reorganization of the DPG group.  The reports are designed
            to give senior management information, however, middle managers may
            find the reports of interest.




     ▲        ‹        ▲        ▲        ▲        ▲        ▲        ▲        ›
[Open Style:InitialCodes][Pg Num Meth:Lev 1;Lowercase Roman][Pg Num Fmt][Pg Num
Pos][HRt]
[HRt]
[Cntr on Mar]Status of Reorganization Report Background[HRt]
[HRt]
[Lft Tab]This report begins a series of monthly reports on the status[SRt]
of the reorganization of the DPG group.  The reports are designed[SRt]
to give senior management information, however, middle managers may[SRt]
find the reports of interest.[HRt]

C:\WPDOCS\REPORT.WPP                              Doc 1 Pg i Ln 1.33" Pos 1"
```

Page numbering codes —

The page numbers will not appear on your page in Text or Graphic Mode. They will appear in Page Mode. Use Ctrl + F3 to switch modes. In all modes, the number appears in the lower right corner of the screen. You can also view the page numbers by pressing ⇧Shift + F7, and then selecting Print Preview.

The following Quick Steps summarize the page numbering process. More details about some of the complex steps follow in later sections of this chapter.

QUICK STEPS   **Using Page Numbering**

1. Place your cursor at the top of a page.

2. Press ⇧Shift+F8, and then select Page. Or select Page from the Layout menu.	The Page Format dialog box appears.
3. Select Page Numbering.	The Page Numbering dialog box appears.
4. Select the options according to the page numbering you want.	
5. Select OK twice and then Close when all page numbering options are set.	

Position on the Page

When it comes to positioning the page number, you are offered a variety of selections. Figure 8.7 illustrates the options. The numbers in the Every Page diagram are simply identifiers for the position you can select. If you are printing pages that will be copied double sided, use the pages shown on the Alternating Pages diagram. Enter the page number on the upper outside (alternating top) of the page or the lower outside (alternating bottom).

Also notice in Figure 8.7 that you can select None. Using this option, you can skip page numbers for one or more pages.

Page Number and Numbering Method

Page Number is WordPerfect's option to allow you to select the page number you want to start with at a given point in the document, along with the method. The numbering method can be numbers (1, 2, 3), Roman numerals (I, II, III), or letters (A, B, C). Roman numerals and letters can be upper- or lowercase.

For example, you might have several WordPerfect documents making up one long, printed document. The first three pages of the first document's introduction are numbered i, ii, and iii, and the next 15 pages in the document can be numbered 1 through 15. You then would want the first WordPerfect page of the second document to be numbered as page 16 with consecutive numbering continuing from there.

Page Number Format

Page Number Format is WordPerfect's option to allow you to enter the page number alone or to enter text along with the page number. As an example, you may want the first three pages of a document to have this text along with the page number:

```
Appendix A--Page 1
Appendix A--Page 2
Appendix A--Page 3
```

On the fourth page, you may want to change to the following format and continue it through the rest of the document:

```
Appendix B--Page 1
```

The text (Appendix) is just one way to use the page number format feature with text and symbols. (You can enter any text up to approximately fifty characters in length.) For instance, you may want to insert:

a date:	`June 10, 1993 (1)`
a copyright notice:	`1994 Alpha / Pg 1`
the author's name:	`By Kate Miller  p. #1`
a confidential notification:	`CONFIDENTIAL: 1`
identify the document as a draft:	`!!!! DRAFT !!!! p. 1`
or just add a decoration to the page number:	`******** 1 ********`

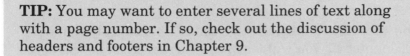

TIP: You may want to enter several lines of text along with a page number. If so, check out the discussion of headers and footers in Chapter 9.

When you set the format in WordPerfect, you enter the text before or after the existing symbol for the page number, that is [page #]. When you enter a new page number format, this type of code is placed in the document:

```
[Pg Num Fmt: Confidential Draft/[page #]]
```

Inserting New Pages After Pages Are Numbered

What if you create a lengthy document with consecutive page numbering, and want to insert pages later? If re-numbering the document would take too long or multiple copies of the existing document have been distributed, add pages in between. For example, pages 17.1 through 17.5 could be added between page 17 and page 18.

You could just type in page numbers for these pages, however, that would leave some pages governed by automatic page number and others with page numbers typed in. If you wanted to print the document later, considerable editing would have to be done first to standardize how page numbers are assigned.

Instead, use WordPerfect's page numbering options to add a new page number with the appropriate format. Continuing the example of adding pages 17.1 through 17.5, enter a code on what is to be page 17.1. Select a new Page Number of 1 (this will become the .1, .2, and so on). Enter a Page Number Format of 17.[page #]. After what is now page 17.5, enter a code with new Page Number set to 18 to return to the correct consecutive page numbering. When you print the pages they will be numbered correctly.

continues

continued

The specially numbered page codes can be easily removed. In Chapter 11 you will learn how to search for codes. If you end up with a document with multiple page changes and you want to remove "inserted" page numbering, just search out the page codes, and edit as you want.

Forcing an Odd or Even Page

You may want to force a page to be odd or even. For example, it is customary for first pages of double sided chapters to be odd pages. This way, the first page of each chapter starts on the right side of the open book. To force an odd or even page, put your cursor on the page. Press ⬦Shift + F8 , and then select Page. Or select Page from the Layout menu. On the Page Format dialog box, select Force Page, and then select Odd or Even.

Controlling Page Number Fonts and Attributes

Whatever fonts and attributes are set prior to a page code affects the appearance of the page number. You can control the font or attributes of the page numbers. Press ⬦Shift + F8 , and then select Page or select Page from the Layout menu. Select Page Numbering. On the Page Numbering dialog box, select Page Number Position. From the Page Number Position dialog box, select Font/Attributes/Color. The Font dialog box appears. Here you can change the font and appearance. For more information about the options on the Font dialog box, consult Chapter 5, "Character Formatting."

Increasing or Decreasing a Page Number

You may want to increase or decrease a page number. This is useful when you want to "skip" a page to make room for a page to be inserted later or to have a page in the document you intend on removing later. For an increase or decrease, place your cursor at the top of the page to affect. Press ⇧Shift+F8, and then select Page. Or select Page from the Layout menu. Select Page Numbering.

Choose Page Number. Check either the **I**ncrement Number or **D**ecrement Number check box.

Inserting the Page Number in the Body of the Page

For reference purposes, you may want to insert the page number in the body of the text. These phrases illustrate two examples:

Return to this page **(page 3)** when you have completed the test.

Remember that the instructions are here on **page 4**.

Use WordPerfect's features for inserting page numbers (instead of typing in the page numbers). That way, if the number of pages changes due to editing, the number that prints will always be correct. You can enter the page number with all formatting or just the page number itself.

To enter the page number with all formatting, follow the next Quick Steps.

Entering the Page Number with Formatting

1. Place the cursor in the body of the text where the page number is to appear.

2. Press ⬆Shift+F8, and then select **P**age or select **P**age from the **L**ayout menu.

The Page Format dialog box appears.

3. Select **P**age **N**umbering.

The Page Numbering dialog box appears.

4. Choose **I**nsert Formatted Page Number.

You are returned to your document. The page number appears in your text along with a code.

TIP: You can also press Ctrl+P to put the formatted page number in your text.

To enter the page number without formatting, follow these Quick Steps.

Entering the Page Number Without Formatting

1. Place the cursor in the body of the text where the page number is to appear.

2. Press `⇧Shift`+`F8`, and then select **P**age. Or select **P**age from the **L**ayout menu.	The Page Format dialog box appears.
3. Select **P**age **N**umbering.	The Page Numbering dialog box appears.
4. Choose **P**age **N**umber.	The Set Page Number dialog box appears.
5. Select the check box for **D**isplay in Document. Choose OK three times and then Close to return to your document.	Only the page number appears in the document.

Suppressing Page Numbers

You may want to suppress a page number on one page. This is sometimes required if you want to place a large graphic on a page or give a different look to the page. When you suppress the page number on a page, that page number remains in the consecutive count. For example, if you suppress the page number on page 3, the pages will be numbered 1, 2, (page 3 will have no page number), 4, 5, and so on.

To suppress a page number, use the following Quick Steps.

Suppressing a Page Number

1. Press ⟨⇧Shift⟩+⟨F8⟩, and then select **P**age. Or select **P**age from the **L**ayout menu.

   The Page Format dialog box appears.

2. Select **S**uppress.

   The Suppress (This Page Only) dialog box appears (see Figure 8.9).

3. Select the **P**age Numbering check box, and select OK.

Figure 8.9

The Suppress (This Page Only) dialog box.

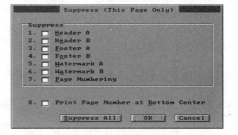

Printing Multiple Pages

Printing multiple pages is simple. When you press ⟨⇧Shift⟩+⟨F7⟩ or select **P**rint from the **F**ile menu, the Print dialog box appears. Choose **M**ultiple Pages. The Print Multiple Pages dialog box appears (see Figure 8.10).

Figure 8.10

The Print Multiple Pages dialog box.

Most often, you will want to print one or more ranges of pages. Select Page/Label Range, and then enter the pages with a dash between the first and last page in the range. Enter individual pages with commas separating each page number. Here are some examples.

1,4-8,12	This entry will cause page 1 to print followed by pages 4 through 8, and then page 12.
2,6-	This entry will print page 2 and then print from page 6 through the end of the document.
-6,22-24	This entry will print from the start of the document through page 6 and then pages 22, 23, and 24.

TIP: Do not enter page numbers randomly (such as 5, 2, 7). Put them in the sequence that they appear in the document (that is, 2, 5, 7). Otherwise, the document will stop printing when the first number out of order is encountered.

TIP: The page numbering you specify with the Page Numbering command must be the same numbers that you specify when you print the document. The number also appears in the status line. For example, if you start the document numbering at page 10, and you want to print the first page, you would specify to print page 10. If you specify page 1 and there is no page numbered 1, a message like the following appears: No Pages Matching Page Range Found.

What Are Headers and Footers?

- A *header* is text that appears at the top of the document page (after the top margin).
- A *footer* appears at the bottom of the page (before the bottom margin).

Add a Header or Footer

1. Press ⬆Shift+F8, and select Header/Footer/ Watermark. Or select Header/Footer/Watermark from the Layout menu.
2. Select Headers or Footers. Change the default Space Below, if you want, and select Header or Footer A or B.
3. Select All Pages, Even Pages, or Odd Pages, then select Create.
4. Enter the text and press F7 or select Exit from the File menu when you are done.

Discontinue a Header or Footer

1. Press ⬆Shift+F8, and select Header/Footer/ Watermark. Or select Header/Footer/Watermark from the Layout menu.
2. Select Headers or Footers. Select Header or Footer A or B.
3. Select Off, OK, and Close.

Adding the Date

1. Press ⬆Shift+F5.
2. Select Insert Date Text or Insert Date Code.

Adding the Name of the File

1. Press ⬆Shift+F8, and then Other. Or select Other from the Layout dialog box.
2. Select Insert Filename.
3. Select Insert Filename or Insert Path and Filename, then select OK twice and Close.

The Professional Touch: Headers and Footers

If you create multiple page documents, such as reports or manuals, you will want to learn about the use of headers and footers. They add professionalism to any document. Better still, they aren't hard to master.

A *header* or *footer* is text that appears at the top (head) or the bottom (foot) of each page. Headers and footers can add a professional touch to a document to give it a first-rate appearance. A header or footer can include the name of a document, version number, notification of status (DRAFT or Confidential, for instance), author's name, page number, chapter or section numbers, graphics, or any other appropriate text you care to include. These are possible sample header or footer lines:

```
Chapter 3                                page 3-16
CONFIDENTIAL from President's office      page 6 of 9
Year End Report         - DRAFT -        by Jim Lindy
1993 Webber Corporation
```

A header or footer can be more than a single line; in fact, it can include up to one pageful of text. This allows you great flexibility in the amount of information you can place in a header or footer. When you create headers and footers, you can use all of WordPerfect's editing features.

When you place the header or footer in the document, a code appears in your document to mark the start of the header or footer. The header or footer is then automatically repeated on each page or on alternating pages, depending on your selection. Every time you enter a new header or footer code, that header or footer is used until you enter another code.

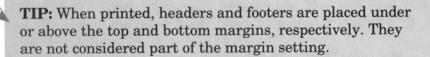

TIP: When printed, headers and footers are placed under or above the top and bottom margins, respectively. They are not considered part of the margin setting.

Here's how to create a header or footer.

1. Place the cursor at the top of the first page for the header or footer (before all codes except Paper Size/Type or Top/Bottom Margin codes).

2. Press ⌂Shift+F8, and select Header/Footer/Watermark. Or select Header/Footer/Watermark from the Layout menu. The Header/Footer/Watermark dialog box appears.

3. Select Headers or Footers. If you want to change the default Space Below the header or above the footer, change it now. Also select whether you want to work with Header or Footer **A** or **B**.

You can place two headers or footers on a page, which is useful if you have entered one header as Header A and then want to add more text to the header. Instead of editing it, you can add Header B. Get in the practice of always choosing Header A or Footer A first. Then, if a Header B or Footer B is necessary, you will know you are adding to the first header or footer on the page.

After selecting Header A or Footer A, a dialog box appears with these options

All Pages

Even Pages

Odd Pages

enabling you to place headers or footers on every page, just on even numbered pages, or just on odd numbered pages. You will probably want the header on every page for most documents. Make the appropriate selection, and select the **C**reate button for a new header or footer. You are taken to the header or footer window (Figure 9.1). Enter header or footer information as you would any WordPerfect text.

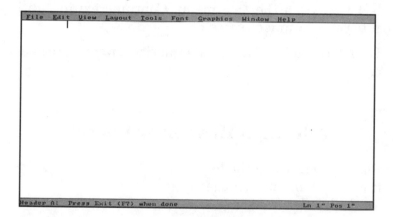

Figure 9.1
Header window.

TIP: To place a page number in the header or footer, press Ctrl + P creating this code [Formatted Pg Num]. Every time this symbol is encountered in a header or footer, WordPerfect will increment the page number by one. To start page numbering with a number other than 1, set the Page Number to the first number you want. Put the new Page Number code in the document before the header or footer code. (See Chapter 8 to review this procedure).

CAUTION   Many of the page numbering options available through `Shift`+`F8` (**L**ayout, **P**age, Page **Num**bering) are not available for headers and footers. For example, you cannot set a new page number in a header and the numbering method cannot be controlled. Also, don't use the Page Number Position option, or you will get two separate page numbers on the same page (one on the regular page and one in the header or footer).

The header or footer screen is just like a regular WordPerfect screen. You can use any editing capability when you are entering the header or footer text. Once you've entered the text, press `F7`, or select Exit from the File menu. Continue exiting until you return to your document screen.

The following Quick Steps summarize how to add a header or footer.

Adding a Header or Footer

1. Place the cursor in the location you want on the page for the header or footer.

2. Press `Shift`+`F8` and select Header/Footer/ Watermark. Or select Header/Footer/ Watermark from the Layout menu.

   The Header/Footer/Watermark dialog box appears.

3. Select Headers or Footers.

   The options for headers or footers become available.

4. If you want, change the default **S**pace Below the header or above the footer. Choose Header or Footer **A** (unless this is a second header or footer on the page).

   A dialog box with new options appears.

5. Select the placement of the header or footer: **A**ll Pages, **E**ven Pages, or **O**dd Pages.

6. Select **C**reate.

You are taken to the header or footer window.

7. Enter the header or footer text just like any WordPerfect text. Press `Ctrl`+`P` for a page number code. When you are done, press `F7`. Or select **E**xit from the **F**ile menu and return to the document screen.

A code for the header or footer is placed in your document.

Safety Checks for Headers and Footers

As you get accustomed to using headers and footers, you may find some surprising results when you print a document. For example, it is easy for a beginner to forget to enter enough blank lines in a header for appropriate spacing between the header text and the body of the document. It is also easy to forget that codes (such as margins or special fonts) entered in the document after the header or footer code will not take effect in the header or footer.

Follow these "safety checks" before you print. Check the Reveal Codes screen to make sure there are no unusual formatting codes accidentally placed around the header or footer. Make certain the header or footer code appears at the top of the page. Consider formatting codes. Are the appropriate codes contained in the header or footer? Finally, check the appearance of the header or footer through `Shift`+`F7` Print Preview. Or look at it through Page Mode selecting `Ctrl`+`F3`, **P**age. Taking a few moments to double-check the setup of your header or footer can save paper and time.

Adding the Date

With WordPerfect, you can automatically enter the current date as text (which doesn't change) or as a code (which reflects the current date). It is handy to use the date in a header or footer when a document will undergo several reviews, that way, the date of the current version is apparent. If you will print a document, the code is useful to indicate the print date.

To insert the date, place the cursor in the location for the date. Press ⇧Shift + F5. On the Date dialog box, select Insert Date Text to insert today's date, as text won't change. Select Insert Date Code to insert a code that will always reflect the current date. To change the format (month, day, year), select Date Format.

Adding the Name of the File

When documents are printed and passed around, it is easy to lose track of the original file and its location. This is especially true in an organization using a large network. To avoid this problem, you can enter the file name or the path and file name in your document. A code is entered that reflects the current file name.

To enter the file name in your document, press ⇧Shift + F8 and then Other. Or select Other from the Layout dialog box. Select Insert Filename. On the Insert Filename dialog box, select Insert Filename (for just the name) or Insert Path and Filename (to include the path). Select OK twice and Close to return to your document. The file name appears in the document, and a code is inserted. If you change the file name, the document is automatically updated.

Adding Graphic Effects

Although headers and footers are typically used to provide information, they can also be used for a pleasing graphic effect. You can use symbols created through WordPerfect's keyboard options (such as underlines or double underlines). Symbols from among the special characters supported by WordPerfect can be used. Or sophisticated graphics (like those covered in Chapter 15, "Graphics") can be placed in headers and footers.

Though creating and inserting graphic effects can take some time, a well designed header or footer can pay off in terms of the professional look of the document and ease of use.

Editing Headers and Footers

Editing a header or footer is a lot like adding one. Follow these steps:

1. Place your cursor on or after the code representing the header or footer you want to edit.

2. Press ⇧Shift+F8, and select Header/Footer/Watermark. Or select Header/Footer/Watermark from the Layout menu.

3. Select Headers or Footers, change the space if you want, and select Header or Footer A or B.

4. Change the frequency, if you want, (All Pages, Even Pages, or Odd Pages). Select the Edit button.

5. Edit the header or footer window as you would any WordPerfect document screen.

6. When you are done, press F7, or select Exit from the File menu until you reach the document screen. The new, edited header or footer takes effect.

Turning a Header or Footer Off

Discontinuing a header or footer is only slightly different from adding and editing one. To turn a header or footer off:

1. Put your cursor after the paragraph containing the header or footer code.

2. Press ⇧Shift+F8, and select Header/Footer/Watermark. Or select Header/Footer/Watermark from the Layout menu.

3. Select **Headers** or **Footers**, and select Header or Footer A or B.

4. Select the **Off** button to discontinue the header or footer. Return to your document. A code like this is placed in your text: [Header B:Off;].

TIP: Once you have turned a header or footer off, you can't turn it back on. If you only want the header or footer turned off for a few pages, block those pages, and then perform the steps to turn the header or footer off.

You can also suppress a header or footer for a single page at a time. To do so:

1. Place the cursor at the top of the page where you want to suppress the header or footer.

2. Press ⇧Shift+F8, and select **Page**. Or select **Page** from the **Layout** menu.

3. Select **Suppress**. The Suppress (This Page Only) dialog box shown in Figure 9.2 appears.

4. Check the appropriate check boxes and return to your document. A code is placed in the document.

Figure 9.2
The Suppress (This Page Only) dialog box.

You can suppress all page numbering (including that in headers and footers) for the page. You can suppress all headers and footers on the page with a single setting. Or you can choose which headers and footers on the page to suppress.

TIP: To delete a header or footer, just delete the code. But be careful to delete the correct one. You can also copy and cut (move) header and footer codes. This is handy if you have developed a fancy header and want to use it in another document. Just copy it to the new document and edit it for that document.

Checking Spelling

1. Press [Ctrl]+[F2]. Or select Writing Tools and then Speller from the Tools menu.
2. Select the amount of text to check: Word, Page, Document, or From Cursor.

Checking the Spelling in a Block of Text

1. Block the text with [Alt]+[F4], or select Block from the Edit menu.
2. Press [Ctrl]+[F2]. Or select Writing Tools and Speller from the Tools menu.

Looking Up a Word

1. Press [Ctrl]+[F2]. Or select Writing Tools and Speller from the Tools menu.
2. Choose Look Up Word.

Getting Document Information

1. Press [Alt]+[F1], or select Writing Tools from the Tools menu.
2. Select Document Information.

Checking Grammar

1. Press [Alt]+[F1] and select Grammatik. Or select Writing Tools and Grammatik from the Tools menu.
2. Select I - Interactive check.

Using the Thesaurus

1. Place your cursor on the word to look up.
2. Press [Alt]+[F1] and Thesaurus. Or select Writing Tools and Thesaurus from the Tools menu.
3. Select an option.

10

Using the Writing Tools

Don't reach for that dictionary! Instead, use WordPerfect's Spell Checker. With it, you can check the spelling of a single word, a page, or an entire document. WordPerfect locates its built-in dictionary, looks up any unrecognized word, and suggests alternative spellings—more than any paper dictionary does. But that's not all; WordPerfect also comes with a handy thesaurus and a sophisticated grammar checking program.

How Does The Spell Checker Work?

WordPerfect's spelling checker consists of a very long list of acceptable words. Every word in your document is checked against this list. If the word is found, WordPerfect goes on to the next word. If the word is not found, it notifies you, and you can skip the word, add it to the list, or make a correction.

In addition to checking spelling, WordPerfect finds double occurrences of a word, which is a common typographical error. In this next sentence the word "the" was entered twice: "Politics is a risky business for the the faint of heart." If you were to spell check a document containing this sentence, WordPerfect would point out the redundant word and enable you to fix the sentence.

Correcting a Word, a Page, a Block, or a Document

To begin the spell check, place your cursor on the word, the page, or anywhere in the document. If you want to spell check a block of text, use Alt + F4. Or select **B**lock from the **E**dit menu to block the appropriate text.

Blocking text is useful when you've already spell checked a document, edited a section, and now want to spell check only that edited section.

Press Ctrl + F2 or select **W**riting Tools and **S**peller from the **T**ools menu. The Speller dialog box appears. Select one of the first four options to check for spelling problems. (If you are checking a block, the spell check begins as soon as you designate the block.)

Word: Checks a word.

Page: Checks the page on which your cursor rests.

Document: Checks the entire document.

From Cursor: Checks from the cursor location to the end of the document.

The spell check begins. WordPerfect skips those words that match words in the dictionary. When WordPerfect hits a word that is not in its dictionary, the Word Not Found dialog box shown in Figure 10.1 appears. The word identified as "misspelled" (mispell) is highlighted. This dialog box suggests spelling alternatives and prompts you for the possible actions to take. You can select a suggested word and press ↵Enter or select from the following actions.

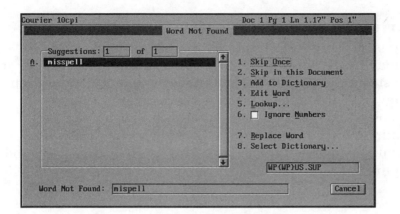

Figure 10.1
Spelling alternatives in the Word Not Found dialog box.

Skip **O**nce: Skips this first occurrence of this word not identified in the dictionary.

Skip in this Document: Adds the word to a Document Specific dictionary so the word will be skipped when this document is checked.

Add to Dictionary: Adds the word to the current supplemental dictionary. Future occurrences of this word will be skipped in this and any other document you spell check, assuming the current supplemental dictionary is used.

TIP: Adding your own name to the supplemental dictionary is a good use of the Add feature.

Edit **W**ord: If you don't like the alternatives WordPerfect presents, you can edit the word (or any part of the document, for that matter). When you select 4, Edit Word, your cursor goes to the document. Make your changes, and press F7 or ↵Enter in order to go back to spell checking.

Lookup: Looks up a different word. The Look Up Word dialog box appears. You can enter a word or word pattern and press ↵Enter. The word you enter is checked.

TIP: Entering a word pattern on a look up takes advantage of WordPerfect's ability to look up on phonetic matches. When you want to look up a word pattern, use an asterisk (*) to stand for multiple characters or a question mark (?) to stand for a single character. For example, looking up *ure will find words such as acupuncture, admeasure, and adventure. Looking up ?ure finds word with a single letter and then "ure", such as cure, lure, and pure.

Ignore **N**umbers: This option skips words with numbers throughout the rest of the editing session. Normally, WordPerfect stops on unusual number combinations.

Replace Word: Replaces the misspelled word with the suggestion highlighted.

A common mistake made when typing is entering double words. If WordPerfect encounters double words, these options are available from the Duplicate Word Found dialog box:

Skip Duplicate Word: Skip the double occurrence.

Delete Duplicate Word: Delete the second occurrence of the word.

Edit Word: Edits the text.

Disable Duplicate Word **C**hecking: Stops finding double words in this spell check session.

When it comes to capitalization, WordPerfect identifies both capitalization differences and irregular case. Capitalization differences are words that are inconsistently capitalized in your document. Irregular case refers to words that have odd capitalization (such as the appearance of the word SinCerely). On capitalization problems, these options come up:

Skip Word: Skips the word once.

Replace Word: Replaces the word with the one you've highlighted in the Suggestions area.

Edit Word: Allows you to edit the text. Press F7 or ↵Enter after editing the text.

Disable Case Checking: Stops locating case problems.

When you have finished spell checking, a message identifies that spell check is complete. Select OK.

TIP: If you want to quit the spell checker before it's finished, just press Esc.

The Quick Steps that follow summarize the steps to spell check, to identify words not in the WordPerfect dictionary, and to respond to the words identified.

Spell Checking

1. If you want, block the text with Alt+F4, or select **Block** from the **Edit** menu. Or place the cursor on the word, page, or document you want to check.	You have identified the text to spell check.
2. Press Ctrl+F2, or select **Writing Tools**, and **Speller** from the **Tools** menu.	If you did not block text, the Speller dialog box appears. Otherwise, spell checking begins (go on to step 4).
3. If you did not block text, select the amount of text to check: **Word**, **Page**, **Document**, or **From Cursor**.	The first unrecognized word is found.
4. Replace the word or make another selection.	Your selection is carried out. Spell checking continues until the final word is checked and you are instructed to select OK to return to document editing mode.

Creating Supplemental Dictionaries

Using supplemental dictionaries opens a whole area of power you might not expect. You can add or change words in supplemental dictionaries. You can also add words to replace others automatically or to supply as alternatives. For example, you may want to type in the acronym HMO but have it replaced by Health Maintenance Organization. You may also want WordPerfect to suggest alternatives to all occurrences of "i.e.". The alternatives might be "that is:" or "such as:".

When you add a word to the dictionary during spell checking, it is saved in a file named WP{WP}US.SUP. As you add words, you are creating a personal supplemental dictionary.

To edit the supplemental dictionary (or create or edit another supplemental dictionary), press Ctrl+F2, or select Writing Tools and Speller from the Tools menu. Select Edit Supplemental Dictionary. Select the dictionary you are using with this document. The Edit Supplemental Dictionary dialog box appears (see Figure 10.2).

Figure 10.2
Edit Supplemental Dictionary dialog box.

Words the user has marked for special treatment.

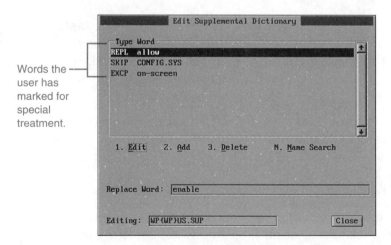

A supplemental dictionary contains three types of words. The types are shown on the left of the dialog box.

REPL:	Words or phrases to be replaced during spell checking with the replacement identified through this dialog box.
SKIP:	Words or phrases to skip during spell checking.
EXCP:	Words or phrases to have exceptions (alternates) identified during spell checking. The exceptions are identified through this dialog box.

On the Edit Supplemental Dictionary dialog box, highlight an existing word, and select Edit to edit the word (including the replacement or alternate words). To delete a word from the supplemental dictionary, highlight it, and select Delete. If you can't find a word, select Name Search to enter the name of the word. To add a word, select Add. When you select Add, these options appear:

Word/Phrase to **S**kip: Skips during spell checking.

Word/Phrase with **R**eplacement: Automatically replaces during spell checking.

Word/Phrase with **A**lternates: Suggests alternatives during spell checking.

WordPerfect prompts you through dialog boxes to enter the word and any replacement or alternates. Select Close when you are done.

Create another supplemental dictionary by selecting the Create New Sup button on the Edit Supplemental Dictionary dialog box. You could, for example, have a supplemental dictionary for legal terms, one for medical terms, and so on. Type in name for the file, and make sure it has the SUP file extension. The file for medical terms may be called MEDICAL.SUP. Press ↵Enter. You can then use the Edit Supplemental Dictionary to edit, add, or delete words. Select Close when you are done.

Looking Up a Word

You can look up a word as you work, rather than performing a full-blown spell check. To look up text you've entered, put the cursor on the word or block the phrase. Press Ctrl+F2 or select Writing Tools and Speller from the Tools menu. Pick Look Up Word. To look up the word or word pattern suggested, press ↵Enter. Or type in a new word or word pattern, and press ↵Enter. Select a suggested word or Cancel to return to your document.

When you enter a word pattern, use an asterisk (*) to stand for multiple characters or a question mark (?) to stand for a single character. (As mentioned earlier, looking up *ure will find words like acupuncture, admeasure, and adventure. Looking up ?ure finds word with a single letter and then "ure", such as cure, lure, and pure.)

Getting Document Information

WordPerfect supplies a good deal of information about your document. From the document, press Alt+F1, or select Writing Tools from the Tools menu. Select Document Information. The Document Information dialog box shown in Figure 10.3 appears.

Figure 10.3

Information available through Document Information.

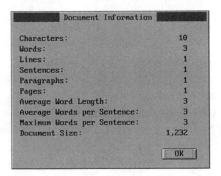

Checking Grammar

WordPerfect comes with Grammatik grammar checker. It will identify sentences that are too lengthy, incorrect tense, omitted words, and other grammar concerns. For example, suppose we use Grammatik to check the grammar on:

```
I never seen him be long to a group before.
```

As shown in Figure 10.4, Grammatik stops at the word "seen" and points out that the sentence doesn't have a main verb. The replacement "saw" is suggested.

Although Grammatik is smart with hundreds of rules built in, it is not your eighth grade language teacher. In our sentence example, Grammatik cannot identify that "be long" is really suppose to be the word "belong." When you use Grammatik, remember that it is giving you suggestions. Use your own judgment in correcting text.

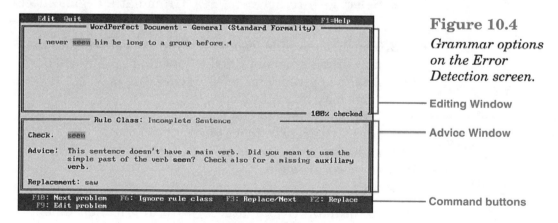

Figure 10.4
Grammar options on the Error Detection screen.

Editing Window

Advice Window

Command buttons

The Error Detection screen is shown in Figure 10.4. The Editing Window shows the portion of your document being checked. The Rule Class indicates the class of the grammar rule being applied. Here, the rules for Incomplete Sentence are applied. You can choose to skip all the rules for a particular problem, if you like, by using the command button for Ignore rule class. The Advice Window includes the word to Check, the Advice, and the suggested Replacement word. The command buttons show your options for continuing.

The following Quick Steps summarize the procedure for checking grammar.

Checking Grammar

1. With your cursor in the document, press [Alt]+[F1] and Grammatik. Or select Writing Tools and Grammatik from the Tools menu.

The opening screen appears.

2. Select **I** - Interactive check.

Grammatik begins checking the document.

3. The first possible grammar problem is identified. Advice is given, and selections may be available. Use the options at the bottom of the screen to make a change, or continue to the next problem.

You are returned to the opening screen when checking is done.

4. When you are returned to the main Grammatik screen, press **Q** to Quit.

You are returned to your WordPerfect document. Any changes you made are placed in the document.

You can choose to skip spell and grammar checking in a particular part of a document. This is helpful if you have text that has already been checked or text that will slow down your work by identifying errors that are not really errors. Place your cursor where you want spell and grammar to stop. Press Alt+F1, or select Writing Tools from the Tools menu. On the Writing Tools dialog box, place a check in the check box before Disable Speller/Grammatik (in this part of the document). To enable spell and grammar checking later, perform the same operation and remove the check from the check box.

Thesaurus

WordPerfect's Thesaurus feature is simple to use and often overlooked. When you say, "that's not quite the word I want," call up WordPerfect's Thesaurus for other suggestions.

The following is a list of the available buttons from within Thesaurus:

Look Up: In the Word text box, type in a different word, and press ↵Enter. Suggested substitutions for that word appear.

View: Allows you to scroll your document. This is especially helpful if you want to see the full context for the word you are replacing. Just press F7 to go back to the Thesaurus screen.

Clear Column: As you work in the Thesaurus, you can look up several words and not only fill all the columns but replace earlier columns of words with later columns of words. This option clears the most recently added columns.

History: Shows you a list of words that have been looked up. Select one to go to the list of words.

Replace: The word in your document is replaced with the one highlighted.

Cancel: To stop using the Thesaurus and return to your document without substituting a word.

If you fill more than the three columns with suggested words, you can press the left or right arrow keys to move from column to column. Or use the mouse, and click on the left arrow or right arrow.

The following Quick Steps detail how to use the Thesaurus.

Using the Thesaurus

1. Place your cursor on the word to look up, and press Alt+F1. Press Thesaurus, or select Writing Tools. Then select Thesaurus from the Tools menu.

   Suggested replacements for the word appear.

2. Select one of the options shown at the bottom of the screen.

   Prompts for the selected operation appear. Follow the prompts to complete the operation.

Search and Replace Rules

- Search and replace occurs from the cursor location forward or backward.
- The character to search for must follow conventions, such as case.
- To extend a search to headers, footers, graphics, and so on, press `Home` before beginning the search or replace.

Searching

- To search forward, press `F2`, or select Search from the Edit menu.
- To search backward, press `⇧Shift`+`F2`, or select Search from the Edit menu. Then check **B**ackward Search on the Search dialog box.

Replacing

1. Press `⇧Shift`+`F2`, or select Replace from the Edit menu.
2. Enter the text and codes to search for, check any check boxes, and select the Replace F2 button.
3. Enter the text and codes to replace, and select the Search F2 button.

Entering Bookmarks

- To enter a QuickMark, press `Ctrl`+`Q`.
- To create and enter a bookmark, press `Alt`+`F5`, and select **B**ookmark. Or select Bookmark from the Edit menu. Select Create and enter a bookmark name.

Searching and Replacing

Searching and replacing characters is a feature that, at first, you may not think you'll use often. Read on. In this chapter, you will learn not only how to use Search and Replace, but you will also gain ideas about how to use Search and Replace creatively to solve problems.

You use WordPerfect's Search feature to find text and codes in a document. You type in the text or codes to search for and WordPerfect finds the first occurrence. If you want, you can then continue searching from that location.

There are more uses for Search than may meet the eye. You can search for text that you believe may be incorrectly entered. Or you can search for a key word in order to find a particular spot in a document. Search is also useful for checking headings, figure numbering, or bulleted text against tables of contents or indexes.

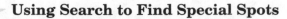

Using Search to Find Special Spots

You may need to go from one part of a lengthy document to another to check information, and then return to your original spot. If so, you can place a Bookmark or QuickMark in your text. Both are described later in this chapter. But, for a quick notation, just enter special text in that special spot.

Here's how to proceed. Place the special text where you want to return. Make sure the characters are unique and won't be used elsewhere in the document. Some users like to use a double asterisk and their name or instructions as a bookmark (such as `**Bill:check this out`). Go wherever you want in your document. Then, when you want to go back to the special spot, simply search out the unique characters. Remember, you are just searching for a series of characters. The down side of this approach is that you must remember to delete all the special text before you are done with the document. Otherwise, the special text will appear in the document when printed. Bookmarks and QuickMarks don't pose this problem.

Figure 11.1 illustrates one use of Search. Here, the document will be checked for "Bennington" being misspelled as "Benningtin." Notice that the Search For: text box shows the text that is sought. The message in Figure 11.2 shows that the spelling is not found. You know that in this document, at least, "Bennington" is not "Benningtin."

The Replace feature goes a step beyond searching. With it, you identify both the text to find and the text to replace the found text. Replace is useful if you realize a proper name is misspelled consistently, a code is incorrectly used, or you want to change formatting. For example, for a bulleted list, you might have entered text with a small "o" (to signify a bullet) followed by a tab. In order to change that to a dash followed by an indent, you could use Replace.

Figure 11.1
Using the Search dialog box to check for Benningtin.

Figure 11.2
Benningtin not found.

Let's take a look at an example. In our letter, bullets are created by a dash followed by an indent. We'll replace those with an indent, a small o, and an indent. Figure 11.3 shows the text that will be searched and the replacement we'll use. We include the indent after the dash because we only want to find occurrences where the dash is followed by an indent (not dashes that might be hyphens, for example). Figure 11.4 illustrates the text after the replacement is made. Notice that the indents and small o's are now included.

Text for which to search   Replacement text

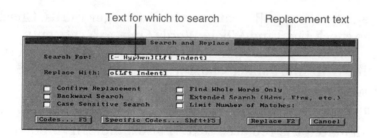

Figure 11.3
The dash and indent entered for the search, to be replaced by an indent, small o, and indent.

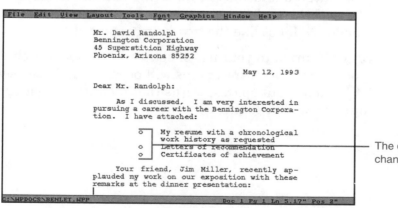

The dashes have changed to bullets.

Figure 11.4
After replacements.

You can check your replacements as you work or let WordPerfect do it alone. If you check replacements, WordPerfect stops at each occurrence. You then identify whether to replace that occurrence or not.

Searching and Replacing Guidelines

When you use Search and Replace, the text you enter is important to identifying what will be found and, potentially, replaced. Here are the rules to keep in mind:

- When you enter the text to search out, the case is ignored unless you check the check box for a case-sensitive search. For example, entering TIme will find time, Time, and TIME. For the search to be case sensitive, you will need to check Case Sensitive Search. Then, the search will yield an exact match to your entry.

- Searched text will locate portions of larger words. Check the check box Find Whole Words Only to locate only complete words not parts of words. For example, entering "like" will find "alike," "businesslike," and "dislike." Selecting for whole words will find only "like."

- When text is replaced, the case used in the replacement will match the replaced text. (For example, if "Merger" is encountered and you are replacing with the word "consolidation," the replacement is entered with the first letter capitalized just like the text being replaced.)

- Pay attention to your use of spaces when you search. If you enter spaces, the spaces will be included in the search. If you leave out spaces, words that include the searched-out text will be found.

TIP: When you search, you can use wild-card characters. Enter an asterisk (*) code to stand for multiple characters. Use a question mark (?) code to stand for a single character. For example, if you want to find "win," "wit," "wicker," and "wicked," search for "wi*." To only find "win" and "wit," search for "wi?" Watch out! You must use the codes using the Codes F5 button. If you enter an asterisk or question mark, those symbols are searched out.

Searching Forward

Searching forward in a document means searching from your cursor location to the end of the document. If you want to search the entire document, press Home, Home, Home, ↑ to move to the top of the document (before any codes).

TIP: When you search forward or backward, only the document text is searched. You can search headers, footers, text boxes, watermarks, footnotes, endnotes, comments, graphics box captions, equations, and Table of Authorities Full Form. Press Home before using F2 or ⇧Shift+F2. Or select Extended Search (Hdrs, Ftrs, and so on) from the Search dialog box.

The following Quick Steps summarize how to search for text forward through a document.

QUICK STEPS

Using Search Forward

1. Position your cursor where the search should begin. Press F2, or select **Search** from the **Edit** menu. — The Search dialog box appears.
2. Enter the text and codes for which you want to search, check any check boxes, and select the Search F2 button. — The text is found.

Searching Backward

To search from your cursor location back to the beginning of the document is referred to as *searching backward*. To search from the end of the document to the beginning, press Home, Home, Home, ↓ to go to the end of the document (after all codes).

The following Quick Steps detail how to search for text backward through a document.

QUICK STEPS

Using Search Backward

1. Position your cursor where the search should begin. Press Shift+F2, or select **Search** from the **Edit** menu. Then check **Backward Search** on the Search dialog box. — The **Backward Search** option on the Search dialog box is checked.
2. Enter the text and codes to search for, check any check boxes, and select the Search F2 button. — The text is found.

Using Search to Block Text

You can block text the old fashioned way . . . or with Search. Suppose you know the last word or phrase you want to include in the blocked text. Press ⬆Shift+F4, or select **Block** from the **Edit** menu to start the block. Press F2, enter the last word or phrase in the block, and choose the F2 Search button. The block is extended to the text in the search.

Searching for Codes

You can enter codes to be searched for or replaced. On the Search and Search and Replace dialog boxes, select the Codes F5 button. When selected, you'll see a list of WordPerfect codes. Select the code to be placed in the area identifying text to search for or replace.

The Specific Codes ⬆Shift+F5 button allows you to search for very specific code information (usually including a measurement or size). For example, rather than just search for every font code, you can identify the font code for Dutch 801 Italic (Speedo). Select the Specific Codes ⬆Shift+F5 button, select the code, and follow the prompts to complete the search. These are the codes that can be made specific:

Bottom Margin

Font

Font Size

Horizontal Advance

Justification

Left Margin

Left Margin Adjustment

Overstrike

Right Margin

Right Margin Adjustment

Style

Top Margin

Vertical Advance

Replacing Text

Replacing text is like searching except that it goes an extra step. You will also notice two check boxes on the Search and Replace dialog box that weren't on the Search dialog box. One is Confirm Replacement that will cause the search to stop and prompt you to confirm the replacement before you continue. If you don't check Confirm Replacement, replacements are made automatically. (Warning: Automatic replacements can be dangerous unless you are sure of what you are replacing.) The other check box is Limit Number of Matches. Check this check box, and enter the number of occurrences that you want WordPerfect to find during the search and replace.

The following Quick Steps detail how to replace text.

Replacing Text

1. Position your cursor where the replace procedure should begin. Press Alt + F2, or select Replace from the Edit menu.	The Search and Replace dialog box appears.
2. Enter the text and codes to search for, check any check boxes, and select the Replace F2 button.	The text and codes to search out appear.

3. Enter the text and codes
to replace, and select the
Replace F2 button.

If you are confirming replacements, you are taken to the first occurrence of the text to replace. A Confirm Replacement dialog box appears. Respond Yes to make the replacement and continue, No to skip the replacement and move on, or Replace All to replace all occurrences without confirmation. When done, a Search and Replace Complete dialog box appears. It includes the number of occurrences found and replacements made.

TIP: As with Search, only the text in the document is searched and replaced. You can search and replace headers, footers, text boxes, watermarks, footnotes, endnotes, comments, graphics box captions, equations, and Table of Authorities Full Form. Press Home before using the Alt + F2 option. Or use the Extended Search (Hdrs, Ftrs, and so on) option on the Search and Replace dialog box.

Bookmarks

Bookmarks allow you to search for a location in a document, regardless of the text or code that the location contains. Bookmarks are especially helpful when you are working on large documents. One type of bookmark is a *QuickMark*. It is a fast way to enter a bookmark, but there can be only one QuickMark in a document.

To enter a QuickMark, put the cursor in the appropriate spot. Press Ctrl + Q. The [Bookmark] code is placed in your document.

You can have multiple bookmarks in a document besides the QuickMark, but each must have a unique name. Press Alt + F5 and select **B**ookmark, or select Bookmark from the **E**dit menu. Select **C**reate, enter a bookmark name, and press OK. The bookmark is placed in your document.

To search for a bookmark code, use the search options and select the Bookmark code. To search out a specific bookmark, press [Alt]+[F5], and select **B**ookmark. Or select Bookmark from the **E**dit menu. Highlight the bookmark to find, and select **F**ind.

Hypertext

Another twist on searching for text involves using *hypertext*. Hypertext is text you identify to link parts of your document to the same document, another document, or to a macro that automatically executes keystrokes and commands. Hypertext is typically a word or phrase that links to the document or macro you identify. The uses of hypertext are ample. Here are a couple of examples to start you thinking. You can jump to reference materials to provide the reader additional information. You can develop instructions to complete forms and run automated forms set up in macros. (To learn more about macros, see Chapter 13, "Macros.")

First, create a link by identifying an existing Bookmark or macro to use with the hypertext. Second, mark the characters as hypertext. Then, set up a link from the hypertext to jump to the Bookmark or to run the macro. When you create a hypertext link, you can choose from these selections:

Go to **B**ookmark: To go to a bookmark in the current document.

Go to **O**ther Document Bookmark: To go to another document or a bookmark in another document. (You'll exit the document with the hypertext you selected.)

Run **M**acro: To run a specified macro. The macro begins running at the hypertext location. If you want to leave the document containing the hypertext, you'll need to build the exit activities in the start of your macro.

You can also identify how you want the hypertext to appear. If you select Highlight Text, you can identify how much highlight is applied to the hypertext. If you select Button Graphic, you can put text or graphics in the button. (Buttons only appear in Text Mode Reveal Codes, Graphics Mode, and Page Mode.)

To create a hypertext link, follow these Quick Steps.

Create a Hypertext Link

1. Block the text to use as hypertext with Alt + F4, or select Block from the File menu.

The hypertext is identified.

2. Press Alt + F5 and select Hypertext, or select Hypertext from the Tools menu.

The Hypertext dialog box appears.

3. Select Create Link.

The Create Hypertext Link dialog box appears.

4. Identify the Hypertext Action (where to link to) and the Hypertext Appearance (Highlighted or Button), and select OK.

A code appears in the document. Repeat steps 1 through 4 to set up as many links as you want.

If you plan on using multiple hypertext links, make it hypertext active first. That way, you can press ↵Enter or click on the hypertext to jump or run. To activate hypertext, press Alt + F5, and select Hypertext, or select Hypertext from the Tools menu. The Hypertext dialog box appears. Check the Hypertext is Active check box, and select OK.

If you only want to make one jump or run, it may be faster to not make hypertext active. Put the cursor on the hypertext. Press

Alt + F5 , and select Hypertext, or select Hypertext from the Tools menu. The Hypertext dialog box appears. Select Jump/Run.

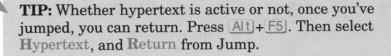

> **TIP:** Whether hypertext is active or not, once you've jumped, you can return. Press Alt + F5 . Then select Hypertext, and Return from Jump.

The Hypertext dialog box can be used for other activities. With the cursor on hypertext, you can choose Edit Link to change the link or format. **D**elete Link(s) can be used to delete the link of the hypertext the cursor rests on or to delete all links in blocked text.

Comments and Hidden Text

Finally, there are two twists on placing and later finding information in your documents. You can use comments or hidden text. Here's how they are different. Comments appear in a text box on your screen but are not printed. Hidden text allows you to display or hide the text. When displayed, it is treated like regular document text and is printed. When it is not displayed, it is also not printed.

To enter a comment, press Ctrl + F7 , and select Comment. Or select Comment from the Layout menu. Select Create, and add the text. Press F7 when done. The text appears in a box, and a code is inserted.

To enter hidden text, press Alt + F5 , and choose Hidden Text. Check the **Hidden** text check box, and select OK. (Notice the check box to control whether hidden text is shown or not.) You are returned to your document where [Hidden On] and [Hidden Off] codes are placed. Type the hidden text between the codes. When you deselect the check box for showing hidden text, the [Hidden On] code remains to let you know the text is still there.

Arranging Document Windows

1. Press `Ctrl`+`F3`, and select Window, or select the Window menu.
2. Select Tile or Cascade.

Switching Between Document Windows

- To move between windows, press `Shift`+`F3`, or select Switch from the Window menu.
- To switch to a particular window, select Switch to from the Window menu, or press `Home`, then `0`.

Using the File Manager

1. Press `F5`, or select File Manager from the File menu.
2. Change the drive, path, and file information, if you want, and select OK.
3. Mark each document with an asterisk, or highlight a single document.
4. Select Copy, Delete or Move/Rename.

Creating a New Directory

1. Press `F5`, or select File Manager from the File menu.
2. Press `=`, enter the drive, path, and name of the new directory, and select **OK**.
3. At the create message, choose Yes.

Finding a File

1. Press `F5`, or select File Manager from the File menu.
2. Press Enter to display the directory's files in the File Manager window.
3. Select Find, Search, or Name Search.

Managing Documents

Experienced WordPerfect users are not the only ones who need to manage multiple documents; even beginners can benefit from WordPerfect's file handling and retrieval capabilities. In this chapter, you'll learn some basic skills for managing your documents, both on-screen and on disks.

Working with Document Windows

Opening several documents at a time has a variety of benefits. You can have several documents readily available for reference or notes, or copy or move text between documents. WordPerfect creates a new *document window* for each document you open.

For example, let's say you need to move the heading information from the document called BENLET.WPP into a document you'll call BENLET-2.WPP. Figure 12.1 shows the heading information in BENLET.WPP (which is the document 1 window). Notice that the lower right corner of the status line indicates Doc 1. Because this is the active window (where the cursor resides), the window is colored (in Graphics Mode) or framed with a double line (in Text Mode). After blocking the appropriate text and then moving it, the text is placed in another window that is document 2. Notice that in Figure 12.2, Doc 2 is the active window. The date has been changed, and the document has been saved as BENLET-2.WPP.

Figure 12.1
BENLET.WPP contents in document 1.

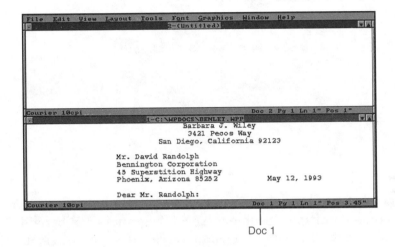

Doc 1

Figure 12.2
BENLET-2.WPP created by moving BENLET.WPP contents to document 2.

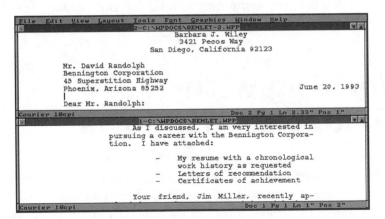

Opening and Closing Document Windows

To create a window, select **N**ew or **O**pen from the **F**ile menu. Or press ⇧Shift+F10, and open a new document. New windows appear full screen and maximized without a frame (a line around the window). To frame the document, press `Ctrl`+`F3`, and select Window and Frame, or select Frame from the Window menu.

To close a window, just close the document by saving it or exiting.

Moving and Sizing Document Windows

As you just learned, you can frame a window by pressing `Ctrl`+`F3`. Framed windows can be moved or sized on the screen, as you'll learn shortly, but first let's take a look at a window frame.

As shown in Figure 12.3, the frame for a window has the title of the document at the top. You can use the keyboard or mouse to control the frame. We'll look at keyboard options first.

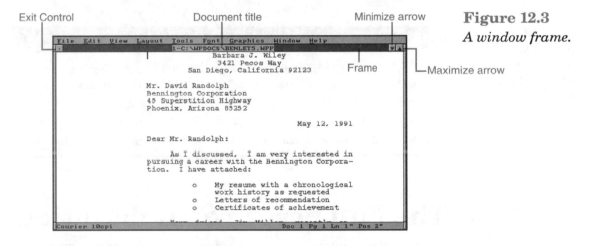

Exit Control   Document title   Minimize arrow

Figure 12.3
A window frame.

Maximize arrow

You can minimize the size of the window or maximize it. Press `Ctrl`+`F3`, select Window and Minimize or Maximize. Or select the Window menu and Minimize or Maximize. Figure 12.4 shows a window minimized.

Figure 12.4
*A minimized
window.*

To move the window, press [Ctrl]+[F3], and select Window Move. The window frame appears as a dotted line. Use the arrow keys to move to the new location. Press [F7] or [↵Enter]. To change the size of a window, press [Ctrl]+[F3], and select Window Size. Use the right and down arrow keys to size the window. Press [F7] or [↵Enter].

To exit a document window, press [F7], or select Exit from the File menu. If you choose Exit WP from the File menu or press [Home] and then [F7], you are prompted through exiting all windows, including WordPerfect itself.

Table 12.1 identifies how to exercise the same control over the window using a mouse.

Table 12.1
*Controlling the
Window Frame
with the Mouse.*

Action	Result
Click the Minimize (down) arrow	Minimizes the window
Click the Maximize (up) arrow	Maximizes the window
Drag the window title	Moves the window
Drag the sides or bottom	Sizes the window
Click on Exit Control (upper left)	Exits the window

The Full Screen Switch Option

Instead of displaying several windows on the screen at once, you can switch between full screen displays of documents. Maximize windows to get the full screen display. To switch to a new display, press [⇧Shift]+[F3], or select Switch from the Window menu. You are taken to the other full screen display. The document number appears in the bottom right corner of the screen, enabling you to distinguish between the documents. Continue to use [⇧Shift]+[F3] to move back and forth between the full screen displays. Or to go to another window, press [Home], [0], or select Switch to from the Window menu.

Copying and Moving Step by Step

Whether you are working with full screen displays or multiple windows on one screen, the method to copy or move text is the same. Create the necessary windows. Then, block the text to copy or move and press `Ctrl`+`F4`. Identify whether to copy and paste or cut and paste the block. Once identified, your screen says: Move cursor; press Enter to retrieve. Then switch to the other document with `⇧Shift`+`F3`. You are then free to press `↵Enter` to complete the copy or move. It's that simple.

Arranging Windows

Because you can open up to nine windows at once, the screen can get messy. Plus, all windows may not be appearing on a single screen. (Remember, when you open a document or create a new document, the window is maximized to full screen with no frame.)

To arrange all windows on one screen, press `Ctrl`+`F3`, and select Window. Or select the Window menu. Select Tile or Cascade. Figure 12.5 shows several windows arranged using Tile. Figure 12.6 shows the same windows organized using Cascade.

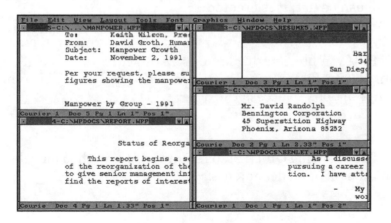

Figure 12.5
Windows in a Tile arrangement.

Figure 12.6
*Windows in a
Cascade
arrangement.*

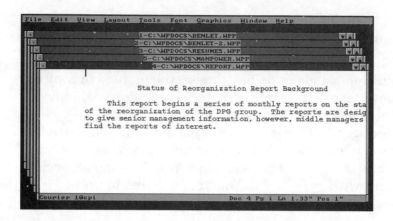

Switching Among Windows

To move from one window to the other, press ⟨⇧Shift⟩+⟨F3⟩, or select
Switch from the Window menu. The current window appears with
a colored or double line as the frame. You can also use these
options from the Window menu to move between windows:

Next: To go to the next window.

Previous: To go to the previous window.

Switch to: To see the Switch to Document dialog box
where you can select the window to go to. If the window
doesn't exist, it is created.

TIP: If you have multiple full screen windows, you can
only switch between two of them with ⟨⇧Shift⟩+⟨F3⟩. Use the
other options to access the other windows.

The following Quick Steps summarize a method for selecting
from a list of open documents.

Switching Among Open Document Windows

1. Press F3, or select Switch to from the Window menu.

A list of open documents appears.

2. Highlight the document to which you want to switch.

3. Press Enter.

The cursor moves to a new window. If there are multiple windows on the screen, the active one appears with a colored or double line as a frame.

CAUTION

If you retrieve the same document into both windows and then edit one of the windows, the edits are not automatically applied to the document in the second window. If you make edits that you want to keep, make sure they are made in one document and that you have that document saved under the appropriate name. The best policy when working with the same document in both windows is to be careful about which document is the "latest and greatest" to save.

Managing Documents on Disks

When you start using WordPerfect, you'll have only a few documents, so managing them is easy. But as you create more documents, you may forget the names or the contents—just locating the document you want can be a problem. Therefore, it's important to have a system for managing your documents.

Following a scheme for naming documents is important so you can readily identify them. If, after creating several documents, you think of a better naming scheme, go ahead and rename the documents. Another important management task is to delete unnecessary documents so you can easily locate the useful documents. This section covers speedy file management procedures that can help you get started with these important tasks.

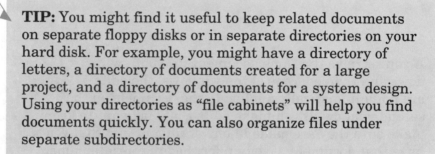

TIP: You might find it useful to keep related documents on separate floppy disks or in separate directories on your hard disk. For example, you might have a directory of letters, a directory of documents created for a large project, and a directory of documents for a system design. Using your directories as "file cabinets" will help you find documents quickly. You can also organize files under separate subdirectories.

A Word About Directories and Subdirectories

To control your files, you need to be familiar with the concepts of directories and subdirectories. Appendix A includes more detail, but we'll hit the highlights here before we start moving around in the File Manager.

Basically, your hard disk can be divided into sections of any size called directories. These sections help you organize your files by use. For example, the WP60 directory contains WordPerfect system files. The WPDOCS directory was created when Word-Perfect was installed and is intended to contain document files. The path (which we've referred to earlier in this book) is a way to identify to your computer how to get to a particular directory, subdirectory, or file. For example, this path indicates the location of a letter called BENLET.WPP. It is stored on drive C, in the WPDOCS directory.

```
C:\WPDOCS\BENLET.WPP
```

The File Manager

The File Manager can't be beat when it comes to handling document management activities. Go to the File Manager by pressing F5 or by selecting File Manager from the File menu. The Specify File Manager List dialog box shown in Figure 12.7 appears.

Figure 12.7
The Specify File Manager List dialog box.

Type in the drive, path, and file identifier you want. (For example, you could type in A:*.WPP to display all the files on the disk in drive A that have the .WPP extension.) Select OK.

TIP: If you type in a path that is not recognized, a message is likely to appear saying you've entered an invalid drive/path specification. Carefully check the punctuation you've used in the path, as well as the validity of the directories and file name used. Usually, some typographical error has occurred.

If you don't know the directory you want to select, select the Directory Tree button or press F8. This takes you to the Directory Tree shown in Figure 12.8. Select the drive and directory you want from those that exist.

Figure 12.8
The Directory Tree.

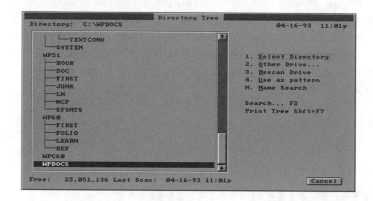

Once you have selected the drive and directory, the File Manager dialog box shown in Figure 12.9 appears.

Figure 12.9
The File Manager dialog box.

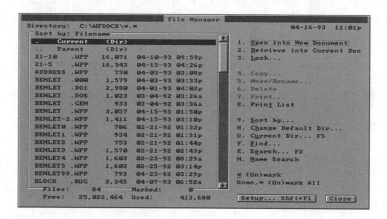

What the File Manager Dialog Box Tells You

Starting at the top of the File Manager dialog box, you are given this information.

- **Directory:** This shows the directory for which documents are displayed.

- **The date and time:** If your computer's internal clock is set correctly, you will see the current date and time at the top of the screen. Each document you create or edit will be time and date stamped. That way, if you have more than one version of a document, you will be able to tell which is the most recent.

> **NOTE:** Most computers have a clock that automatically enters the date and time for you. If yours does not, use DOS's DATE and TIME commands before using WordPerfect (see your DOS manual for information about these commands).

- **Sort by:** Indicates how the files that follow are sorted. In this example, the files are sorted by file name.

- **The directories (such as** . Current <Dir>)**:** The directory you are using appears along with other available directories. To display the files for another directory, highlight it, and press Enter.

- **The files:** This listing shows each file name, extension, and size (in bytes), as well as the date and time last saved.

- **Files:** This identifies the number of files in this directory.

- **Marked:** This identifies the number of documents in the directory that are marked with an asterisk.

- **Free and Used:** This shows the amount of unused space (in bytes) on your disk, as well as the amount used in this directory. When you mark a file (possibly to copy), the amount used is the total amount of space consumed by the file marked.

NOTE: A *byte* is approximately equal to one character.

CAUTION   Never allow the free space to dwindle to less than 10% of the total space on your drive. If space becomes short, move documents to another disk or delete unneeded documents.

The options you have for manipulating files appear on the right of the dialog box. We covered the first two options (**O**pen into New Document and **R**etrieve into Current Document) in Chapter 3. The **P**rint option was covered in Chapter 6. (To print the list of files in the directory selected on the File Manager dialog box, select the Print List option.) We'll cover the remaining options in this chapter.

Marking Files

The File Manager allows you to work with one document or several. If you are working with one document, highlight it and perform the needed operation.

To work with multiple documents, highlight one of the documents, and press the asterisk key (using ⇧Shift+8 on most keyboards). An asterisk appears before the file name. Continue to mark as many files as you want. Figure 12.10 shows three files marked with an asterisk. To eliminate the asterisk from a file name, highlight the document name, and type * again. To mark or unmark all files in the directory, press Home and then *.

If the number of documents on the List Files screen fills more than one screen, press PgUp or PgDn to move from screen to screen. To leave the File Manger dialog box, select Close.

Documents marked with asterisks.

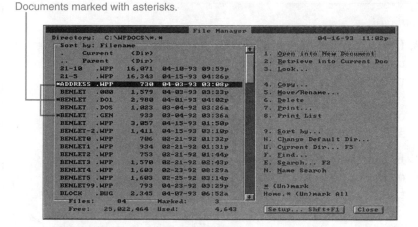

Figure 12.10
Three documents marked for work.

Copying Documents

You will want to copy documents to create backups, in case a document becomes damaged or lost. One way to copy a document is to save it under another name or to save it to another disk. Another way to copy documents is to use the File Manager. The benefits of this procedure are that you can copy a file on disk (instead of having to retrieve it to your screen), and you can copy more than one document in a single operation.

The following Quick Steps identify how to copy documents.

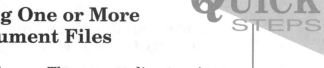

Copying One or More Document Files

1. Press F5, or select File Manager from the File menu.

   The current directory is displayed in the Specify File Manager List dialog box.

2. Change the drive, path, and file information, if you want, and select OK.

   The File Manager dialog box appears.

continues

continued

3. If you want to copy more than one file, type `*` to mark each file name with an asterisk. To copy just one file, highlight it. Then select Copy.

The Copy dialog box appears.

4. Enter the drive and path of the disk to which to copy the files, and select OK.

If the files don't already exist, they are copied. A replace message appears for your response if the files are already on the disk (for example `Replace A:BENLET.WPP`).

5. If prompted for replacement, select Yes to copy over the existing file.

6. Unmark the files, if necessary, by typing `*`.

FYI IDEAS

Estimating How Much You Can Copy to a Diskette

As mentioned, the File Manager copy command is often used to create diskette backups of documents. But, how many documents can you copy to a diskette before you get a disk full message?

To see how much space is free on the diskette, press `F5`, or select File Manager from the File menu. Enter the drive of the diskette, and select OK. Jot down the amount of space Free shown at the bottom of the File Manager dialog box.

Next, mark the files to copy on the File Manager dialog box. As you mark them, the number Marked and the spaced Used by the marked files appears under the list of files. Compare this to the free space on the diskette, and you'll know how close you're coming to filling the diskette.

Moving or Renaming Documents

You can move or rename documents through the File Manager. As you'll see, though these features are handled through the same selection, the results are very different.

When you rename a file, the existing name is replaced with the new name you suggest. Renaming a file is useful when you determine a better way to organize existing files. For example, you may have created these three versions of a document:

DEARPT.WPP

DREPORT.WPP

DRT.WPP

You could rename these files to suggest the order in which they were created:

DERPT1.WPP

DERPT2.WPP

DERPT3.WPP

When you move a file, it is removed from the current disk location and placed at a new location you have indicated. For example, you might move a file from one disk to another when the original disk is getting full or if you want to sort the file on a disk you use less often.

CAUTION   Don't confuse moving a file with copying a file. When you move, the original location of the file is lost. When you copy, the original location of the file is preserved and a duplicate of the file is made.

TIP: You can rename files only one at a time. You can move files only by marking them with an asterisk.

The following Quick Steps detail how to move or change the names of documents.

Moving or Renaming Documents

1. Press F5, or select File Manager from the File menu.	The current directory is displayed in the Specify File Manager List dialog box.
2. Change the drive, path, and file information, if you want, and select OK.	The File Manager dialog box appears.
3. Highlight a single file to rename. Or mark one or more files to move with an asterisk by typing an * for each. Select Move/Rename.	The Move/Rename dialog box appears.
4. Follow the prompts.	The highlighted file is renamed or the fields marked with asterisks are moved.

Deleting Files

Deleting a document is useful when you are sure you will not want that version of the document again. For example, let's say you've created several different versions of BENLET.WPP for internal review. When one version is selected, you may want to delete the other versions. This not only saves space but saves possible future confusion about which version was used.

> When deleting, always proceed carefully. Check and double check the file you want to delete to make sure you will never again want the document. Once a document is deleted, it cannot be recovered through WordPerfect.

CAUTION

The following Quick Steps explain how to delete one or more files.

Deleting One or More Files

1. Press F5, or select File Manager from the File menu.

The current directory is displayed in the Specify File Manager List dialog box.

2. Change the drive, path, and file information, if you want, and select OK.

The File Manager dialog box appears.

3. To delete multiple files, mark each with an asterisk using *. To delete one file, highlight it.

The files to delete are identified.

continues

continued

4. Select **D**elete. — A message to confirm the delete appears.

5. Respond **Y**es to the delete messages when they appear. — The file or files are deleted.

Changing the Default Directory

When WordPerfect is installed, the default directory for your documents is set up to be WPDOCS. You can change the directory to a new default for the editing session. This is useful if you will be creating new documents and want to save them to a different directory without typing in the entire path.

To change the default directory, press F5 or select File Manager from the File menu. Type in an equal sign (=). The Change Default Directory dialog box appears. Type in the new directory, and select OK. You can also use the Directory Tree button or the QuickList button to locate the new directory. (Another alternative is to change the default directory on the File Manager dialog box by using the Change Default Dir option.)

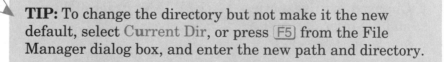

TIP: To change the directory but not make it the new default, select Current Dir, or press F5 from the File Manager dialog box, and enter the new path and directory.

Creating Directories and Subdirectories

You can use the File Manager to create a new directory or subdirectory to store the files you have saved (or are about to save).

Decide on the drive, path, and unique name for the new directory. Press F5, or select File Manager from the File menu. The Specify File Manager List dialog box appears. Enter an equal sign (=). The Change Default Directory dialog box appears. Enter the drive, path, and name of the new directory, and select OK. A message to confirm the creation of the directory appears. Select Yes to create the directory.

> **TIP:** Once you have created a new directory, you can confirm its creation by looking at the Directory Tree. Press F5, and select the Directory Tree button. You may need to use the Rescan Drive option on the Directory Tree dialog box for the newly created drive to appear.

To delete a subdirectory, make sure all the files are deleted from the subdirectory. Press F5, or select File Manager from the File menu. Go to the parent directory of the subdirectory to delete. Highlight the subdirectory to delete, and select Delete. You are asked to confirm the removal of the directory. Respond Yes, and the subdirectory is deleted.

Finding a File

The ability to find a file by file name or a word in a file is invaluable.

The easiest way to find a file by file name is to press [F5], or select File Manager from the File menu. Enter the directory with the file, and, on the File Manager dialog box, select Name Search. Begin typing in the letters of the file name, and your highlight goes to the file.

This approach is only useful if you know the name of the file. What if you don't know the full name of the file or only know the file contents you seek? You can use the Find option. Find allows you to search by precise file name or word(s), or use an asterisk to stand in place of one or more letters of which you are unsure. Use a question mark to stand in place of a single letter.

For example, suppose as a convention you use "let" in the file name of letters and .WPP as the extension on all WordPerfect document files. You could look for all letters by entering this text:

```
*LET.WPP
```

Names like those that follow appear for you to narrow down your selection:

BENLET.WPP

JIMLET.WPP

STARLET.WPP

MALLET.WPP

Use Find to find a file by full or partial file name or to create a list of files that contains a word or phrase. To proceed, press [F5], or select File Manager from the File menu to display the files you want to look through. If you want to go through only certain files, identify each with an asterisk. Otherwise, all files in the directory will be considered.

Select Find to display the Find dialog box. Choose among these options to find a name, word, or pattern:

Name: To look for a file name. From the File Manager dialog box, you can also use Search ([F2]) to search for a file name. For more information about WordPerfect's Search capability, see Chapter 11.

Document Summary: To look through Document Summaries to find a word or pattern.

First **P**age: To look through first pages of documents only.

Entire Document: To look through the entire contents of documents.

Conditions: To add conditions to limit the find operation. Figure 12.11 shows the File Manager Find Conditions dialog box from which you can work.

QuickFinder: QuickFinder File Indexer is used to quickly search indexes. To use this option, you must create an index in a document.

Undo: Once the find is complete, select Undo to return the File Manager to the state it was in prior to the find operation.

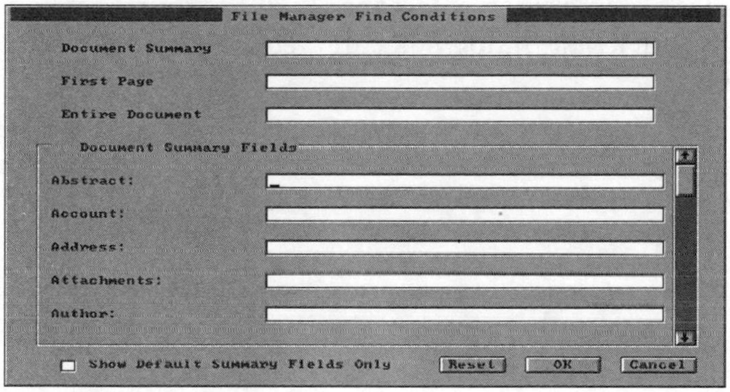

Figure 12.11
The File Manager Find Conditions dialog box.

File Manager Setup

You can control the setup of the File Manager through the Setup button on the File Manager dialog box. This takes you to the File Manager Setup dialog box (see Figure 12.12). On it, you can identify how you want the list of files sorted and displayed. The check boxes allow you to select **D**escending Sort (Z–A, 9–1), **W**P Documents Only, and Compressed **P**rint for List. (The latter causes a small font to be used when Print List is selected from the File Manager dialog box.)

Figure 12.12

The File Manager
Setup dialog box.

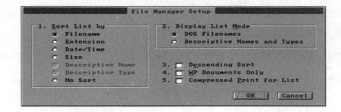

QuickList

If you use a set of directories and files often, you may want to set up a QuickList for quick access. To do this, press F5, or select File Manager from the File menu. Choose the QuickList F6 button. On the QuickList dialog box, select Create. Enter a Description. If you're adding a directory, enter in Filename/Directory, or select it from the Directory Tree. If you're adding a document, type in the path and file name. Select OK. Continue to add other items to the QuickList. To use the QuickList, select the QuickList button when it appears. (The QuickList dialog box can also be used to edit or delete QuickLists.)

Recording a Macro

1. Press Ctrl+F10. Or select Macro and Record from the Tools menu.
2. Type in a name, or press Alt and any letter. Press ↵Enter.
3. Enter the keystrokes for the macro.
4. When done, press Ctrl+F10. Or select Macro and Stop from the Tools menu.

Playing a Macro

- Press Alt plus the letter, if the macro has this type of name.
- Press Alt+F10, or select Macro and Play from the Tools menu. Type in the macro name, and select OK.

Editing a Macro

- Edit Macro screen: Press Ctrl+F10. Or select Macro, and Record from the Tools menu. Enter the macro name, check Edit Macro, and select OK.
- WordPerfect document editing: Press ⇧Shift+F10 or select Open from the File menu. Enter the file name, and select OK.
- To switch methods during editing, press Ctrl+PgUp, and select or deselect Macro Record Document.
- To exit, press F7, or select Exit from the File menu.

Automating with Macros

In this chapter, you will learn how to automate your activities to save time and effort. With an investment of just a little time, you'll discover a slick way to make WordPerfect automatically perform tasks specific to your own needs.

Macros: Why and When

A *macro* is a special file you can create with WordPerfect to store your keystrokes and commands. Any time you want to replay the contents of the macro, just call it up with one or a few keypresses, and the rest is automatic.

When can you use a macro? There are plenty of opportunities. You may want to create a macro to automatically type in your return address, your name, or other names and addresses you commonly use. Or you may want to use a macro to store formatting codes you commonly use. For example, if you often create letters with 1.5' margins and with justification off, you can enter those commands once in a macro and then replay them in any document.

Another good use of macros is to store your common headers or footers. You can have a macro that stores all the keystrokes required to create a header or footer, or you can have a macro that stores all the keystrokes required to exit the header or footer.

Macros save time. By placing header or footer activities in a macro, you save yourself from trying to remember exactly how you set up the header or footer the last time. Without the macro, you might find yourself looking for old documents—wasting time rummaging through files. In addition, macros save you from extra keyboard activity.

How do you know what macros to create? That's easy. Just watch what you do. Especially pay attention to those activities you perform over and over, those that seem tedious, and those that could be faster or more pleasant if you let WordPerfect do them for you. Since virtually any WordPerfect keystrokes can be in a macro, your limit is your imagination and your mastery of the steps to create and use macros.

FYI IDEAS

Don't Reinvent the Wheel

If you work in an office, other people may have created macros that they're willing to share. Set up some means to pool macros with others in the office. You may want to go so far as to identify common naming conventions and encourage very precise descriptions. Create a master list of macros and their descriptions along with where to access the macros. Make this list available to everyone. If you work on a network, this list can be kept up-to-date in a document to which everyone has access.

Some work environments have one or two "macro masters" who have become very expert at developing timesaving macros and are willing to share their expertise. Find these people and set up a means by which everyone can benefit from their skill.

Recording a Macro

The easy way to get started using macros is to create one by entering keystrokes and recording them as you go. Creating a macro in this way is referred to as "recording" the macro.

Let's look at an example. Suppose you often use your return address centered on the page. A macro is a good way for you to store and replay the text.

To create the macro, press Ctrl+F10, or select Macro and Record from the Tools menu. The Record Macro dialog box appears. In the Macro: text box, name the macro. You will enter this name when you want to use the macro. There are two options for naming it. Use the approach with which you feel most comfortable.

Option 1:   Type in eight or fewer letters. (You don't include an extension with macros. WordPerfect automatically adds .WPM to the end, for "WordPerfect Macro.") Select OK.

Using this naming approach allows you to enter a descriptive name. Our example might be called BRETADD for "Barbara's RETurn ADDress."

Option 2:   Hold down Alt, and type in any letter. What appears in the Macro: text box is ALTB (Alt and the letter you pressed). Select OK.

The benefit of this naming approach is that you only have to make two keypresses when you later use the macro. For example, you could press Alt and B (for Barbara's return address). The problem with this approach is that you could end up with a lot of macros you can't identify later. Or you could wind up wanting to use the same Alt+letter combination for another macro.

If you accidentally enter a name for a macro that you've already used, a message like this appears:

```
BRETADD.WPM already exists
```

You can choose among the Replace, Edit, or Cancel buttons.

To quit defining the macro and begin again with a different name, just press the Cancel button. If you want to completely replace the macro keystrokes with different keystrokes, select **R**eplace. Selecting **R**eplace takes you immediately to recording the new macro keystrokes. There is no second warning. The **E**dit option is covered later in this chapter.

After entering the name for the macro you are recording and selecting OK, the following prompt appears in the lower left corner of the screen, to remind you that any keystrokes you enter will be placed in the macro.

```
Recording Macro
```

Type in the text and WordPerfect key combinations. You can use most WordPerfect keyboard and mouse editing capabilities. (You cannot use a mouse, however, to position the cursor within a macro.)

As you enter the keystrokes, you can make a typographical error or press an incorrect command. If you make a mistake that you can correct, first finish the macro keystrokes. WordPerfect corrects simple mistakes for you in the macro. Or, if it is a mistake WordPerfect doesn't pick up, you can either use the macro with the mistake and its correction (if no harm is done), or you can edit the macro contents (covered later in this chapter). An example of a mistake WordPerfect will correct is typing in this text when recording a macro:

```
San Dieb
```

To correct, you'd press (◆Backspace) to get to:

```
San Die
```

Then you'd complete the correct keystrokes before continuing:

```
San Diego
```

Once the macro text is entered, just press [Ctrl]+[F10], or select Macro and Stop from the Tools menu. As the macro is prepared for use, a compiling message appears briefly and the `Recording Macro` message goes away. Then, you are returned to regular WordPerfect editing.

The following Quick Steps summarize the process of recording a macro.

Recording a Macro

1. Press [Ctrl]+[F10]. Or select Macro, and Record from the Tools menu.

   The Record Macro dialog box appears.

2. Type in an eight-character (or less) name, and press [↵Enter]; or press [Alt] and any letter.

   This message appears in the lower left corner of the screen: `Recording Macro`.

3. Enter the keystrokes for the macro. When done, press [Ctrl]+[F10]. Or select Macro and Stop from the Tools menu.

   A compiling message appears briefly, `Recording Macro` disappears, and you are returned to Word-Perfect editing.

A good way to display the names of macros that have been recorded is to press [F5] or select File Manager from the File menu. You're taken to the Specify File Manager List dialog box. Enter the drive, path, and `*.WPM` as the file extension in order to display only macro files. For example:

```
Directory: C\WP60\*.WPM
```

A screen like that in Figure 13.1, displaying only macro files, would appear.

Figure 13.1

*Macro files shown
on the File
Manager dialog
box.*

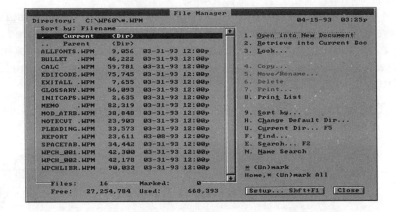

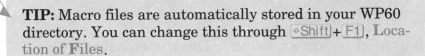

TIP: Macro files are automatically stored in your WP60 directory. You can change this through ⇧Shift + F1, Location of Files.

As you create macros, it can be useful to keep your own list of macro names, descriptions, and uses. That way, you can easily remember the use of each macro.

Playing a Macro

Once you have recorded a macro, you can use it. This is called *playing* a macro. (Breathe easy. The work's in the recording, not the playing.)

It is a good practice to play a new macro right after you've recorded it. That way, you can test to see whether it works the way you intended. If it doesn't, you can record it again (select Replace when that option appears) or edit the macro (described later in this chapter).

TIP: It is a good habit to save your document before playing a macro. That way, if you have valuable text and a macro that doesn't execute properly, you don't lose the text.

The following Quick Steps show how to play a macro.

Playing a Macro

1. Press the Alt +*letter* key combination.	The macro keystrokes are played.
or	
Position the cursor where the macro should play and press Alt + F10 . Or select **M**acro and **P**lay from the **T**ools menu.	The Play Macro dialog box appears.
2. Type in the macro name and select OK.	The macro keystrokes are played.

Editing a Macro

There are two ways to edit a macro. One is editing while recording and the other is as a WordPerfect document. You can easily switch between these two methods.

Using either approach displays macros like that shown in Figure 13.2. As you can see, all the keystrokes appear and each WordPerfect command appears. For example, the Center command (⇧Shift + F6) appears as Center, and a press of the ↵Enter key appears as HardReturn. Text you have typed in appears after the word Type, in parentheses and quotes. For example, Barbara J. Wiley's name appears as:

```
Type("Barbara J. Wiley")
```

Figure 13.2
Edit Macro screen.

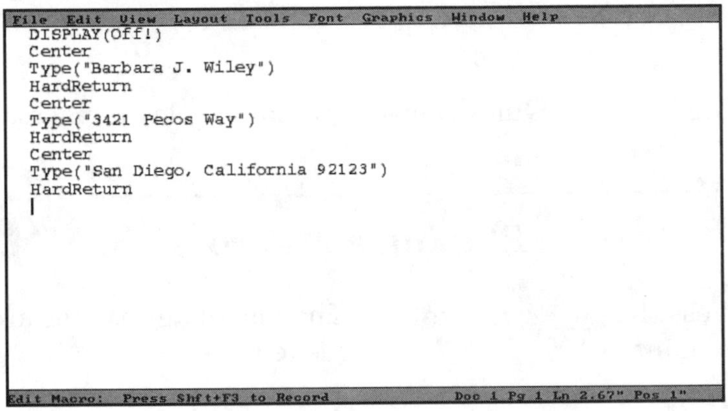

```
 File  Edit  View  Layout  Tools  Font  Graphics  Window  Help
  DISPLAY(Off)
  Center
  Type("Barbara J. Wiley")
  HardReturn
  Center
  Type("3421 Pecos Way")
  HardReturn
  Center
  Type("San Diego, California 92123")
  HardReturn
  |




Edit Macro:  Press Shft+F3 to Record          Doc 1 Pg 1 Ln 2.67" Pos 1"
```

Editing While Recording

To edit while recording, press Ctrl+F10. Or select **Macro** and **Record** from the **Tools** menu. You are taken to the Record Macro dialog box. Enter the name of the existing macro you want to edit, which can be an Alt+letter combination. To select the macro, use the drop-down list. Once the macro name is entered, place a check in the check box for Edit Macro, and select **OK**. If you forget to check the Edit Macro check box, a message like this appears. Select the **Edit** button.

```
BRETADD.WPM already exists
```

The prompt Edit Macro: Press Shft+F3 to Record appears in the lower left of the screen. This means you can position your cursor where you want additions made and press ⇧Shift+F3. The keystrokes you enter are automatically added at the spot of your cursor.

Let's look at an example. In Figure 13.2, the cursor was placed after the last hard return. Barbara's phone number will be

added to the address after the city, state, and zip code line. Press
⟨⇧Shift⟩+⟨F3⟩ to switch to the Recording Macro screen (which looks
much like a blank editing screen). All keystrokes entered on this
screen are automatically recorded as part of the macro at the
cursor location on the Edit Macro screen. Type and center the
phone number and press ⟨↵Enter⟩, and then press ⟨⇧Shift⟩+⟨F3⟩. We
see that the phone number has been added at the cursor position
on the Edit Macro screen (see Figure 13.3). Press ⟨F7⟩ to save the
macro.

```
File  Edit  View  Layout  Tools  Font  Graphics  Window  Help
DISPLAY(Off!)
Center
Type("Barbara J. Wiley")
HardReturn
Center
Type("3421 Pecos Way")
HardReturn
Center
Type("San Diego, California 92123")
HardReturn
Center
Type("619-546-9980")
HardReturn




Edit Macro:  Press Shft+F3 to Record              Doc 1 Pg 1 Ln 3.17" Pos 1"
```

Figure 13.3

Edit Macro screen after adding the phone number.

On the Edit Macro screen (not the Recording Macro screen),
you can also delete, copy, and move commands and text. Be careful
when you do because WordPerfect is picky about how commands
and text appear. For example, don't leave out the quote and
parenthesis at the end of text that has been copied.

TIP: You cannot type in command names or text using
parentheses and quote marks on either the Edit Macro or
Recording Macro screens. If you do and try to save the
macro, you will be given a syntax error message. Instead,
use the WordPerfect Document editing option to type in
commands and text.

Editing a Macro As a WordPerfect Document

Editing a macro as a WordPerfect document allows you add or change commands and text. Just open and make changes to the macro file like any other WordPerfect document.

Press ⇧Shift+F10, or select **O**pen from the **F**ile menu. Enter the file name (including the .WPM extension). Select OK. You make changes to the file including typing in commands and text in the form WordPerfect understands.

The *syntax* of a command refers to the form in which a command or text must be entered for WordPerfect to recognize the action to take. The easiest way to learn the syntax of a few commands is to record them and then look at their appearance. As you do this, you'll see that different commands have different syntax.

Each keystroke to a command is not shown. For example, to change the top margin to 2", there are no keystrokes about pressing ⇧Shift+F8, and so on. Instead the command is:

```
MarginTop(2")
```

The command name appears first. Sometimes, that is all that is needed (HardReturn, for example). After the command name, parameters that are the added information needed to specify the command appear. They are always in parentheses. In the MarginTop example, (2") is a parameter. After the parameters, there may be *separators* that allow the macro to make multiple selections. Separators are semicolons (;). For example, they might be used to separate variables such as variable1; variable2.

Switching Between Edit Macro and WordPerfect Document Editing

As mentioned earlier, you can switch between editing while recording and editing as a WordPerfect document. From either method, press Ctrl+PgUp to see the Macro Control dialog box. Check the Macro **R**ecord Document to record keystrokes. Or deselect the check box to go to WordPerfect document editing. Choose OK. Confirm the mode in the lower left of your screen.

Exiting Once the Macro Is Edited

Whether you are editing while recording or editing as a WordPerfect document, saving and exiting are the same. When you are done making changes, press F7, or select Exit from the File menu. Choose to save the file. (Or don't save the file if you want to lose the edits.) If you chose to save the file, the macro is compiled. Play the macro to make sure your edits perform as expected.

If you enter a command or text incorrectly, you won't be able to save the macro. Instead, you'll get a Macro compiler error message stating syntax error. This simply means the form of commands or text in the macro is not correct. Select the Edit button to return to the macro and fix any errors.

Fields and Records in Data Documents

- Data documents contain fields grouped in records.
- To name fields, press ⇧Shift+F9, or select Merge and Define from the Tools menu. Then select Field Names.
- To end a field, press F9.
- To end a record, press ⇧Shift+F9, or select Merge and Define from the Tools menu. Select End Record.

Fields in Form Documents

- Form documents contain boilerplate text and field codes.
- To identify a field to merge, press ⇧Shift+F9, or select Merge and Define from the Tools menu. Select Field. Type in the name for the field.

Merging Form and Data Documents

1. Press Ctrl+F9 and Merge, or select Merge and Run from the Tools menu.
2. Type in the name of the Form File and Data File. Complete other options, if you want.
3. Select the Merge button.

Sorting a List

1. Press Ctrl+F9, and select Sort. Or select Sort from the Tools menu.
2. Identify the From (Source) and To (Destination) locations and select OK.
3. Complete the options describing the sort, and select Perform Action.

14

Merging Documents and Sorting

WordPerfect allows you to merge the contents of one document with a list of data in another document. The data can comprise any small bits of information, such as names, addresses, telephone numbers, product numbers, sales regions, contributions, booth assignments, office numbers, birth dates, and so on.

If you ever need to send out form letters or use the same data in multiple documents, the Merge feature will save you a great deal of time and enable you to produce more personalized letters and documents. For example, you can merge a list of names, addresses, and phone numbers of members of a professional group, a work team, or a scout troop. Then you merge that data with a notice today, a letter tomorrow, or to make a list next week. Or you could create a document containing raw product data and then pull out the data you need according to the requirements of the immediate document. Virtually any time you have a body of data that you will be using repeatedly, Merge is the way to go.

Elements of a Merge

Each piece of data in a merge is referred to as a *field*. A field may be a first name, last name, phone number, ZIP code—any single bit of information. All the related fields are organized into a *record*. For example, all the fields for one person (first name, last name, address, phone number) are organized into a record for that individual.

Three documents are involved in a merge:

- **The form document:** This is the "boilerplate" text that will be used in the merged document. Type it in as regular WordPerfect text. In this document, you also identify what data you want "plugged in." By entering codes for the fields, you tell WordPerfect what to put where.

- **The data document:** This document contains the data, organized in a way that lets WordPerfect identify what's what. For example, the fields in each record are listed in the same order, and the records are clearly separated. This way, WordPerfect knows what type of field comes first, second, third, and so on. And, WordPerfect knows where one record ends and another begins.

- **The merged document:** This is the result of merging the form and data documents. The data from the data document is entered at the appropriate spots according to the instructions in the form document.

Let's take a look at an example of each type of document. We'll use Barbara Wiley's notice to the members of her professional group. Figure 14.1 shows the form document. Notice that each field to be inserted during the merge is identified:

```
FIELD(first name)
```

In the Reveal Codes screen, you'll see

```
[MRG:FIELD]first name[mrg:field]
```

that reminds you that the field is to be merged.

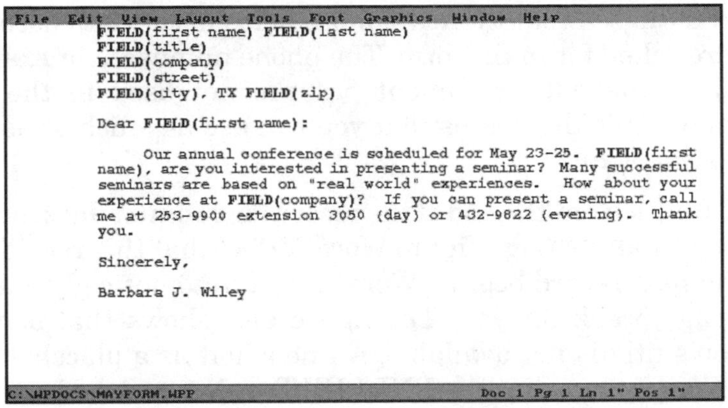
File Edit View Layout Tools Font Graphics Window Help
FIELD(first name) FIELD(last name)
FIELD(title)
FIELD(company)
FIELD(street)
FIELD(city), TX FIELD(zip)

Dear FIELD(first name):

Our annual conference is scheduled for May 23-25. FIELD(first name), are you interested in presenting a seminar? Many successful seminars are based on "real world" experiences. How about your experience at FIELD(company)? If you can present a seminar, call me at 253-9900 extension 3050 (day) or 432-9822 (evening). Thank you.

Sincerely,

Barbara J. Wiley

C:\WPDOCS\MAYFORM.WPP Doc 1 Pg 1 Ln 1" Pos 1"

Figure 14.1
Form document.

Figure 14.1 illustrates that the order of the fields is not important. The numbers of the fields simply let WordPerfect match up with the proper data in the data document. Also, fields do not need to be represented an equal number of times in the form document: the first name is used three times and the company name is used twice.

Now let's take a look at the data document. Figure 14.2 shows the full screen display of two records. Notice that each field (such as first name) is entered on its own line and ends with:

```
ENDFIELD
```

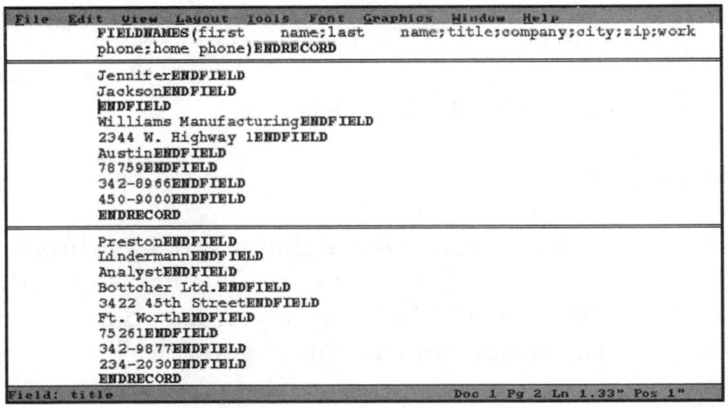
File Edit View Layout Tools Font Graphics Window Help
FIELDNAMES(first name;last name;title;company;city;zip;work phone;home phone)ENDRECORD

JenniferENDFIELD
JacksonENDFIELD
ENDFIELD
Williams ManufacturingENDFIELD
2344 W. Highway 1ENDFIELD
AustinENDFIELD
78759ENDFIELD
342-8966ENDFIELD
450-9000ENDFIELD
ENDRECORD

PrestonENDFIELD
LindermannENDFIELD
AnalystENDFIELD
Bottcher Ltd.ENDFIELD
3422 45th StreetENDFIELD
Ft. WorthENDFIELD
75261ENDFIELD
342-9877ENDFIELD
234-2030ENDFIELD
ENDRECORD

Field: title Doc 1 Pg 2 Ln 1.33" Pos 1"

Figure 14.2
Full-screen display of records in a data document.

You can see that there are more fields in the data document than are called for in the form. The phone numbers, for example, appear in the data document but are not used in the form document. This illustrates that you can use as much or as little data as you want.

Take a look at the end of the record for Jennifer Jackson. The notation ENDRECORD signifies to WordPerfect that this record ends and the next record begins. WordPerfect automatically enters a hard page break for you. The figure also shows that Jennifer Jackson's title is not available. A line is left as a placeholder to alert WordPerfect, but the ENDFIELD code is entered anyway.

Look at the order of the data in each record: the first name is always first, then the last name, title, company and so on. The order in which your fields present data does not matter (for example, the last names could make up the first field). However, all records must have the fields in the same order by type and the same number of field lines. When the merge code is in the form document

```
FIELD(first name)
```

the first name data is merged.

Figure 14.3 shows the codes as shown in the Reveal Codes screen. This code

```
[MRG:END FIELD]
```

marks the end of each field. The code

```
[MGR:END RECORD]
```

marks the end of each record. Notice that a hard page break [HPg] is also entered after the end of a record. The name of each field appears in the lower left of the corner. (If you don't name the fields, WordPerfect assigns numbers. In this chapter, we'll cover how to name fields.)

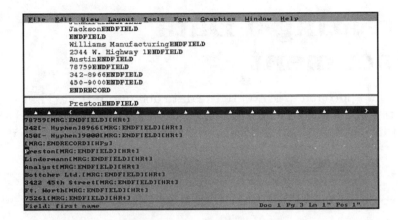

Figure 14.3
*Data document
Reveal Codes.*

Figure 14.4 shows the first document (for Jennifer Jackson) fully merged, and it shows the beginning of the merging of the second document (for Preston Lindermann). The result of the merge, then, is one or more documents with the applicable fields from each record in the data document merged into the form document. You can edit or print the merged document.

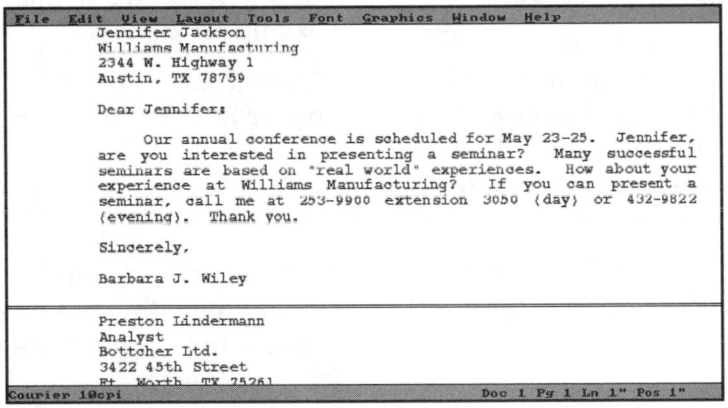

Figure 14.4
Merged documents.

Creating a Data Document

A sound approach is to create the data document first. That way, when you create the form document, you have established the field names in the data document. Follow these Quick Steps.

Creating a Data Document

1. Name the fields by pressing ⇧Shift + F9, or select Merge, and Define from the Tools menu. If necessary, identify this as a Data document, and select OK.

   The Merge Codes (Text Data File) dialog box appears.

2. Select Field Names.

   The Field Names dialog box appears.

3. Type in the first field name, and press Enter. Continue until all field names are entered in order. Select OK.

   The FIELDNAMES codes appear in your document.

4. Enter the data for the first field, and press F9.

   ENDFIELD appears, and you are on a new line to enter another field. The name for the new field appears in the lower left corner of the screen.

5. Enter all the fields for a record following the process in step 4. On the line after the last field for the record, press ⎇Shift+F9, or select Merge and then Define from the Tools menu. Select End Record.

ENDRECORD and a hard page break are entered.

6. Enter the field for the next record. Or if you are done, save the document like any WordPerfect document.

After saving the data document, you can use it in a merge.

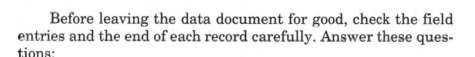

TIP: If you need to add to or delete field names, just edit the field names between the codes to reflect the data in the file. Then, save and exit the document and retrieve it. The changes will have taken effect.

Before leaving the data document for good, check the field entries and the end of each record carefully. Answer these questions:

- Does each record have the same number of fields?
- Are the types of fields in the same order in each record?
- Is there an ENDFIELD mark at the end of each field?
- Is there an ENDRECORD mark at the end of each record (including the last record)?
- Are there unnecessary blank lines, spaces, or text that should be deleted?

CAUTION

When entering the end field and end record codes, do not type in the letter that makes up ENDFIELD or ENDRECORD. You must use the appropriate WordPerfect keypresses or menu selections.

FYI IDEAS

Saving Data Entry Time

Entering the end field and end record codes can become tedious. Also, some records may include similar information (such as addresses containing common city, state, and ZIP information). To save time and reduce the tedium, use the Copy command.

Enter the sample record. Block it with Alt+F4, or Block from the Edit menu. Copy using Alt+F4 and Copy and Paste or by selecting Copy and Paste from the Edit menu. Press ↵Enter to complete the copy at the location you want. Copy the text as needed to accommodate your data. Finally, go back and add or delete text in the records to meet your needs. The development of the document is simplified.

A more sophisticated approach is to create a macro. With some study, you can have the macro pause to allow you to enter field data.

Creating a Form Document

To create a form document, type in the boilerplate text. When you want to reference a field, press ⇧Shift+F9, or select Merge and Define from the Tools menu. The first time you make this selection, you have to identify you are working with a Form document and select OK. On the Merge Codes (Form File) dialog box, select Field. Type in the name assigned to the field (in the data document), and select OK. The entry looks like this:

```
FIELD(first name)
```

Again, do not type in FIELD from your keyboard. If you do, that text will print, and you will not be calling data from the data document. You must use the WordPerfect keypresses or menu selections.

Continue to type in the boilerplate text and enter fields as you want. Fields need not be entered in order, and you can use all of the fields in the data document or only a few. When you are done creating the form document, save it like any other WordPerfect document.

Using Data Documents More Than Once

Don't forget that the information in data documents can be used for more than one form document. For example, you may have a customer list in a data document. One form document might be used to generate a form letter thanking customers for their business. Such a document would be for 8.5" x 11" letterhead. Another form document could be used to generate envelopes for the form letter. This form document would include the paper size/type for envelopes. Another form document might create a postcard-size sales notice. A form document would be needed to generate mailing labels to be used with the postcard. Need other ideas? How about customized holiday greetings for the customers on the list? As you can see, the use of form documents is limited only by your imagination.

The following Quick Steps summarize creating a form document.

Creating a Form Document

1. Type in the boilerplate text. When you want to insert a field from the data document, press `⇧Shift`+`F9`, or select **Merge** and **Define** from the **Tools** menu. Identify you are working with a **Form** document (first time only), and select OK.

   The Merge Codes (Form File) dialog box appears.

2. Select **Field**. Type in the name assigned to the field (in the data document), and select OK.

   A code like this appears in your text: FIELD(field name).

3. When all text and fields are entered, save the document.

   The document is saved.

Be sure to check your document before saving, asking these questions:

- Have you entered each field with the correct number?

- Is the punctuation placed appropriately around the field data that will be inserted?

Merging

Once you have completed the form and data documents, you can merge them. Follow these Quick Steps.

Merging Documents

1. Start with a blank WordPerfect screen.

2. Press `Ctrl`+`F9` and then Merge. Or select Merge and Run from the Tools menu.

   The Run Merge dialog box appears.

3. Type in the name of the Form File and Data File (include the drive and path, if necessary).

4. Leave the Output as Current Document.

5. Select Data File Options, and under Blank Fields in Data File, select Remove Resulting Blank Line to avoid having blank lines entered when data is missing.

6. Identify whether you want a Page Break Between Merge Records or whether you want to limit the Data Record Selection.

7. Once the information is entered, select the Merge button.

   The merge begins.

TIP: The form file and data file are accessed from the disk. You must have saved the files and any edits. If you edit the documents on screen but do not save them, the changes will not be used in the merge.

The documents are merged and appear on your screen. Check to make sure the result is as you expected. Save the document. You can edit it and print it as you would any WordPerfect document.

You can use a database or other file (other than one created with WordPerfect) for the data file. If this is the case, the file must have "DOS delimiters," which are special characters that separate the fields and records. (See the manual for the database or other package to determine which delimiter characters the program uses.) If you are using a DOS delimited file, when the prompt for the data document appears, enter the name of the ASCII file. WordPerfect will identify that the file is not a WordPerfect file and ask you to identify it as DOS Delimited Text. When you do, the Delimited Text Options dialog box appears. Enter the symbol for the **F**ield Delimiter, **R**ecord Delimiter, and select OK. You are returned to the Run Merge dialog box where you can select **M**erge to begin the merge process.

CAUTION   When you begin using merge, your first results may not come out as you want. This is pretty normal. Call up the data document and check each record and field carefully. Then look at your form document and check each field carefully. Pay special attention to the fields and records where the data did not print appropriately. After making corrections, try again.

Inserting the Current Date

WordPerfect has a variety of commands that you can use for merging. The date command is especially helpful. Place it in your form document, and the current date will print in place of the code.

To use the date command:

1. Place your cursor in the form document where you want the date placed.

2. Press ⌖Shift+F9 and then the **M**erge Codes ⌖Shift+F9 button. Or select Merge Codes and **D**efine from the **T**ools menu. The Merge Codes dialog box appears.

3. Select Merge Codes. Figure 14.5 shows the All Merge Codes dialog box with DATE highlighted for selection.

4. Once you have entered or selected DATE, press ⏎Enter. DATE appears in your document, and [MRG:DATE] appears in Reveal Codes. When you merge the form document, DATE is replaced with the current date set in your computer.

Figure 14.5
The All Merge Codes dialog box with Date is selected.

Sorting

WordPerfect allows you to sort lists alphabetically or numerically. This is particularly useful when creating a data merge document.

To sort, simply select the text to sort. If you don't make a selection, the contents of the entire document will be sorted. For example, Figure 14.6 shows a list to sort.

Figure 14.6
A list to sort.

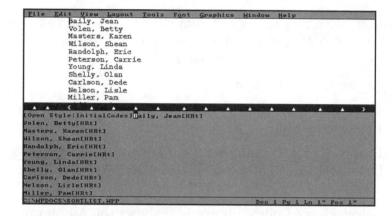

> **CAUTION**
>
> Before you sort, always save a copy of your document. That way, if the result of the sort is different than you imagined, you still have the original document to try the sort again.

Press Ctrl + F9 and select Sort. Or select Sort from the Tools menu. The Sort (Source and Destination) dialog box appears. For From (Source), check Document on screen or File, and type in a file name. For To (Destination), check Document on Screen or File, and enter a file name. Select OK. The Sort dialog box appears in the lower part of the screen (see Figure 14.7).

Figure 14.7
The Sort dialog box to define the sort.

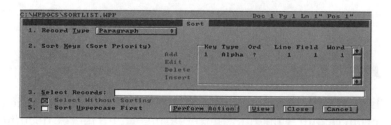

On the Sort dialog box, you have several selections. We'll cover each in some detail. (As you complete the dialog box, you can select the View button to look at the text in the upper half of the screen.)

First, enter the Record Type. You can identify Line (to sort records that are a line in length), Paragraph (to sort records that are a paragraph long), Merge Data File (to sort data merge records), Parallel Columns (where each record is a row of columns), or Table (where each record is a row of cells).

Next, enter the Sort Keys. They specify which piece of the record you want to sort by first (Key 1), second (Key 2), and so on. For example, the criteria for sorting on Key 1 takes precedence over Key 2. The Type indicates whether the characters to sort on are Alpha or Numeric. Next, the Order of sorting for the key can be Ascending (an arrow pointing up for A–Z or 1–9) or Descending (an arrow pointing down for Z–A or 9–1).

The Field is identified next. Fields in lines or paragraphs are separated by tabs or indents. Fields in merge records are separated by ENDFIELD codes and those in table rows are separated into cells. Fields are considered to be numbered from left to right. Finally, the Word is identified. Words are separated by spaces, forward slashes, and hard hyphens (and are also numbered from left to right within in the field).

For example, you can have a list of product item numbers, the item description, and size in line records with two fields separated by tabs like this:

```
546890          Shirt/M
435677          Shirt/XL
435677          Shirt/M
435677          Shirt/S
```

The first Key (Key 1) to sort on could be the product item number. To find this field and word for the sort, WordPerfect needs the following Key information. That is:

```
Key     Type      Order       Field   Word
1       Numeric   Ascending   1       1
```

The product item is in the first field (there are two fields separated by tabs) and is the first and only word in the field.

The second Key (Key 2) to sort on is a little more tricky. We want to sort by size. The Key information is:

Key	Type	Order	Field	Word
2	Alpha	Ascending	2	2

The Field is 2 because the first field in the record is the product number and the second field is the product description and size. The fields are separated by a Tab. The Word is 2 because the product description (Shirt) is the first word. A forward slash separates it and the second word, which is the size (the word on which we want to sort).

The result of this sort would be as follows. The first key (the product number) is sorted first. Then, the size is sorted within each product number group.

```
435677          Shirt/M
435677          Shirt/S
435677          Shirt/XL
546890          Shirt/M
```

Once the Sort Keys are set up, you can choose Select Records if you want the result to be limited to records with certain criteria. For example, to only sort shirts that are Mediums (Key 2), the value Key2=M would be entered. If you enter selection criteria and decide to try the sort without the criteria, you can check Select Without Sorting.

Finally, you can check Sort Uppercase First to put keys with uppercase letters before those with lowercase.

Once the Sort dialog box is complete, select the Perform Action button to begin the sort.

The result of the name sort is shown in Figure 14.8. Notice that the lines were sorted in ascending alphabetical order. No code is placed in the document.

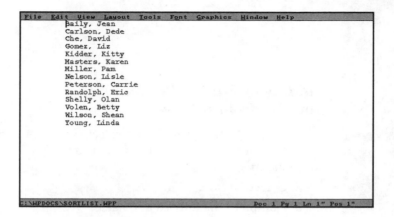

Figure 14.8
A sorted list.

The following Quick Steps summarize how to sort a list.

Sorting a List

1. Press `Ctrl`+`F9` and Sort. Or select Sort from the Tools menu.	The Sort dialog box to enter the source and destination appears.
2. Enter the From (Source) and To (Destination) locations. Select OK.	The Sort dialog box to define the sort appears.
3. Complete the Sort dialog box values, and select Perform Action.	The document is sorted.

Adding or Editing Vertical and Horizontal Lines

1. Press `Alt`+`F9`, and then select Graphics Lines. Or select Graphics Lines from the Graphics menu.
2. Select Create.
3. Complete the entries and select OK.

Adding Page Borders

1. Press `Shift`+`F8`, and select Page. Or select Page from the Layout menu.
2. Select Page Borders.
3. Complete the options, and choose Select.
4. Choose Close, OK twice, then Close again.

Adding Graphics Borders

1. Identify the text. Press `Alt`+`F9` or select the Graphics menu.
2. Select Borders.
3. Select Paragraph (for a paragraph or table), Page, or Columns.
4. Complete the option and select OK.

Creating a Box

1. Press `Alt`+`F9`, or select the Graphics menu.
2. Select Graphics Boxes and then Create.
3. Complete the options on the Create Graphics Box dialog box, and select OK.

15

Using Graphics in Your Documents

Whether you have a printer that handles sophisticated graphics or you have a simple printer that produces basic results, there are graphic features you can use in your documents. This chapter will get you up and running.

NOTE: Not all printers handle all line and graph options. You will need to experiment to see what your printer can produce.

Adding and Editing Vertical and Horizontal Lines

WordPerfect is like the slogan from "The Outer Limits" that went, "You control the horizontal. You control the vertical."

You can add horizontal or vertical lines in your document for a pleasing effect. The lines can be black or a shade of gray, and you can set the width of the lines. For example, the sample resumé shown through Print Preview in Figure 15.1 is dressed up with horizontal and vertical lines. Even though no fancy fonts are used, the resumé is much more striking with the simple addition of lines.

Figure 15.1

A sample resume with lines added.

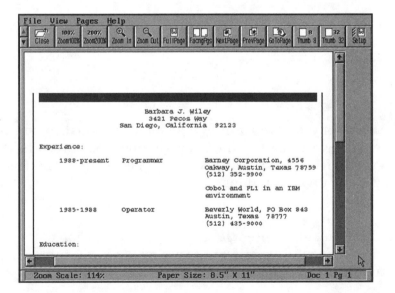

Adding a Line

Before adding lines or any graphic effects, always save a version of your document before you begin. That way, if the result is not as you anticipated, you can go back to your "clean" document. After you've saved your work, follow these Quick Steps to create a line.

Creating a Graphics Line

1. Press Alt+F9 then select Graphics Lines, or select Graphics Lines from the Graphics menu.

2. Select Create.

The Create Graphics Line dialog box appears (Figure 15.2).

3. For Line **O**rientation, enter whether you want to create a horizontal or vertical line.

4. Identify the position of the line by entering the **H**orizontal Position and **V**ertical Position of the line from the top and left of the page, respectively.

5. Enter the **T**hickness and **L**ength of the line.

6. Select a Line St**y**le and **C**olor.

The Color can be a percentage of black to achieve gray tones. (Not all printers handle Gray Shading. You may want to test yours.)

7. Enter the **S**pacing to maintain above and below a horizontal line or the spacing between the vertical line and the edge of the page.

8. Select OK to return to your document.

Figure 15.2

*The Create
Graphics Line
dialog box.*

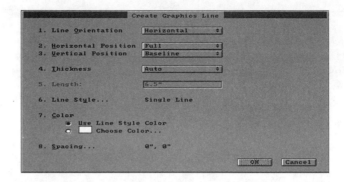

A code for the line appears in your document. When you
return to your document, a code like the following is placed in your
document:

```
[Grph Line:Edit Num 1;Horiz;Single
Line;Full;Baseline;6.5";0.25"]
```

It is full of abbreviations and numbers but easy to interpret.
It indicates the number of the line for editing purposes, whether
the line is horizontal or vertical, the style of the line, the horizontal
position, the vertical position, the length of the line, and the
thickness.

The horizontal lines shown in the resumé in Figure 15.1 were
set with the Horizontal Position at Full, Vertical Position at
Baseline, Thickness of the line at .25', Line Style at Single Line,
and the Color as black with shading at 50%.

The vertical lines in Figure 15.1 were set up with the
Horizontal Position (for each vertical line) at Left Margin for one
line and Right Margin for the other. For both lines, the Vertical
Position was set to Full page (extending from the top to the bottom
margin), the Thickness of the line set to 0.013', Line Style at Single
Line, and Color set at black with 100% shading.

TIP: Experiment with lines. Use Graphics and Page
Modes with Ctrl + F3 to look at the images. Also, don't
forget about Print Preview. Press ⇧Shift + F7 and select
Print Preview, or select Print Preview from the File menu.

Editing A Line

Once you see the line on the page, you may realize that it needs some modification. Follow these Quick Steps.

Editing a Line

1. Place your cursor on or after the code for the line.

2. Press Alt+F9 or the Graphics menu. Select Graphics Lines and then Edit.

3. On the Select Graphics Line To Edit dialog box, choose the line to edit.

   You can enter a Graphics Line Number or choose the next or previous line.

4. Select the Edit Line button.

   The Edit Graphics Line dialog box appears.

5. Enter your changes, and select OK.

TIP: From Graphics and Page Modes, you can move and size a line with the mouse. With the tip of the mouse pointer on the line, click the line to select it. A dotted line with box "handles" appears around the line. You can drag the line to a new location or use the handles on the line to enlarge or reduce the line.

WordPerfect also has a Line Draw feature that turns your arrow keys into drawing tools. Place your cursor where you want to begin drawing. Press Ctrl+F3, and then select Line Draw. Or select Line Draw from the Graphics menu. Just move the arrow keys to begin drawing. To change the style of the line while in Line Draw mode, make a selection 1 through 3. To change the type of line graphic in selection 1, 2, or 3, select 4 Change and pick a new line graphic. To move your cursor without drawing a line (and without leaving Line Draw mode), select 6 Move. To erase a portion of the line, position your cursor and use 5 Erase.

Page Borders

Want a border around the page? If so, WordPerfect has a special feature for you. You can place a border around the page and enter fill (the shade inside the bordered area). Follow these Quick Steps.

QUICK STEPS

Putting a Border on a Page

1. Press ⇧Shift+F8, and select Page. Or select Page from the Layout menu.

   The Page Format dialog box appears.

2. Select Page Borders.

   The Create Page Border dialog box appears.

3. Select a Border Style and a Fill Style. The Fill Style determines the shading on the page inside the border. For example, a 10% fill gives a light gray appearance. Select OK.

   A page border code, like this, appears in your document:
   ```
   [Pg Border:Single Border;
   20% Shaded Fill]
   ```

To delete the border, delete the code. To stop the border from appearing later in the document, return to the Create Page Border dialog box. Set the options to None.

Graphics Borders

You can enter a variety of borders from the Graphics menu. The Border option allows for borders to be added to paragraphs, pages, tables, and columns.

The first step is to tell WordPerfect what you want a border around. To add a border to a single paragraph, table, or column, place your cursor in the paragraph, table, or column. To add a border to several paragraphs, columns, or tables, select the text. If you are adding a border to a page, place your cursor on the first page.

Once the cursor identifies the text to be in the border, press Alt + F9, or select the Graphics menu. Select Borders. Select **P**aragraph (for a paragraph or table), **P**age, or **C**olumn. Enter **B**order Style and **F**ill Style. To customize the border's appearance further, select Customize, and make changes. Select OK, and return to our document when all options are complete. A code is placed in your text.

You can control the style of the border by pressing Alt + F9 or choosing the Graphics menu. Select Borders. Select Styles. Complete the options.

A border can be turned off. Position your cursor, or block the text to include. Press Alt + F9, or choose the Graphics menu. Select Borders. Select the type of border to turn off, and then select the Off button.

Graphics Boxes

A graphic border is simply a design placed around a word or paragraph (such as text) to dress it up. A graphics box is important—graphics boxes are WordPerfect's way of handling figures, equations, and other special graphic elements. WordPerfect places each special graphic element in its own box, so the element can be easily manipulated. You can also create a graphics box and put text in it, to lend your text the same flexibility of movement.

WordPerfect allows you to choose from eight different types of graphics boxes. In this chapter, we'll cover details about text boxes (designed to contain text) and figure boxes (which are useful for clip art images, drawings, and charts). The same dialog box is used for creating each type of box. It is the Create Graphics Box dialog box shown in Figure 15.3.

Figure 15.3

The Create Graphics Box dialog box.

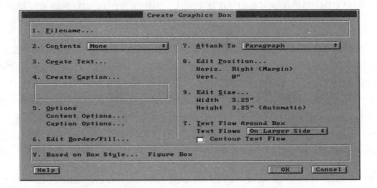

As an overview, these are the options on the Create Graphics Box dialog box that you can control for boxes. Read the next sections of this chapter for a detailed walk-through of the text and figure boxes.

Y. Based on Box Style: This is the first selection you'll make to identify the type of box you will create. The defaults for that type of box are set.

1. Filename: To enter a path and file name containing text for a box or a graphic.

2. Contents: To select the type of box contents (such as text, image, or equation).

3. Create Text: To go to the editor to edit text as you would any WordPerfect text.

4. Create Caption: To enter the text for the caption on the box, if one is wanted.

5. **O**ptions: To enter Content Options such as the horizontal and vertical position of the box contents. Or to enter Caption Options such as the position of the caption and its size.

6. Edit **B**order/Fill: To identify the border style, color, spacing, appearance, and fill (shading) inside the box.

7. **A**ttach To: To identify how you want the box handled when the surrounding text is edited. Select Fixed and the position will remain fixed, regardless of how the page content changes. Select Paragraph and the box will be kept with the surrounding text, even if you move the text. Select Page and the box will be kept on the specified page. Choose Character Position for the box to be handled as a character on the line containing the cursor.

8. Edit **P**osition: Enter the horizontal and vertical position (the options vary depending on the Attach To setting). If you select Set to enter measurements, the position is measured from the top left edge of the page.

9. Edit **S**ize: Identify how to set the width and height of the box. You can select Set Width or Set Height and have WordPerfect automatically set the other dimension. You can set both the width and height. Or you can have WordPerfect make both the width and height selection.

T. **T**ext Flow Around Box: Identify how you want text to flow around the box or through the box. In some cases, you can choose Contour Text Flow to have the flow follow the shape of the graphic. It's a sophisticated look.

Enclosing and Editing Text in a Box

To see how to set up a box, we'll look at a text box first. Entering text in a box is good to emphasize it or set it apart from the body of the text. Figure 15.4 shows a simple use of this feature.

Figure 15.4

Text placed in a box.

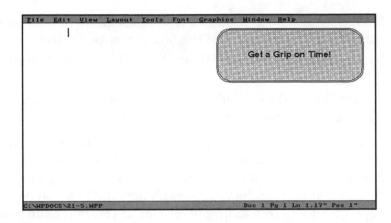

Don't Forget Headers and Footers

A good use of text boxes is in headers or footers. Instead of simple text, a box around the text and shading can add interest.

To place text in a box, press Alt+F9, or select the Graphics menu. Select Graphics Boxes and then Create. The Create Graphics Box dialog box (see Figure 15.3) appears.

Select Based on Box Style, and select the Text Box option. Notice that Text is selected in the Contents option. This indicates that text only will be the contents of the box.

Next, identify the text for the box. There are two ways to do this. The first way is to select Create Text. You are taken to the text editor, which works very much like regular WordPerfect document editing. Type in any text, and select the features you want. In the example, text was typed in and a font selected. When the text and formatting is entered, press F7. The second way to identify the text to hold in the box is to retrieve an existing file by selecting Filename and entering the file path and name.

Finally, you can make other selections to control the visual appearance of the text box. In the example, Edit Border/Fill was selected. Border Style was set to Double, the Corners were set to Rounded, and the Fill was set at 20%. The Edit Size was set.

Select OK when all settings are complete. A code like the following is placed in the document at the cursor location.

```
[Para Box:Edit Num 1;Text Box;Get A Grip On Time!]
```

Para Box indicates the box is attached to a paragraph. The Edit Num in the code is the text box number that WordPerfect assigns. If you have more than one text box in a document, WordPerfect numbers them sequentially. The type of box appears next, and because this example is for a Text Box, text in the box appears.

Because the text was allowed to flow around the box, we can type text around the text box. Figure 15.5 shows the document with text added outside the text box. Notice in Reveal Codes there are no hard returns in the paragraph. Text just wraps around the text box.

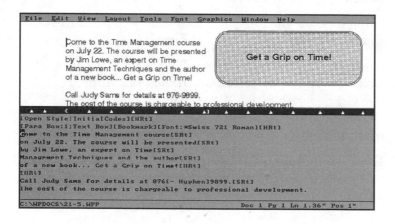

Figure 15.5

Text wrapped around the text box.

To delete a box, delete the code for the box. To edit the contents of a text box, press Alt + F9, or select the Graphics menu. Select Graphics Boxes and then Edit. The Select Box to Edit dialog box appears. Enter the number of the box you want to edit, or select the next or previous box. Select Edit Box. You are taken to the Edit Graphics Box dialog box. The options are identical to the Create Graphics Box dialog box. Make any changes you like, and select OK.

Steps to Create and Edit a Box

Now that you've seen an example, the steps for creating a box should make more sense. The following Quick Steps summarize how to create and edit a box. These steps apply to any one of the eight types of boxes that can be created with WordPerfect.

QUICK STEPS

Creating and Editing a Box

1. Press Alt + F9, or select the Graphics menu. Select Graphics Boxes and then Create.

   The Create Graphics Box dialog box appears.

2. Complete the options, and select OK.

   A code is placed in your document.

3. To later edit the box, press Alt + F9, or select the Graphics menu. Select Graphics Boxes and then Edit.

   The Select Box to Edit dialog box appears.

4. Enter the number of the box you want to edit, or select the next or previous box. Select Edit Box.

   The Edit Graphics Box dialog box appears.

5. Complete the options, and select OK.

   The box is edited per your instructions.

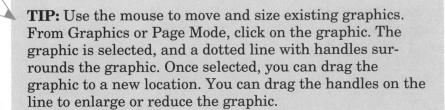

TIP: Use the mouse to move and size existing graphics. From Graphics or Page Mode, click on the graphic. The graphic is selected, and a dotted line with handles surrounds the graphic. Once selected, you can drag the graphic to a new location. You can drag the handles on the line to enlarge or reduce the graphic.

Adding and Editing Figures

WordPerfect comes with a number of graphics that you can insert in flyers, memos, newsletters and so on. You can use the graphic files in virtually any document that calls for a little pizzazz.

While most printers will handle lines and text boxes, not all will print the graphics supplied with WordPerfect. Test your computer to see if this fancy feature will work for you.

Using or Creating Custom Graphics

You can use graphics from third party sources or create your own custom graphics with products like Microsoft Windows Paintbrush. This opens up a wide variety of effects and options. You can be very specific in designing your own letterhead, business cards, birthday cards, invitations, brochures, or advertisements.

Before you buy a graphics product, make sure it is compatible with WordPerfect. You can check your WordPerfect Reference for compatible file formats. Or you can check with the manufacturer of the product you are considering to find out if the product is compatible with WordPerfect.

If you try to use a graphic file that is incompatible, you may have luck using WordPerfect's graphic conversion program to convert the file to WordPerfect graphic format. Check your WordPerfect Reference for specific instructions on graphic file conversion.

Let's walk-through adding a figure box. Press Alt + F9, or select the Graphics menu. Select Graphics Boxes and then Create. The Create Graphics Box dialog box appears. First, check the Based on Box Style setting and make sure Figure Box is selected.

Select Filename, and enter the path and file name of the graphic to place in the figure. If you don't know the file name, you can select Filename , and then select the File List F5 button and search for the file. To find WordPerfect's graphic files, search for

.WPG files in the WP60\GRAPHICS directory. Just list the files for this path: C:\WP60\GRAPHICS.WPG. In the example shown in Figure 15.6, the file named HOTROD.WPG (a WordPerfect supplied graphic) was used.

Figure 15.6
The HOTROD.WPG file is selected.

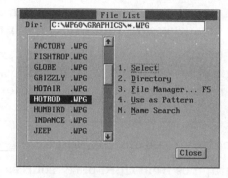

From the Create Graphics Box, you can select Image Editor to change the appearance of the contents of the figure. The Image Editor is shown in Figure 15.7. Use this screen to change a variety of size and appearance settings. Press F7 to return to the Create Graphics Box dialog box when you are done editing.

Figure 15.7
Editing WordPerfect's HOTROD.WPG graphic file.

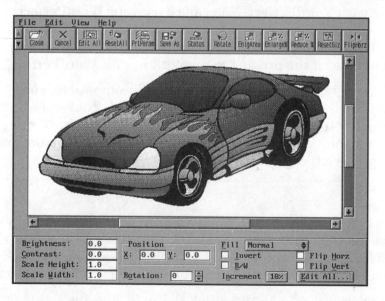

In the example, the Edit **B**order/Fill option was used. The Based on Border Style option was set to Spacing Only (No Lines).

The Edit **P**osition Horizontal option was set at Centered between the margins. Finally, for the **T**ext Flow Around Box option on the Create Graphics Box dialog box, the Text Flows was set to On Both Sides, and **C**ontour Text Flow was checked to contour the edge of the text to match the contours of the hot rod. Select OK to leave the Create Graphics Box dialog box. A code is placed in the document.

Figure 15.8 shows the results after text is added. The first three lines were controlled with hard returns to prevent text from going on the right side of the hot rod. The paragraph was allowed to flow around the car graphic.

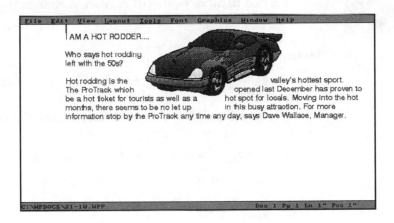

Figure 15.8

The figure with text added.

Creating a Style

1. Press `Alt`+`F8` or select Styles from the Layout menu.
2. Select Create.
3. Complete the Style **N**ame and Style **T**ype fields. Check the check box, if you want. Select OK.
4. Enter the Description and Style **C**ontents. Choose to Show Style **O**ff codes and change the **E**nter Key Action, if you want. Select OK.

Using a Style

1. Press `Alt`+`F8` or select Styles from the Layout menu.
2. Highlight the style you want, and choose Select.

Style Contents and Control

- Styles can include codes, text, and graphics.

16

Styles

Creating and Using Styles

If you develop reports, newsletters, or other documents with special font, graphic, or text effects, you will want to learn about Styles. Using Styles allows you to save many keystrokes by automating common formatting options.

The What and When of Styles

A style is usually thought of as a collection of formatting instructions that you identify based on your own needs. However, you can also include graphics and text, as well as formatting codes, in a style. Then, use the style whenever you want to insert that set of codes, graphics, or text into your document. Styles both save time (because you don't have to continually re-enter the formatting codes) and increase accuracy (because the style is tested, you know it is correct).

When should you create a style? Create a style for any special formatting, text, or graphics that you use over and over. For instance, you can create company reports, develop organization newsletters, or create letters or memos with varying formatting elements. Using styles will speed the more repetitive tasks in developing such documents and free you to concentrate on the more creative aspects of your work.

The real beauty of styles comes when you want to change a style. Suppose you have a 50 page document with multiple occurrences of a heading. Changing the style once affects all headings. If formatting were entered manually or with a macro, each occurrence of the heading would have to be changed individually.

> **TIP:** You can include in a style any codes, graphics, or text that can be put in a regular WordPerfect document. This includes figures, lines, names, addresses, special fonts, formatting, index or table of contents codes, column on and off settings, and so on.

The example in Figure 16.1 shows the Print Preview of a monthly flyer describing company news. It includes five customized styles with different fonts that account for the unusual spacing of text. The five styles created for this example are:

Figure 16.1

Monthly flyer with five customized styles.

Flyer heading

Major heading

Body

Minor heading

Article divider

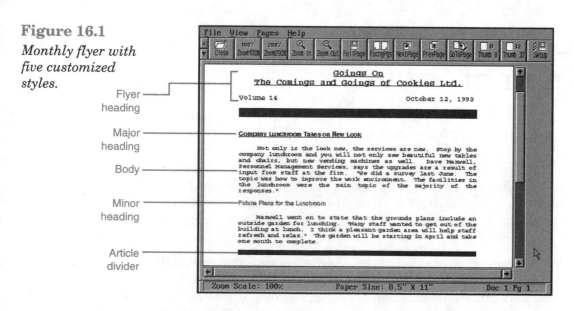

- **Flyer heading:** Includes the font codes, title of the flyer, and the solid line.

- **Major heading** for company flyer body: Contains font and underline codes.

- **Minor heading** for company flyer body: Contains font.

- **Body** of company flyer: Contains font and tab codes.

- **Article divider** for company flyer: Contains the line code.

Styles and Graphics

If you find yourself defining graphics options often, you may want to set up a style for each of the different option settings you use. This way, you will not have to redefine the options each time you want to switch. Just insert the new style and away you go.

Types of Styles

When you create and use a style, the style can be one of three types:

Paragraph Style: Affects paragraph at the cursor or in text you've blocked.

Character Style: Affects text that has been blocked or text you are about to enter.

Open Style: Affects all text from the cursor to the end of the document.

A code is placed in your document at the beginning of each style. Figure 16.2 shows character style codes in place for the flyer.

Figure 16.2
Character codes.

Codes for
article divider

Codes for flyer body

Codes for
major heading

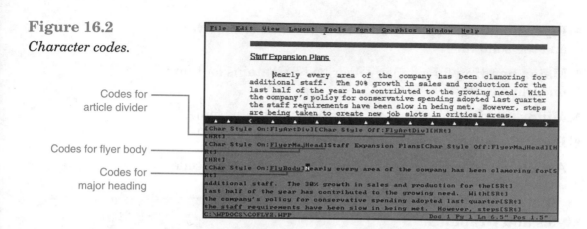

Creating a Style

To create a style, press Alt + F8, or select Styles from the Layout
menu. The Styles List dialog box appears. Select Create. The
Create Style dialog box appears (see Figure 16.3).

Figure 16.3

*The Create Style
dialog box.*

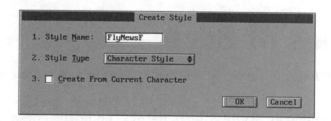

Type in a name for the style. Select a Style Type. If you
selected Paragraph Style, check the Create From Current Paragraph check box to include the paragraph containing the cursor.
If you selected Character Style, check the Create From Current
Character check box to create the style from the font attributes
for the character at the cursor location.

CAUTION
Always use a unique name when you create a
style. Otherwise, you may inadvertently replace
an existing style.

Select OK. You are taken to the Edit Style dialog box. Select **D**escription to enter a descriptive phrase for the style. Enter a description that distinguishes the style from other styles (such as the use or the font type).

Choose Style **C**ontents to enter the codes and text that make up the style, and press F7 when done. This takes you to the Edit Style dialog box shown in Figure 16.4.

Figure 16.4
The Edit Style dialog box.

In Figure 16.4, the font is identified, followed by a center code, and then the standard text to be used every time the style is used. A hard return is entered, followed by a new font and the code for center justification.

> **TIP:** You can cut or copy codes from your document into Style Contents. Use Alt+F4 to block the text. Then press Ctrl+F4. Select Cut and Paste or Copy and Paste. Go into the Style Contents, and press ↵Enter to retrieve the cut or copied text. Be careful not to press ↵Enter before getting into Style Contents.

Next, for Paragraph and Character styles, you can check a check box to Show Style **O**ff Codes. A code showing where the style ends will be placed in your document. If you want to change the action of the ⏎Enter key when in a Paragraph or Character Style, check the **E**nter Key Action check box and make a selection. These are the options:

Insert Hard Return: When you press ⏎Enter, a hard return is placed in your document. Because this is the "status quo," it is a popular setting. With this setting, you need to remember to move your cursor past style off codes, if entered.

Turn Style Off: When you press ⏎Enter, your cursor goes past the style. This option is useful for headings.

Turn Style Off and Back On: Pressing ⏎Enter moves the cursor past the style then turns the style on again. This is useful for bulleted lists or situations where you want to insert text between styles later.

Turn Style Off and Link to: Pressing ⏎Enter moves the cursor past the style and turns on the style you indicate here.

Once you have completed the contents of the style, select OK to leave the Edit Style dialog box.

The style is created, and the style becomes available for use in the Styles List dialog box. Select the Close button to return to your document.

The following Quick Steps summarize how to create a style.

Creating a Style

1. To create a style, press [Alt]+[F8], or select **S**tyles from the **L**ayout menu.

   The Styles List dialog box appears.

2. Select **C**reate.

   The Create Style dialog box appears.

3. Complete the Style **N**ame and Style **T**ype fields, and check the check box, if you want. Select OK.

   The Edit Style dialog box appears.

4. Enter the Description and Style **C**ontents. Choose to Show Style **O**ff codes and change the Enter Key Action, if you want. Select OK.	The style is added to the Style List dialog box.
5. Select Close.	You are returned to your document.

Using a Style

To use a style, just press Alt + F8, or select Styles from the Layout menu. The available styles appear on the Style List dialog box. Highlight the style you want, and choose Select. The style codes are placed in your document. Figure 16.5 shows the result of turning on the NewsFlash style and entering text. In this example, the cursor was placed on the code for the NewsFlash.

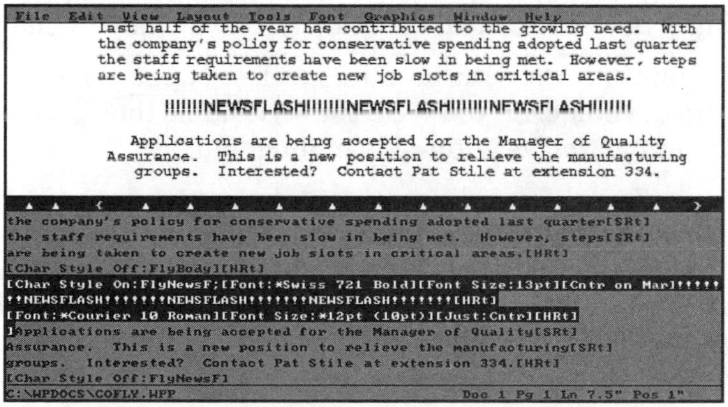

Figure 16.5
The NewsFlash style with text entered.

Any formatting you enter in your document takes priority over the formatting in the style. That way, if you want to turn off or add style attributes for a single occurrence, you can do so. For example, you can have a style that includes a font code and margin codes but doesn't include underlining of text. You can add the underline code in the document and use the remaining codes from the style.

The following Quick Steps detail how to use a style.

Using a Style

1. Press Alt + F8, or select Styles from the Layout menu.

   The available styles appear on the Style List dialog box.

2. Highlight the style you want, and choose Select.

   The style codes are placed in your document.

Other Style Options

You may have noticed some other options on the Styles List dialog box. Among these options are ways to edit, delete, save, or retrieve existing styles. You can also look up a style quickly by the name.

To find a style with its name, select Name Search. Begin typing in the name. As you type, the style name that is the closest match to what you've entered is highlighted.

When you select Edit on the Style List dialog box, you are taken to the Edit Style dialog box, which allows you to change any element of the selected style. The edits affect all occurrences of that style in your current document. (To affect another document, you must make the document active and then retrieve the new, edited style. A description of this retrieve function appears later in this section.) When you are done editing, the name for the new style appears on the Style List screen. The name of the style you edited is gone.

To delete a style for a single section of text, delete the styles code in Reveal Codes. Use the **D**elete option on the Style List dialog box to delete all occurrences of a style in a document. Just highlight the style to delete, and select Delete. The Delete Style dialog box appears. Identify if you want to delete:

Including Codes: Deletes the style and all related codes in your document. Use this option if you want all traces of the style formatting removed from your document, as well as the style removed.

Leaving Codes: The style is deleted, and the style codes are removed from your document, but the codes that made up the style remain. Use this option if you no longer want to use the style but you don't want the formatting of the document altered.

Styles are saved with the active document. However, you can save the styles you create for a document to a file and then retrieve that style file to use with other documents. This is useful if you have developed some all-purpose styles. To save styles, select Save from the Style List dialog box. The Save Styles dialog box appears. Enter the file name. (Use the .STY extension to easily identify the style file). Select OK. To later retrieve the styles to use with an active document, select Retrieve from the Style List dialog box, enter the file name, and select OK.

TIP: Styles are saved in the directory set up according to the Location of Files dialog box. This is usually C:\WP60. To check, press ⇧Shift+F1, or select Setup from the Files menu. Select Location of Files. Check (and change if you want) the location of the Style Files.

Exporting a File

1. Press `F10` or select Save As from the File menu.
2. Enter the Filename and Format from the list, and then select OK.

Importing a File

1. Press `Shift`+`F10` or select Open from the File menu. Or, use Retrieve from the File menu.
2. Identify the file to open or retrieve, and choose OK.
3. On the File Format dialog box, identify the format and choose Select.

Linking Spreadsheet Information

1. Place the cursor where the data will be placed.
2. Press `Alt`+`F7`, and select Spreadsheet. Or select Spreadsheet from the Tools menu. Select Create Link.
3. Enter the options, and then select Create Link.
4. Specify the spreadsheet name, then choose Link & Import.

Getting Information from and to Other Sources

Using the clipboard, which you'll learn about in Chapter 19, is one way of sharing information between programs. This chapter covers several other methods of transferring information into and out of WordPerfect.

Moving information into WordPerfect is called *importing*. Saving a WordPerfect file in a format that another program can use is called *exporting*. Importing text is useful if you have text in another format (such as a spreadsheet) to put in a WordPerfect document. Exporting is handy if you need to share a WordPerfect file with someone using another word processor or if you need to send information over the phone lines via a modem.

Exporting a Document

To export a WordPerfect document to another format, press [F10], or select Save As from the File menu. Enter the name you want to give the exported version, including the proper extension for the format into which you're exporting. (For example, MS Word uses .DOC for its files, so if you are exporting in MS Word format, you might call your file NEWFILE.DOC.)

Once the name of the file is entered, select Format. A drop-down list (shown in Figure 17.1) appears. This list shows the formats in which a WordPerfect document can be saved. The default selection is WordPerfect 6.0. However, the list also includes other popular word processing program formats, as well as all-purpose formats including ASCII text, Navy DIF Standard, Rich Text Format (RTF), and Spreadsheet DIF.

Figure 17.1
Save dialog box with format options.

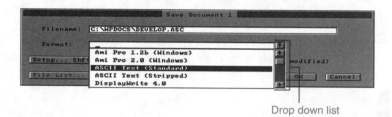

Drop down list

Exporting Plain Text

Plain formats like ASCII Text export the file without its formatting (such as margins and italics). Why would you want to export into a format like that? Here's an example. Let's say you're using an electronic publishing program and find that the specific file format for that program is not listed. In this case, you could save the WordPerfect file in the ASCII format (sometimes known as the DOS text format). Then, import the ASCII file into your electronic publishing package. Some format settings may be lost; however, the time saved retyping text is usually well worth any changes that need to be made.

Once you have selected the file format, select OK. The new file is created.

> **TIP:** Always save the document in WordPerfect format too so you'll have the document to refer to later. Use the regular File Save command.

Importing Documents from Other Programs

Users of WordPerfect version 6.0 will be happy to learn that files from other versions of WordPerfect can be exchanged. When you retrieve a document created in WordPerfect 5.1 for DOS or WordPerfect 5.1 or 5.2 for Windows, no conversion is needed, and your formatting is maintained.

WordPerfect is set up to handle popular "brand name" word processing file formats (such as files for MS Word and Ami Pro). It also handles industry standard personal computer formats common to word processing, spreadsheet, and database programs (such as Spreadsheet DIF, Rich Text Format (RTF), and ASCII).

> **TIP:** File format names may sound foreign to you. If you are unsure about the format used by a program, consult the manual for the program. It should identify the format that the files are saved in and whether you can convert from that program to other common formats. The program may even convert files directly to WordPerfect format!

To import a document, press ⇧Shift + F10, or select Open from the File menu. Or use Retrieve from the File menu to insert the file contents where your cursor rests. Depending on your choice, the Open Document or Retrieve Document dialog box appears. Enter or select the file to open or retrieve.

In the process of inserting the file contents, the File Format dialog box appears and lists the format from which the file will be converted. This format is WordPerfect's "best guess." If the format shown is incorrect, select another format. Figure 17.2 illustrates the File Format dialog box with ASCII Text (Standard) selected. Once the correct format to convert from appears, select OK. The file is converted and appears.

Figure 17.2
File Format dialog box.

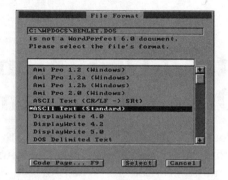

Importing Graphics

Some WordPerfect users may wonder what graphic files can be used other than those supplied by WordPerfect Corporation. WordPerfect supports the graphic files created by most programs, including CGM, DXF (AutoCAD), EPS, GEM, PCX, PIC (Lotus), TIFF, and more. Your WordPerfect Reference lists the types of graphic files that are automatically converted when they are brought into WordPerfect using Alt + F9 or the Graphics menu (see Chapter 15).

Working with Spreadsheets

The procedure for importing spreadsheet data is the same as the procedure covered under "Importing Documents" earlier in this chapter. (You can export to spreadsheet files in the same way as you export documents too; see "Exporting Documents.")

Spreadsheet data can also be combined into existing WordPerfect documents. Two Spreadsheet alternatives are available: *importing* and *linking*.

- Importing spreadsheet data is useful for including a spreadsheet in memos, reports, and letters that will be generated once.

- Linking spreadsheet data means the spreadsheet information can be automatically updated in both files when a change is made in the spreadsheet file. Links are useful for documents that have life over time, such as lists and regular reports.

In both cases, you can import or link the whole spreadsheet or a range (a portion) of spreadsheet data.

CAUTION

The Import and Link features were designed to work with the most popular spreadsheets on the market, including most versions of Lotus 1-2-3, Excel, and Quattro Pro. Check with WordPerfect Corporation if your spreadsheet data does not seem to be importing or linking as described. You may have a spreadsheet that is not supported by this feature.

Importing Spreadsheet Data

Importing spreadsheet data brings the data into the file exactly as it is at the moment. If you make changes to the spreadsheet in the future using your spreadsheet program, the WordPerfect document will not be affected.

You can import an entire spreadsheet or a part of one (using the **R**ange option), and you can import it either as text (with tabs) or in a WordPerfect table. To import a spreadsheet, use the following Quick Steps.

Importing a Spreadsheet

1. Place the cursor where the data will be imported.

The position for importing the data is identified by the cursor.

2. Press Alt + F7, and select Spreadsheet. Or select Spreadsheet from the Tools menu. Select Import.

The Import Spreadsheet dialog box appears (Figure 17.3).

3. Make the necessary selections to enter the path and name of the file, the range of the file to import, and the format type for display of the imported text. Then select Import.

The spreadsheet is imported.

Figure 17.3

The Import Spreadsheet dialog box.

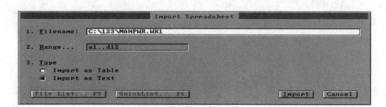

Select Import when the settings are all made. The spreadsheet data is imported. Figure 17.4 shows a spreadsheet imported into a document. Notice that the spreadsheet (imported as text rather than a table) has tabs inserted.

```
File  Edit  View  Layout  Tools  Font  Graphics  Window  Help
        Per your request, please supplement my earlier report with these
        figures showing the manpower growth for the first quarter.

        Manpower by Group - 1991

                    January    February   March

        Group 1        45         47        47
        Group 2        21         25        28
        Group 3        26         29        31
 [▲        ▲ ▲       ▲▲        ▲ ▲        ▲                              ]
figures showing the manpower growth for the first quarter.[HRt]
[HRt]
[Tab Set][+Tab Set][Rgt Tab][Lft Tab][Rgt Tab][Lft Tab][Rgt Tab][Lft Tab][Rgt Ta
b][Ignore:Lft Tab][HRt]
Manpower by Group - 1991[Rgt Tab][Lft Tab][Rgt Tab][Ignore:Lft Tab][Ignore:Lft T
ab][Ignore:Lft Tab][Ignore:Lft Tab][HRt]
[Rgt Tab][Lft Tab][Rgt Tab][Lft Tab][Rgt Tab][Lft Tab][Rgt Tab][Ignore:Lft Tab][
HRt]
[Rgt Tab][Lft Tab]January[Rgt Tab][Lft Tab]February[Rgt Tab][Lft Tab]March[Rgt T
ab][Ignore:Lft Tab][HRt]
[Rgt Tab][Lft Tab][Rgt Tab][Lft Tab][Rgt Tab][Lft Tab][Rgt Tab][Ignore:Lft Tab][
C:\WPDOCS\MANPOWER.WPP                        Doc 1 Pg 1 Ln 2.67" Pos 1"
```

Figure 17.4

The result of importing the spreadsheet.

Linking Spreadsheet Data

When you import spreadsheet data into an existing WordPerfect document, the information in your document is not updated when you update the spreadsheet. However, if you link the spreadsheet data, the linked document can be updated when you update the spreadsheet.

The procedure for linking is very similar to that of importing, except that you must choose between **L**ink and **L**ink & **I**mport. With **L**ink, the spreadsheet is linked to the WordPerfect document but does not appear immediately in the document. With **L**ink and **I**mport, the spreadsheet is linked and appears in the document.

Follow these Quick Steps to link a spreadsheet.

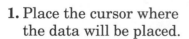

Linking a Spreadsheet

1. Place the cursor where the data will be placed.

The position for spreadsheet data is identified by the cursor.

continues

continued

2. Press ⌊Alt⌋+⌊F7⌋, and select **S**preadsheet. Or select **S**preadsheet from the **T**ools menu. Select **C**reate Link.

The Create Spreadsheet Link dialog box appears (Figure 17.5).

3. Enter the options you want for **F**ilename, **R**ange, and **T**ype; then select Link & **I**mport.

The spreadsheet data is linked.

Figure 17.5

The Create Spreadsheet Link dialog box.

An example of a completed link is shown in Figure 17.6. The beginning of the link is displayed on the screen in boldface. The information includes the path and file name and is included along with the range. This information is also shown in Reveal Codes.

```
[Link:C:\123\MANPWR2.WK1;A1..F12]
```

At the end of the link, another visual display is placed in your document stating Link End, and a [Link End] code is shown in Reveal Codes.

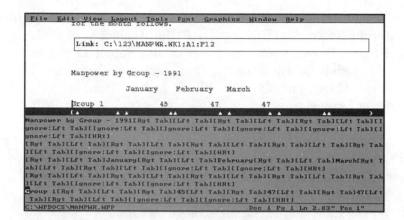

Figure 17.6
Result of link.

Spreadsheet Options and Editing

If you don't like the on-screen display of the link beginning and end, press Alt+F7, and select Spreadsheet. Or select Spreadsheet from the Tools menu. Select Link Options. The Spreadsheet Link Options dialog box appears. Deselect the check box Show Link Codes.

The Spreadsheet Link Options dialog box also has a check box for Update on Retrieve. Check this check box if you want WordPerfect to automatically update the spreadsheet when the WordPerfect document is retrieved. If you leave the check box blank, you can manually update the spreadsheet information. To manually update it, select the Update All Links button.

If you want to delete the link (but not the spreadsheet information), delete either the beginning or ending code in Reveal Codes.

To edit a single link, place your cursor between the beginning and ending link codes. Press Alt + F7, and select Spreadsheet. Or select Spreadsheet from the Tools menu. Select Edit Link. The Edit Spreadsheet Link dialog box appears. You can change **F**ilename, **R**ange, or **T**ype (Table or Text). Then, select Link & Import or Import.

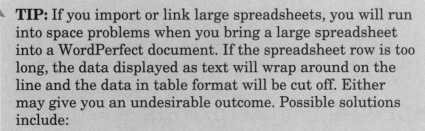

TIP: If you import or link large spreadsheets, you will run into space problems when you bring a large spreadsheet into a WordPerfect document. If the spreadsheet row is too long, the data displayed as text will wrap around on the line and the data in table format will be cut off. Either may give you an undesirable outcome. Possible solutions include:

- Reduce the column width in the spreadsheet program (if the columns can be made smaller without losing the contents). See the documentation for the spreadsheet program for instructions on how to change the width, resize, or reduce columns.

- Change the base font affecting the imported spreadsheet information in WordPerfect. Press Ctrl + F8, or select Font from the Font menu. Select a small font.

- Change the margins in WordPerfect by selecting Shift + F8 and then Page. Or select Page from the Layout menu. Select Paper Size/Type.

- If the spreadsheet is imported as a table, size the table to fit between the margins. Press Alt + F7, and select Table Edit, or select Tables and then Edit from the Layout menu.

- Set up the WordPerfect document for printing in land-scape mode ("sideways" on the page). Select ⎗Shift + F8 and then **Page**. Or select Page from the Layout menu. Select Paper Size/Type. Select a Paper Name listed as Landscape that works with your printer and allows for a long paper length.

Read about these options and hints for handling more complicated import and export tasks in an advanced WordPerfect text.

Creating a Table of Contents and Index

1. Mark each entry.
2. Define the Table of Contents and Index.
3. Generate the Table of Contents and Index.

Marking a Table of Contents or Index Entry

1. Block the entry with Alt+F4 or by selecting Block from the Edit menu.
2. Press Alt+F5, and select Table of Contents or Index. Choose OK.

Defining a Table of Contents or Index

1. Place your cursor where the table of contents or index should appear.
2. Press Alt+F5, select Define and Index. Complete the Define Index dialog box, and choose OK.

Generating a Table of Contents or Index

1. Press Alt+F5, and select Generate.
2. Choose OK to confirm.

Creating an Outline

1. Press Ctrl+F5, or select Outline from the Tools menu. Choose Begin New Outline, and complete the Outline Style List dialog box.
2. Use Tab and ⇧Shift+Tab to control the outline entry.
3. Press Ctrl+F5, or select Outline from the Tools menu. Choose End Outline.

Tables of Contents and Indexes

Creating Tables of Contents, Indexes, and Outlines

WordPerfect has a wealth of organizational features to make your job easier. Among them is the capability of WordPerfect to automatically generate tables of contents, indexes, and outlines. This chapter details how it works.

The Benefits of "Automated" Tables of Contents and Indexes

The "old-fashioned" way of creating a table of contents or an index is to identify the text manually in your document after all page numbers have been assigned and then type in each entry along with the page number. If the document is edited and the page numbers change, the table of contents and index have to be updated manually.

However, with WordPerfect, the process of creating tables of contents and indexes is greatly simplified. In the document, you mark the text that is to be included in the table of contents or index. Then when you give the signal, WordPerfect generates the table of contents or index automatically. When the document is edited, just ask WordPerfect to generate the references again. There's no manual record-keeping of what's in the index and table of contents and no manual updating of the table of contents and index. And there is no chance of a page numbering error.

Creating a Table of Contents or Index

To create a table of contents or index, follow these basic steps:

1. Mark the text you want to include in the table of contents or index: This identifies to WordPerfect the entries for the table of contents or index.

2. Define the characteristics of the table of contents or index: You can identify the location and appearance of a table of contents and the location for index words.

3. Generate the table of contents or index: WordPerfect finds each occurrence of the text marked for a table of contents or index and creates the references.

TIP: Always plan your table of contents or index before you start writing the document. Have an idea of how detailed you want the table of contents or index to be so you are consistent throughout the document. Also consider how many levels you want reflected. For example, the index in this book could have a single level "index" to cover index information or more detailed entry with two levels:

index
   generating
   marking and defining

The procedures for marking and defining tables of contents and indexes are slightly different, so we'll discuss them separately in the following sections. The procedure for generating them is the same; you'll learn how near the end of the chapter.

Marking and Defining a Table of Contents

You can create a table of contents with one to five levels. Each additional level is a "sublevel." Figure 18.1 shows part of a table of contents for a document created by Barbara J. Wiley. It has only one level. Figure 18.2 shows a portion of Wiley's table of contents, this time with two levels. Each new sublevel in a table of contents is indented to the next tab stop.

Figure 18.1

Table of contents with one level.

Developing a Computer System
By Barbara J. Wiley and Paul G. Otto

Table of Contents

Figure 18.2

Table of contents with two levels.

Developing a Computer System
By Barbara J. Wiley and Paul G. Otto

Table of Contents

The first step in creating a table of contents or index is marking each item in the document that needs to be included. The following Quick Steps show how to mark an entry for a table of contents.

Marking a Table of Contents Entry

Quick Steps

1. Block the entry with Alt+F4, or select **Block** from the **Edit** menu.

The entry for the table of contents is identified.

2. Press Alt+F5, and then select Table of Contents. Or select Table of Contents and then **Mark** from the **Tools** menu.

The Mark Table of Contents dialog box appears with the level.

3. Enter the level number (1, 2, 3, 4, or 5), and select OK.

Codes are placed around the text. For example, these codes show that the word "Coding" is a level 1 table of contents entry:
```
[Mrk Txt ToC
Begin:1]Coding[Mrk Txt ToC
End:1]
```

Once all of the table of contents entries are marked, you must define the table of contents.

1. Place your cursor where you want the table of contents to appear. Typically, you will want it at the beginning of the document on its own page. (To create a page, enter a hard page break with Ctrl+Enter.) You can also enter a heading, such as "Contents."

2. Press Alt+F5, select **Define**, and then select Table of Contents. Or select Table of Contents and then **Define** from the **Tools** menu. The Define Table of Contents dialog box appears (see Figure 18.3).

Figure 18.3

The Table of Contents dialog box.

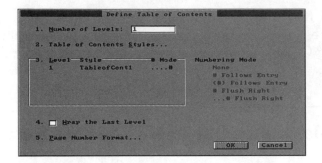

3. Identify the number of levels by selecting Number of Levels and typing in a number 1 through 5.

4. Select Level to choose how page numbers are to be displayed. The selections with examples of each numbering mode follow:

   O - **No**ne (no page numbers):

   Major Tasks

   F - Page Number **F**ollows Entry:

   Major Tasks 1

   (- Page Number in Parentheses Follows Entry:

   Major Tasks (1)

   R - Page Number Flush **R**ight:

   Major Tasks 1

   L - Page Number Flush Right with Dot Leaders:

   Major Tasks..............................1

5. Leave the check box Wrap the Last Level unchecked. (Otherwise the levels wrap around as if they are part of one paragraph.)

6. For **P**age Number Format, leave it as is for the pages to be the same as the document. Or select it, and identify how you want the page numbers different. (See Chapter 8 for information on page numbering.)

7. Select OK when you are done. A code like this appears in your document:

```
[Def Mark:TofC,3:Dot Ldr #]
```

The code starts with the Definition mark for the table of contents. There are three levels and the page numbering on each level will have dot leaders.

Once you have marked the table of contents entries and defined the table of contents, you can generate it, which is discussed in "Generating the Table of Contents and Index" later in this chapter. Because you generate both the table of contents and index at the same time, you may want to mark and define an index first.

Marking and Defining an Index

When you create an index, you can use headings and subheadings. Figure 18.4 shows a portion of an index with headings and subheadings. Notice that the subheadings are indented under the associated heading. The tab stops are used for indentation.

Index	
ABC Approach	2
Benefits to Users	1
BITTLE Company Experience	54
Coding	19
Common Problems and Solutions	24
Handling DSD Changes	21
Managing the Coding Activity	25
Methods to Code	22
Cutting Costs	42

Figure 18.4
Index with headings and subheadings.

To mark a single word as an index entry, place your cursor on that word. To mark several words making up one entry, block the words using Alt + F4 or by selecting Block from the Edit menu. Positioning the cursor marks the text to use to identify the page number. As you will see, you can change the actual wording of the index entry, if you like.

Press Alt + F5, and choose Mark Text, and then Index. Or select Index and then Mark from the Tools menu. The Mark Index dialog box appears. The words you've identified appear in the Heading: text box. Use the text as marked, or type in your own index entry. (For instance, you may want different capitalization, a different tense, or entirely different text.)

If you don't want a subheading, leave the Subheading: text box empty. If you want one, either type in a subheading or just accept the one shown. Select OK. Codes are placed in your document around the marked words. Here is an example:

```
[Index:Coding;Common Problems and Solutions]
```

In Figure 18.4, the heading is Coding and the subheading is Common Problems and Solutions.

The following Quick Steps summarize the process of marking an index entry.

Marking an Index Entry

1. Place your cursor on the word or block the words for the entry using Alt + F4, or select Block from the Edit menu.

   The location of the index entry is identified.

2. Press Alt + F5, Mark Text, and then Index. Or select Index and then Mark from the Tools menu.

   The Mark Index dialog box appears.

3. Accept the Heading or enter a new one; accept the subheading or enter a new one. Select OK.	Codes appear in the document. The following code indicates the word "Shoes" is an index entry: `[Index:Shoes].`

There is one other method you can use in identifying words for an index. You can create a *concordance file*, which is a list of words you want in the index. WordPerfect looks for and marks these words in your document. You can check each mark, adding and deleting marks as you want. For more information on using a concordance file, see your WordPerfect Reference.

Once all index entries are marked, define the index. To do this:

1. Place your cursor where you want the index to appear in your document.

2. Press Alt + F5, select Define, and select Index. Or select Index and then Define from the Tools menu. The Define Index dialog box appears (see Figure 18.5).

Figure 18.5
Define Index dialog box appears.

The selections are identical to those used when defining a Table of Contents. The only additional selection is Combine Sequential Page Numbers (Example: 51–62). Check the box to combine page numbers, or deselect it to write out each page number (such as 51, 52, 53, and so on). Select OK. A code like this is placed in your document:

```
[Def Mark:Index,Dot Ldr #;]
```

This identifies where the index will be placed and the type of page numbering.

Generating the Table of Contents and Index

The procedure for generating a table of contents and an index is the same. In fact, if you have marked entries for both, both will be generated when you follow these steps.

1. Press Alt + F5 , and select Generate. Or select Generate from the Tools menu.

2. The Generate dialog box appears with this message: Existing tables, lists, and indexes will be replaced if you continue. Select OK.

A Generation in Progress message appears. When it goes away, the table of contents and index have been generated. The table of contents or index appears after the appropriate [Def Mark:...]. Following the table of contents or index, this code appears:

    [End Gen Txt]

CAUTION   Never delete the [Def Mark] or [End Gen Txt] codes. If you do, WordPerfect will not know where to put the table of contents or index if you generate it again. Only delete these codes if you are deleting the entire table of contents or index.

Once the table of contents or index has been generated, you can edit it like any document text. For example, you can add your own headings, blank lines, or change tab settings to alter the indentation.

The page numbers in the table of contents and index remain the same until you generate them again. As a result, when you edit a document, the page numbers in the table of contents and index do not change automatically. When you are done making changes in the document, use Alt + F5 and Generate, or select Generate from the Tools menu, and proceed.

TIP: You will usually want to generate your table of contents and index after spell checking but before printing your document. This way, all editing will be complete, and the page numbers will be stable. Sometimes, however, it is useful to generate the table of contents or index as you work. Doing so provides a reference to see the structure of the document and the location of particular material. You can generate a table of contents and index again and again.

Creative Uses of Tables of Contents and Indexes

Don't let names fool you. You can use Table of Contents and Index functions for applications other than generating tables of contents and indexes. The Table of Contents feature can be used to create any list that places the items in the list in the order they appear in the document. The Index feature places items in alphabetical order and can be used to associate subordinate items to a superior item. Consider their use in putting together any kind of list.

For example, one clever user composed a narrative of her family and used the Index feature of WordPerfect to automatically generate a family tree. (Children were marked as subordinate items to parents.) Open your mind. Create vocabulary lists, short narrative summaries, lists of figures or graphics, or any form of list using the Table of Contents and Index features.

Creating Outlines

Outlining is another useful organizing technique WordPerfect makes easy. You can switch to the outline mode, and the text you type will be automatically numbered and indented; you don't have to remember what number or letter comes next or how far to indent. Also, numbers and letters are automatically updated when you edit the outline. Figure 18.6 illustrates part of an outline created using WordPerfect.

Figure 18.6

An outline created with WordPerfect.

Talk for Data Processing Professional Group

By Barbara J. Wiley

I.   Background of presenters

II. Why computer systems haven't met needs

III. Benefits of a better approach

IV. Major Tasks

    A. Specifications

        1. The stated and hidden goals

        2. Getting user requirements

        3. Story of BITTLE

        4. MIS role (new and old)

    B. Design

To develop an outline, first follow these Quick Steps to begin using the Outline feature.

Beginning a New Outline

1. Place the cursor where the outline will start.

2. Press Ctrl+F5, or select Outline from the Tools menu.   Outlining options appear.

3. Choose **B**egin New Outline.	The Outline Style List dialog box appears.
4. Select an outline style.	Codes for outlining and paragraph style appear. The first level number, letter, or symbol also appears.

Text you enter will be in outline form. As you can see, certain keypresses give different results in Outline mode than when you are in regular editing mode.

Type in text or, to go to the next level, press `Tab ↹`. To go back a level, press `⇧Shift`+`Tab ↹`. Continue using these keys while you create your outline. Table 18.1 is a summary of the keys to press and the results.

Key to press	Result
`Tab ↹`	To go "in" (right) one level
`⇧Shift`+`Tab ↹`	To go "out" (left) one level

Table 18.1
*Keys to Press
While Outlining*

When you insert a level number, a code for paragraph style appears in the text:

```
[Para Style:Level 1;]
```

For example, to recreate the outline in Figure 18.6, follow these steps:

1. After the outline title and Barbara J. Wiley's by-line, begin an outline (as shown in the previous Quick Steps). Select Outline as the outline style. The first line will automatically be numbered I.

2. Type in the text. Press `↵Enter` at the end of the line. A II appears. Type in the next line, doing the same for lines III and IV. Press `↵Enter` at the end of each line.

3. To go to a new level, press Tab⇄. The number V disappears and is replaced with the letter A.

4. Type Specification, press ⏎Enter and Tab⇄ to go to a new level, the number 1.

5. From the line marked 1 through the line marked 4, type in a line, and press ⏎Enter at the end of each line.

6. After line 4, 5 appears. Press ⇧Shift + Tab⇄ to move left one tab setting. The 5 is replaced with the letter B.

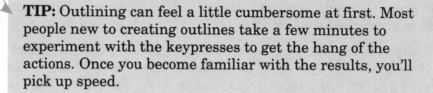

TIP: Outlining can feel a little cumbersome at first. Most people new to creating outlines take a few minutes to experiment with the keypresses to get the hang of the actions. Once you become familiar with the results, you'll pick up speed.

When you are done creating the outline, press Ctrl + F5, then select End Outline. Or select Outline and then End Outline from the Tools menu. You are returned to regular editing mode. Codes are placed in the document.

This description of outlining will get you started. Consult your WordPerfect Reference if you use outlining often and want to learn a few tricks. For example, there are keypresses that move you more than one level at a time and to the most recent occurrence of the same level. You can select the Outline Bar from the View menu to provide a quick route to outline options. Also, you can use the Cut/Copy/Delete options to control a level of the outline and all subordinate levels. Finally, you can create your own level styles.

Displaying the Button Bar

- To see a Button Bar, select Button Bar from the View menu.

Creating and Editing a Button Bar

1. Select Button Bar Setup from the View menu, and choose Select.
2. Choose Create, name the Button Bar, and select OK. Or highlight the Button Bar to edit, and select Edit.
3. You can add, delete, and move buttons. Select OK when done.

Selecting a New Button Bar

1. Select Button Bar Setup from the View menu.
2. Choose Select.
3. Highlight the Button Bar you want, and choose Select.

Starting Shell from DOS

1. From DOS, change the drive, if necessary, by entering the drive number and a colon (C:).
2. Change directories, if necessary, by using a command like this: cd\wpcdos60.
3. Type in shell, and press ↵Enter.

Using the Clipboard

1. If necessary, block the text with Alt+F4, or select Block from the Edit menu.
2. Press Ctrl+F1, or select Go to Shell from the File menu.
3. Change the Clipboard Number, if necessary.
4. Select Save to, Append, or Retrieve.

Other Tools

In addition to the features you've been working with so far, WordPerfect offers several handy tools for getting work done faster and easier. You'll learn about them in this chapter. The Button Bar is, by far, the most versatile of the special tools; it enables you to select many of the most common commands with a simple click on a button. Other tools you may find a use for include the clipboard, an electronic holding area for bits of a document, and a task-switching program new to version 6.0 called Shell.

Button Bars

Button Bars can be used to quickly perform any operation you want with a click of the mouse—whether it is a command, a series of commands, or a macro. Because you set up the operation, you control what the Button Bar performs. You can create any number of Button Bars and edit them at any time.

> **TIP:** When to use a Button Bar? If you have a macro you often use, put it on a Button Bar. If you use operations regularly, they are good candidates for the Button Bar. For example, you may have several boilerplate documents with
>
> *continues*

continued

common formatting setups for, perhaps, a memo, a letter, a standard report, or a status report. If you set up opening each document in a macro, and then assign the macro to a Button Bar, you can quickly get to these frequently used documents.

Displaying and Using a Button Bar

To see a Button Bar, select Button Bar from the View menu. The Button Bar command is marked, and the current Button Bar will display until you change the selection (even if you leave and return to WordPerfect).

WordPerfect comes with a general use Button Bar already set up for you. The Button Bar shown in Figure 19.1 appears when you first select Button Bar from the View menu. The selections of this Button Bar are outlined in Chapter 1.

Figure 19.1
Button Bar.

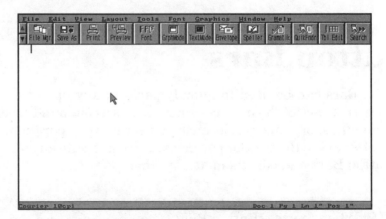

Creating and Editing a Button Bar

Once you get used to the quickness of the Button Bar, you will want to customize your own Button Bar. For example, if you work with graphics often, you may want a Button Bar just for graphics. You may also want to edit existing Button Bars. The steps for creating and editing Button Bars are similar.

To create or edit a Button Bar, select Button Bar Setup from the View menu. Then, choose Select. The Select Button Bar dialog box appears. Choose Create, give the Button Bar a name, and select OK. Or highlight the name of the Button Bar to edit, and choose Edit. When creating or editing, the Edit Button Bar dialog box shown in Figure 19.2 appears.

Figure 19.2
The Edit Button Bar dialog box, with several buttons already added.

You can use the Edit Button Bar dialog box to perform several types of additions to the Button Bar. Select one of the following:

Add Menu Item: Use this to choose items from a pull-down menu. The button appears in the Button Bar, and the button name appears in the Edit Button Bar dialog box. Continue adding buttons, and press F7 when you are done.

Add Feature: Choose this option to select from a long list of WordPerfect features. Many of these features could be selected via menus, however this approach is faster.

Add Macro: Use this option to select an existing macro to be run when the button is selected. The button is given the same name as the macro. When saved, macros are stored according to the file location set up through ⇧Shift+F1, **L**ocation of Files. The default is C:\WP60. This is also the directory to which Button Bars are saved with the .WPB file extension.

Add **B**utton Bar: Choose this to select an existing Button Bar. The name of the Button Bar is added as a button. You'll be able to activate the Button Bar by selecting the button.

TIP: If you add a button on a Button Bar to go to a new Button Bar, it is a good idea to add a button on the destination Button Bar so you can return.

If you enter a button you want to delete, highlight the button description in the Edit Button Bar dialog box, and select the description of the Button Bar. Select Delete Button.

You may not like the order of the buttons on the Button Bar. If so, use the Edit Button Bar dialog box to move the button. Highlight the button name to move and choose Move Button. Select another button name in the list and Paste Button. The button you moved appears before the last selected button name. You can also paste the button at the bottom of the list.

Figure 19.2 shows a Button Bar being created with several buttons already added. Notice that the buttons listed in the Edit Button Bar dialog box appear in the Button Bar area as they are added.

CAUTION   As you build the Button Bar, don't select the same option twice. Although WordPerfect will let you, it is a waste of good button space.

Once the Button Bar is created, it is selected for use until you change the selection. Figure 19.3 illustrates the completed Button Bar including a button for the BRETADD macro. Notice the arrows on the Button Bar. These arrows may be clicked to expose other buttons.

Arrow changes Button Bar display.   BRETADD macro

Figure 19.3
*The completed
Button Bar.*

TIP: If you add more buttons than can appear on a Button Bar, the Button Bar extends off the screen. Later, when you want to access buttons that are off the screen, you can click on the arrows in the Button Bar to move the Button Bar and expose the button you want.

The following Quick Steps summarize how to create or edit a Button Bar.

Creating or Editing
a Button Bar

1. Select Button Bar Setup from the View menu, and choose Select.

   The Select Button Bar dialog box appears.

2. Choose Create, name the Button Bar, and select OK. Or highlight the Button Bar to edit, and select Edit.

   The Edit Button Bar dialog box appears.

3. Add, delete, and move buttons as you want. Select OK when you are done.

   The Button Bar is available for use.

> **TIP:** If you are editing the current Button Bar, you may select Button Bar Setup from the View menu, and choose Edit. You are taken directly to the Edit Button Bar dialog box.

Selecting a Different Button Bar

Once you have created one or more new Button Bars, you may want to switch between Button Bars. To do this, select Button Bar Setup from the View menu. Choose Select. Highlight the Button Bar you want, and choose Select. The Button Bar is now available when displayed.

Renaming a Button Bar

Sometimes, you'll edit a Button Bar so that the original name is no longer descriptive of the buttons. Or you may decide to split the functions on a Button Bar into multiple Button Bars. Rather than start from scratch, you can rename an existing Button Bar to make life easier. Select Button Bar Setup from the View menu. Choose Select. Highlight the Button Bar you want to rename, and choose Rename. Enter in a new Button Bar name, and select OK.

Button Bar Options

You may have noticed the Button Bar Options command. It allows you to change the position and style of the Button Bar. To use the options, select Button Bar Setup on the View menu. Select Options. The Button Bar Options dialog box appears. Select the Position of the Button Bar on the screen. The options are **T**op, **B**ottom, **L**eft Side, and **R**ight Side. Then, select the Style. The options are **P**icture and Text, Picture **O**nly, and Te**x**t Only. (The Picture and Text option and the Picture Only option are not available when using Text Mode.) Select OK.

Figure 19.4 illustrates our Button Bar on the bottom position with Text Only. This Button Bar takes up considerably less screen space. However, it is not as graphical.

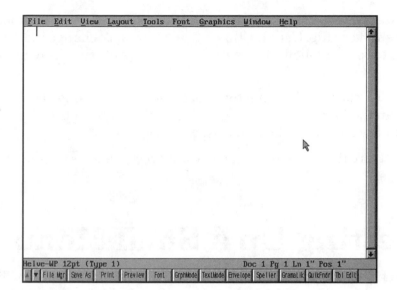

Figure 19.4
Button Bar on bottom of screen with text only.

WordPerfect's Shell Program

Do you find yourself switching between programs often (such as WordPerfect and a spreadsheet like Paradox)? Do you want to be able to share information easily and often between programs? Would it be helpful to be able to save information to one of 80 clipboards and retrieve it later? If so, take a look at the Shell.

Shell is a separate program that comes with WordPerfect 6.0. It lets you place programs and commands into menus. It allows you to switch between programs without leaving the original program. Shell also includes a clipboard. The clipboard allows you to swap information between programs running under Shell. You may also temporarily store information for use in WordPerfect.

Starting Shell

Shell can be added to your AUTOEXEC.BAT file. That way, each time you start your computer, Shell is started. If added, you will not need to start Shell from DOS as described in this section.

If the Shell menu does not appear when you start your computer, you will need to start it at the DOS prompt (usually c:).

To start Shell, change the drive and directory to the one that holds the shell.exe file. Usually, this is `C:\WPC60DOS`. To change the drive, just type it in followed by a colon, and press enter—for example, `C:`.

To change the directory, use the DOS Change Directory command followed by a backslash and the name of the directory with the shell.exe file, like this: `CD\WPC60DOS`.

Once the drive and directory is correct, type `shell`, and press `⏎Enter`.

Setting Up a Shell Menu

The first time you start up Shell, the Getting Started dialog box appears (see Figure 19.5). Here, you are asked to create the menu that includes the programs to display. To find and select programs on your system, choose Select Programs. From the List Programs dialog box, leave Program **T**ype set to Common Programs. Next, identify the directories to search. If you are working on a stand-alone machine, this will be your hard drive (probably `C:`). Select the Search...F2 button.

Figure 19.5

The Getting Started dialog box.

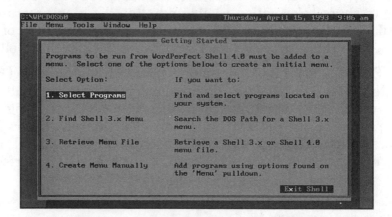

The search is complete and the List Programs dialog box appears. Mark each program for your menu with an asterisk (*), and then select the Add to Menu button. On the Menu Description dialog box, type in the Description for the menu that will appear at the top of the menu, and select OK. A menu like the one shown in Figure 19.6 appears. Notice that WordPerfect 6.0 is one of the options on the menu. Also notice the menu bar for controlling Shell options across the top of the screen. This screen is referred to as the Shell desktop.

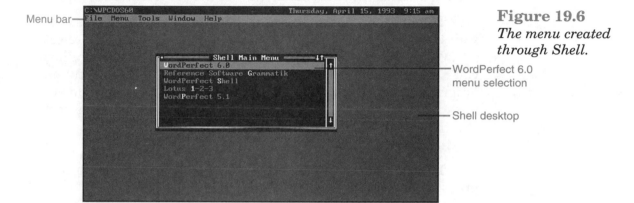

Menu bar

WordPerfect 6.0 menu selection

Shell desktop

Figure 19.6
The menu created through Shell.

Using the Shell Menu

The procedure for making Shell menu selections is identical to WordPerfect menu selections. Use the arrow keys to highlight a selection, and then press ⏎Enter. Double-click on a selection with the mouse. Or press the highlighted letter in the selection. When you select a program, you are taken to that program. Exit the program, and you are returned to the Shell menu.

Control the menu window like any WordPerfect window. (See Chapter 12 to learn about document windows.)

To exit Shell and return to DOS, press F7, or select Exit from the File menu. If files and programs are open, you are asked to confirm saving the file information and exiting the program.

Changing the Menu

You can change the Shell menu. This is especially important if a program has been overlooked when the menu was created. To add a program, highlight the spot for the new program name to appear above. Press Ins, or select Add Item(s) from the Menu menu and then Program. Complete the Description including a tilde (~) before the character to be the *mnemonic* (the mnemonic is the highlighted letter to press to make the menu selection). Complete the Filename (including the path) to start the program, and enter the Directories to set as the default in the program. Select OK.

To edit a menu selection, highlight it, and press F6. Or select Edit Item from the Menu menu. Complete the changes, and select OK. While editing an item, you may enter a hot key. Hot keys allow you to press Ctrl+Alt+(letter or number) to switch between programs and skip returning to the Shell menu. You may add hot keys when adding or editing Shell menu selections. Just select Hot Key, and enter the letter or number to be pressed with Ctrl+Alt.

To delete a program, highlight the program on the menu, and press Del, or select Delete from the Menu menu.

TIP: When setting up mnemonics or hot keys, make sure each mnemonic or hot key is unique for that program. Otherwise, you won't get the desired result.

Using Shell from Inside WordPerfect

You may use Shell from within WordPerfect to go to another active program, use the clipboard, or use DOS. Press Ctrl+F1, or select Go to Shell from the File menu. The Shell dialog box shown in Figure 19.7 appears.

An *active* program is one that has been selected from the Shell menu or with a hot key. To select an active program, select Active Programs from the Shell dialog box. Select the program.

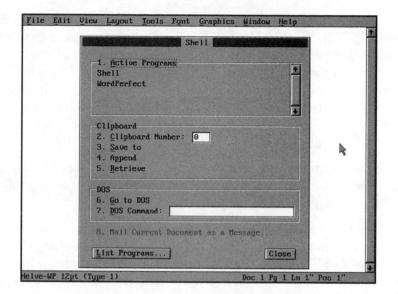

Figure 19.7
The Shell dialog box.

To use DOS, select Go to DOS from the Shell dialog box. You are taken to the DOS prompt. To return to WordPerfect, type in `Exit`, and press `⏎Enter` at the DOS prompt. To enter a DOS command from the Shell dialog box, select DOS Command, enter the command, and select Close.

Using the Clipboard

The clipboard allows you to store information that can be retrieved in WordPerfect or another program. You can create up to 80 clipboards. When you exit Shell, the contents of all clipboards are deleted.

TIP: To use the Shell feature in another program, it must be a Shell aware program or have a Screen Copy or Screen Paste feature. To learn whether your programs have these features, consult the manual for each program.

To save text to a clipboard from WordPerfect, select the text with Alt+F4, or select **Block** from the **E**dit menu. Press Ctrl+F1, or select **G**o to Shell from the **F**ile menu. From the Shell dialog box, note the **C**lipboard Number. This is the clipboard to which the information will be saved. Change the number of the clipboard, if you like, by selecting **C**lipboard and entering a new number. Once the **C**lipboard Number is set, select **S**ave to. The blocked text is saved to that clipboard.

You may have noticed the **A**ppend option on the Shell dialog box. Use it to add the blocked information to the end of the information saved in the clipboard.

To retrieve information from a clipboard, place your cursor where you want the information retrieved. Press Ctrl+F1, or select **G**o to Shell from the **F**ile menu. Make sure the number of the clipboard you want to retrieve from is identified, and then select **R**etrieve.

The following Quick Steps identify how to use the clipboard from WordPerfect.

QUICK STEPS — Using the Clipboard

Steps	Result
1. If you are saving or appending text, block the text with Alt+F4, or select **B**lock from the **E**dit menu.	The text is identified.
2. Press Ctrl+F1, or select **G**o to Shell from the **F**ile menu.	The Shell dialog box appears.
3. Change the **C**lipboard Number, if necessary.	The number of the clipboard you will save to or retrieve from appears.
4. Select **S**ave to, **A**ppend, or **R**etrieve.	The operation is complete.

Don't Get Confused

Having up to 80 clipboards can become confusing. If you
forget what clipboard contains which contents, you may
view the contents of your clipboards. Exit the program and
return to the Shell desktop. Press ⟨Alt⟩+⟨F1⟩, or select
Clipboard from the File menu. The contents of the last
selected clipboard appear. To view the contents for anther
clipboard, select Number from the Clipboard dialog box,
and enter the number. Select Cancel to return to the Shell
desktop.

FYI
IDEAS

Getting Ready to Use WordPerfect

You may want to fire up your computer and begin punching keys right now, however, if you spend just a few moments picking up some basic concepts, you'll avoid confusion later. Once you have the "big picture," you can fill in the details. This appendix will help you understand how WordPerfect works with your computer, how DOS fits into the picture, and how a WordPerfect document is created.

What is Word Processing?

Word processing is the term used to describe the development of letters, reports, and other documents with a computer. Word processing offers many advantages over handwriting or typing documents. Speed is a primary advantage. Because most people write by hand at about twelve words per minute, you don't have to be a speed demon on a keyboard to improve your efficiency with word processing. Another advantage you gain with word processing is the ease of entry, editing, and printing your work. You replace the cumbersome "cut, paste, and retype" approach with copying, moving, and deleting words instantly. A final, printed copy is only a few keystrokes away. The printed copy is clean and free of erasures and correction fluid.

WordPerfect is one brand of word processor. WordPerfect has been a bestseller for years because of its simplicity and power. At first, you'll probably create small, straightforward documents. But once you get up and running and want to go on to more sophisticated word processing, WordPerfect won't hold you back.

The written works you create using WordPerfect are called *documents*. A document can be any written item you create, such as a letter, a report, a memo, an expense sheet, a bill, or a list (to name just a few). You can combine elements in one document (such as following a letter with a bill). You decide how many documents you want to create and the contents of each document.

Computer System Components

WordPerfect is available in many versions, each one designed to run on a specific type of computer. This book describes using WordPerfect with an IBM-compatible microcomputer (also known as a DOS-based personal computer). IBM compatible is the standard set by IBM which other (often less expensive) computers match in specifications.

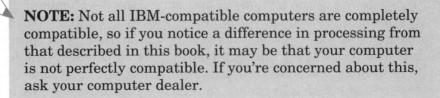

NOTE: Not all IBM-compatible computers are completely compatible, so if you notice a difference in processing from that described in this book, it may be that your computer is not perfectly compatible. If you're concerned about this, ask your computer dealer.

Your computer system includes hardware and software. *Hardware*, the "physical" part, is made up of the computer parts you can see and touch, while *software* consists of the operating system and the programs you run—the "logical" part.

Hardware Components

Your computer is made up of many hardware components, which work together to provide a fully functional unit. Figure A.1 illustrates some common hardware components:

Keyboard: The component that resembles the keys on a typewriter with a few added. You'll enter commands and type documents by pressing keys on the keyboard.

Monitor: The component that looks like a television screen. The text you type appears here, as well as special messages from WordPerfect that prompt you to press certain keys.

Central Processing Unit (CPU): The CPU is the brains of the computer, where all the processing takes place. As you work, the WordPerfect program and the documents you type are stored in random-access memory (RAM). RAM is temporary; its content is cleared when the computer is turned off. That's why it is so important to save your work to a disk.

Hard Disks, Floppy Disks, and Disk Drives: When you save your work, it is transferred from RAM to a disk for permanent storage. Once your work is saved on a disk, you can turn off your computer and retrieve the document from the disk when you use WordPerfect again. The disk may be a hard disk (fixed in the computer's case) or a removable 5 1/4-inch or 3 1/2-inch floppy (flexible) disk.

Printer (optional): You can use WordPerfect without a printer, but if you do, you can only view your documents on the monitor. You cannot get a hard copy of your work without a printer.

Mouse: You can use a mouse to point to and select WordPerfect options as a substitute for making selections from the keyboard. However, you will still use the keyboard for typing text and for some WordPerfect functions. Many WordPerfect users prefer a mouse because it seems to be easier and faster to use than the keyboard.

Figure A.1
*Computer
components.*

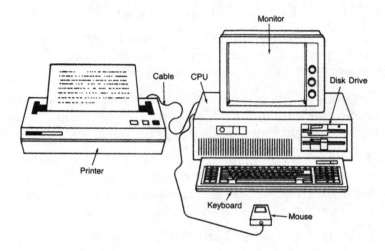

Software Components

Software refers to a computer program stored on a disk. Different programs have different functions. The software that enables the WordPerfect program to interact with your computer hardware is called the *operating system*. On an IBM-compatible PC, your operating system is DOS, which stands for Disk Operating System. The WordPerfect program is another kind of software: an *application*. While the operating system simply keeps the computer up and running, application software helps you perform a task, such as word processing.

Many files make up the WordPerfect application, each one carrying a specific set of instructions to the computer. There are many different types of files, and each file has a unique, descriptive name. Each WordPerfect document that you create can be stored individually on disk, too, with its own unique name.

DOS Fundamentals

You do not have to know much about DOS in order to use WordPerfect, but understanding a few basic principles will help you get the most out of your word processing sessions. Two key concepts you should understand are directories and formatting.

Using DOS Directories

A disk can be divided into parts called *directories*. Directories are especially useful on hard disks to keep certain types of files separate so that you can easily find what you need.

Directories take on the structure of an upside-down tree. The first level is called the root, and is represented by a backslash (\). Off the root, typically, is a directory for your operating system, along with a directory for each of your applications. In Figure A.2, the operating system is DOS, and the applications installed are WordPerfect (WP60) and Windows (WINDOWS). There is also a directory underneath the Windows directory called SYSTEM that is used to store special system files used by that program.

> **NOTE:** Chapter 12 in this book explains how to use WordPerfect to create directories and copy documents between directories.

When you use WordPerfect's File Manager, F5, you may be asked to enter the path. The path indicates how to get from where you are to the desired directory. For example, this is the path to a WordPerfect document called MYDOC.WPP:

```
C:\WPDOCS\MYDOC.WPP
```

First, `C:` identifies the drive. Then, a backslash (\) identifies the root. `WPDOCS` shows the directory, and then the name of the document follows. The directory and document names are separated by a backslash.

Formatting Disks

When you buy a floppy disk, it could be used by many types of computers and operating systems. *Formatting* a floppy disk makes that disk ready to be used by your operating system and your computer.

NOTE: An exception to this is preformatted floppy disks. These disks, while more expensive, are ready to use with DOS and do not require formatting.

Because you will be using a hard disk or working on a network, you will want to format floppy disks to store additional backup copies of your documents. You don't need these to install WordPerfect, but it's always a good idea to have several extra formatted floppy disks on which you can save your work.

CAUTION   When you format a floppy disk, all the information on the disk is erased. Never format a floppy disk if you want to save the information on the disk.

To format a floppy disk using DOS:

1. Start from the system prompt for the drive where DOS resides. (Exit from any application program you are running.) The system prompt is usually the drive letter followed by a colon or other symbols—for example, C> or C:\>.

2. At the system prompt, type in the command to format the disk: FORMAT. Follow it with a space, the drive letter for the disk to be formatted, and a colon. For example, you would use the following command to format the floppy disk in drive A:

   FORMAT A:

3. Press ⏎Enter). DOS will ask you to place the floppy disk to be formatted in the drive that you specified in the command. If there's already a floppy disk in that drive, remove it and insert the disk to be formatted.

At the drive C system prompt, never type FOR-MAT without specifying a drive letter, or DOS will assume that you want to format the current drive-your hard drive.

4. When you are sure you are formatting the correct disk, press ⏎Enter) to begin the format process.

5. Now you just wait while the computer processes. You can tell it is working by the lights and the sound of the machine.

6. A message similar to Format another disk? appears when the process is complete. Press Y for Yes to format another disk or N for No to stop formatting disks.

NOTE: There are two disk densities: double-density and high-density. DOS will normally format a disk at the highest density that the disk drive supports. You can format a double-density disk in a high-density drive by using special command line parameters; see your DOS manual for details.

Using Your Keyboard with WordPerfect

The computer keyboard lets you communicate with WordPerfect. The keys on the keyboard are shown in Figure A.2. Many keyboard keys are the same as those on a typewriter; others are special-use keys that access powerful features or shortcuts.

Figure A.2
A typical keyboard.

The following is a description of each group of keys found on the keyboard. Find these on your own keyboard.

- The Letter/Number/Symbol keys are common to computers and typewriters. Press these to type letters, numbers, and symbols. Press ⬆Shift to type capital letters, symbols, or punctuation marks found on the top half of these keys.

- The Function keys are labeled F1 through F10 (F12 on some computers). They are used to perform special WordPerfect functions. They may be used alone or in conjunction with other keys including Alt, Ctrl, or ⬆Shift. This book uses illustrations of keys and places a plus (+) between two key names, such as ⬆Shift+F1, to indicate you are to press the two keys simultaneously.

- The cursor arrow keys are used to move the cursor. You can use the cursor arrow keys to move across existing text without changing the text. On most computers, pressing the key marked Num Lock first will produce the numbers on these keys instead of the arrows.

- The Spacebar is used to enter spaces or blank out text.

- The Home, PgUp, End, and PgDn keys are used for special WordPerfect movements.

- The Tab, ⬅Backspace, Ins, and Del keys are used for special functions described later in this book.

Diagram of Typewriter Keyboard
(Horizontal Method)

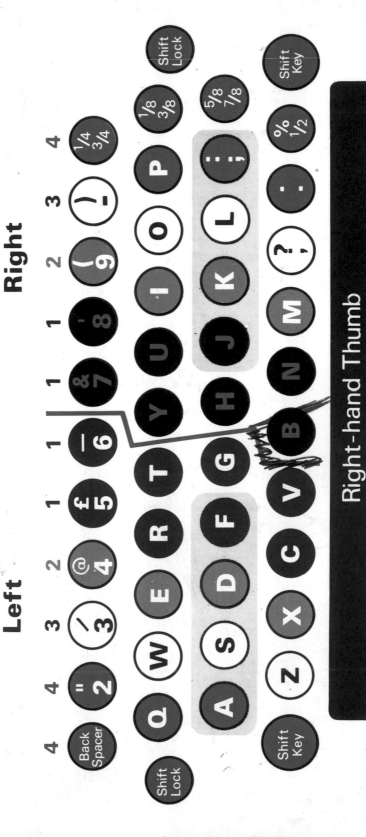

Left

Right

Right-hand Thumb

The correct fingering is indicated by figures and colours

PITMAN (Q.848:31)

Using A Mouse with WordPerfect

If you have never used a mouse before, some of the terminology used in this book may seem strange to you. Here's a quick summary of the mouse techniques you need to know.

- **Point:** To move the mouse until the pointer on-screen points to a specified item.

- **Click:** To press and release the left mouse button.

- **Double-click:** To press and release the left mouse button twice in a row quickly.

- **Drag:** To hold down the left mouse button while you move the mouse.

Practice these techniques until you become familiar with them; if you use a mouse with WordPerfect, these skills will be very important.

B

Installing WordPerfect

Before you can use WordPerfect for the first time, you must prepare the program to run on your computer. This is called *installing*, because a working copy of the program is placed on your hard disk during the procedure. Installing is a one-time operation; once WordPerfect is available, you can use it again and again.

Because the folks at WordPerfect have you—the first-time user—in mind, the installation process is almost entirely automated. You only need to know a little about the type of computer you are using and how to use your keyboard to respond to the screens WordPerfect shows you.

TIP: During installation, you will be given the option of network installation. Installing WordPerfect on a network is usually considered a fairly advanced task. WordPerfect walks you through installing the *server*, the primary computer with the hard disk to which other computers are attached. It also helps you install the computers, called *workstations*, that are hooked to the server. If you run into problems when you install, don't hesitate to seek help from your dealer or another knowledgeable source.

Starting the Installation

To begin installing WordPerfect, place the WordPerfect disk with the word "Install #1" on the label in drive A of your computer. Type:

```
A:install
```

and press `⏎Enter`.

A screen appears inquiring whether you have a color monitor. If you can see colors (versus shades of grey or green), press `Y` for **Y**es. Otherwise, press `N` for No. Anytime you see a letter in bright (bold) text, you can just press it to select the option instead of typing the entire word.

Next, you're taken to the WordPerfect 6.0 Installation screen. Select an installation option based on your needs.

- If you're a beginner, select **S**tandard Installation—it's the easiest.

- If you're an advanced user, select **C**ustom Installation; it gives you more control.

- If you want to install WordPerfect on a network, select **N**etwork Installation. (Check with your network administrator first, though.)

I'm going to assume that you're choosing Standard Installation; that's the option that's best for beginning users.

After making your WordPerfect 6.0 Installation screen selections, you are walked through a series of screens. WordPerfect tells you when to replace the disk in the drive with another disk. Note the name of the disk WordPerfect requests, find the disk with that label, and place it in the drive.

CAUTION

Never remove or replace a disk in a drive when the drive light is on, or you might damage the disk.

WordPerfect explains each feature as you install it. If you aren't sure that you want to install a particular feature, go ahead and select Yes to install it. Having features you don't use only takes up some space, but failing to install a feature you later want costs you time and causes confusion when you have to install that feature alone. Plus, until you understand WordPerfect, it is difficult to distinguish which features you won't need. So, installing each feature early in your WordPerfect experience can only help you.

One of the final features you install is the link to your printer. When you get to the printer screen, the operation is a little more complex than just selecting yes or no.

The printer screen lists all the printers with which WordPerfect will work. First, determine the brand and model of your printer. Then, press PgUp and PgDn until you see that printer and model. Highlight it, and press ⏎Enter. This installs the files for that printer only. Continue following the messages.

TIP: If you can't find the brand or model of your printer, select the printer most like your own. Consult your printer dealer or the dealer that sold you WordPerfect.

When installation is done, you're returned to the DOS prompt. Information about your installation appears.

TIP: If you change printers later, you can use the installation program to install a new printer. From the Installation screen, select 4 - Device (Files, Sound, Graphics, Fax, Printer) Files. Select the new printer just like you did during installation.

Once WordPerfect is installed, place the original disks from WordPerfect Corporation in a safe, temperate environment. These are your final backup copies so you don't want anything to happen to them.

What's New in WordPerfect 6.0?

In two words . . . WordPerfect 6.0 is "more" and "better". Even though WordPerfect 5.1 was hard to beat, version 6.0 brings more capability. Plus, those features that were already a familiar part of WordPerfect have been improved. Let's see how.

Button Bars: Button Bars allow you to make quick selections with a click of the mouse. WordPerfect comes standard with Button Bars, and you can make your own. Chapter 1 introduces them, and Chapter 19 goes into more depth on Button Bars.

Enhanced Screens: WordPerfect for DOS is getting the "Windows" feel in more ways than one. The first thing you'll notice is the Windows-like use of dialog boxes, radio buttons, and check boxes. Chapter 1 provides the introduction.

Windows: The next "Windows" feel you get is through windows themselves. Chapter 12 covers how to use the nine windows WordPerfect now offers.

Ease of Installation: The installation process has been made easier. In addition, WordPerfect now sets up a WPDOCS directory off the root which is the default directory when saving documents. No need for the novice user to have to create directories right away. Appendix B covers the details.

File Manager: The File Manager provides a host of new options to make life easier. A directory tree, along with enhanced sort and search capabilities, aid in finding documents quickly. QuickList and QuickFinder help the user get right to often-needed work. Chapter 12 covers the File Manager.

Formatting Options: Some WordPerfect enhancements seem small but make for big-time savings. Here's an example. Instead of going to one screen to set top and bottom margins and another to set left and right margins, the margin settings are on one dialog box. This is just one example of small formatting enhancements in WordPerfect 6.0 that will make for smoother sailing. There are more options for justifying text, more ways to align text, you can add borders to text, and on and on. Chapter 4 covers setting margins and Chapters 5 and 6 cover other formatting options.

Mailing Labels and Envelopes: Instead of guesswork, WordPerfect 6.0 provides you features designed just for creating mailing labels and envelopes. These aren't covered in this book, but you can find information about them in your WordPerfect documentation.

Fonts: WordPerfect comes with fonts. See Chapter 5 for details on how to put them to use.

New Print Features: There are more print options including an improved Print Preview, the capability to print double sided, more output options, and even Fax services. Many of these features are covered in Chapter 6.

Ribbon: The ribbon provides quick access to font features and other features. Check it out in Chapter 5.

Text, Graphics, and Page Modes: Text Mode is the familiar screen look. Use Graphics and Page Modes for a "what you see is what you get" look. You'll be pleased with the outcome. Chapter 1 covers these modes.

Handling Pages: You can now use Secondary Page, Chapter, and Volume page numbering. You can also subdivide a page, easily creating tri-fold brochures or booklets. See Chapter 8 for the scoop.

Grammar Checking: WordPerfect 6.0 gives you a grammar checker . . . no, a *sophisticated* grammar checker. Chapter 10 tells you how to get started using Grammatik.

Spelling Enhancements: The speller has been improved. For example, you can now set up automatic replacements for words you typically mistype or acronyms you use often. You can also set up suggested words for those you commonly overuse. Look at Chapter 10.

Bookmarks and Hypertext: You can set up bookmarks and then use them with Hypertext to shoot from one document to another or from one spot within a document to another spot. Macros can be started, as well. Check out Chapter 11.

Macro Editing: Wow, is it easy now! You can swiftly switch between editing a macro as a regular WordPerfect document or editing in the familiar "recording" mode. An equally easy "how to" is waiting for you in Chapter 13.

Merging and Styles: While both merging and styles will seem very familiar on the surface, enhancements await. Check them out in Chapters 14 and 16.

Graphics: WordPerfect is giving you increasingly fine control over graphics, along with new features, such as interesting border and appearance options. Chapter 15 covers the details.

The Shell and Clipboard: Set up the Shell to move quickly from WordPerfect to another program. Use the Clipboard feature to access up to 80 clipboards to store text. You access them from within WordPerfect or a "Shell aware" program. Take a look at Chapter 19 for more.

Index

350 *First Book of WordPerfect 6*

Quick Command Reference (*continued*)

Function	Menu Selections	Quick Keys
Margins, Set	Layout, Margins	⇧Shift+F8
Maximize a Window	Window, Maximize	Alt+W, M
Minimize a Window	Window, Minimize	Alt+W, I
New File, Creating	File, New	Alt+F, N
Print	File, Print/Fax	⇧Shift+F7, R
Print Preview	File, Print Preview	⇧Shift+F7, V
Retrieve a File	File, Retrieve	⇧Shift+F10, ⇧Shift+F10
Reveal Codes	View, Reveal Codes	Alt+F3
Save	File, Save	Ctrl+F12
Save As	File, Save As	F10
Sort a List	Tools, Sort	Ctrl+F9
Spelling	Tools, Writing Tools, Speller	Ctrl+F2
Style, Create	Layout, Styles, Create	Alt+F8, C
Tabs	Layout, Line, Tab Set	⇧Shift+F8, T
Table, Create	Layout, Tables, Create	Alt+F7, T, C
Undelete	Edit, Undelete	Esc
Underline	Font, Underline	Ctrl+F8, U
Undo	Edit, Undo	Ctrl+Z

Quick Command Reference (Menu and Keystroke)

Function	Menu Selections	Quick Keys
Alignment	Layout, Alignment	`Alt`+`L`,`A`
Block	Edit, Block	`Alt`+`F4`
Bold	Font, Bold	`F6`
Columns	Layout, Columns	`Alt`+`F7`,`1`
Create Directory	File, File Manager, =	`F5`,`=`
Display Button Bar	View, Button Bar	`Alt`+`V`, `B`
Display Ribbon	View, Ribbon	`Alt`+`V`, `R`
Envelope	Layout, Envelope	`Alt`+`F12`
Exit WordPerfect	File, Exit WP	`Home`, `F7`
Export a File	File, Save As, (Name), Format	`F10`, (name), `R`
File Manager	File, File Manager	`F5`
Font, Change	Font, Font, 1	`F8`, `1`
Frame a Window	Window, Frame	`Alt`+`W`, `F`
Graphics Box, Create	Graphics, Graphics Boxes, Create	`Alt`+`F9`, `B`, `C`
Graphics Box, Edit	Graphics, Graphics Boxes, Edit	`Alt`+`F9`, `B`, `E`
Graphics Lines, Create	Graphics, Graphics Lines, Create	`Alt`+`F9`, `L`, `C`
Graphics Lines, Edit	Graphics, Graphics Lines, Edit	`Alt`+`F9`, `L`, `E`
Help, Getting	Help	`F1`
Import a Text File	File, Open	`Shift`+`F10`
Import a Spreadsheet	Tools, Spreadsheet	`Alt`+`F7`, `S`, `I`

continues